牛津社会语言学丛书

Multilingualism and the Periphery

语言的多元化与边缘化

Sari Pietikäinen & Helen Kelly–Holmes 编

上海外语教育出版社
外教社 SHANGHAI FOREIGN LANGUAGE EDUCATION PRESS
www.sflep.com

图书在版编目(CIP)数据

语言的多元化与边缘化／(芬)莎莉·派提凯能，(爱尔兰)海伦·凯丽-霍尔姆斯编. —上海：上海外语教育出版社，2017
(牛津社会语言学丛书)
ISBN 978-7-5446-4982-7

Ⅰ.①语… Ⅱ.①莎… ②海… Ⅲ.①社会语言学-英文
Ⅳ.①H0

中国版本图书馆 CIP 数据核字(2017)第 156825 号

图字：09-2016-736

出版发行：上海外语教育出版社
　　　　　　(上海外国语大学内)　邮编：200083
电　　话：021-65425300 (总机)
电子邮箱：bookinfo@sflep.com.cn
网　　址：http://www.sflep.com.cn http://www.sflep.com
责任编辑：奚玲燕

印　　刷：上海华教印务有限公司
开　　本：787×1000　1/16　印张 15.5　字数 258千字
版　　次：2018 年 1 月第 1 版　2018 年 1 月第 1 次印刷
印　　数：2 100 册

书　　号：ISBN 978-7-5446-4982-7
定　　价：50.00 元
　　　　本版图书如有印装质量问题,可向本社调换

出版说明

　　社会语言学是研究语言与社会多方面关系的学科,它从社会科学的不同角度,诸如社会学、人类学、民族学、心理学、地理学和历史学等去考察语言。自20世纪60年代发端以来,社会语言学已经逐渐发展成为语言学研究中的一门重要学科,引发众多学者的关注和探究。

　　"牛津社会语言学丛书"由国际社会语言学研究的两位领军人物——英国卡迪夫大学语言与交际研究中心的教授 Nicolas Coupland 和 Adam Jaworski(现在中国香港大学英语学院任教)——担任主编。丛书自2004年由牛津大学出版社陆续出版以来,推出了一系列社会语言学研究的专著,可以说是汇集了这一学科研究的最新成果,代表了当今国际社会语言学研究的最高水平。

　　我们从中精选出九种,引进出版。所选的这些专著内容广泛,又较贴近我国学者研究的需求,涵盖了当今社会语言学的许多重要课题,如语言变体与语言变化、语言权力与文化认同、语言多元化与语言边缘化、语言与族裔、语言与立场(界位)、语言与新媒体、语用学与礼貌、语言与法律以及社会语言学视角下的话语研究等等。其中既有理论研究,又有方法创新;既有框架分析建构,又有实地考察报告;既体现本学科的前沿和纵深,又展现跨学科的交叉和互补。

　　相信丛书的引进出版能为从事社会语言学研究的读者带来新的启示,进一步推动我国语言学研究的发展。

Multilingualism and the Periphery

Edited by Sari Pietikäinen

and

Helen Kelly-Holmes

CONTENTS

ACKNOWLEDGEMENTS

This volume emerged out of a series of discussions we were fortunate to have in different locations. It began as an invited seminar on Northern Multilingualism in 2010 Inari, Finland and continued, with a larger set of participants, at the Sociolinguistics Symposium 18 in 2010 Southampton. Finally, in 2011, the research project called *Peripheral Multilingualism*, funded by the Academy of Finland (2011–2015) was launched. This volume is part of this research project (http://www.peripheralmultilingualism.fi).

We are grateful for these opportunities, and for the many conversations in and out of these meetings. We owe a debt to all the contributors for their engagement and enthusiasm throughout the process.

We would also like to acknowledge the support of the Academy of Finland. The actual preparation of the volume has greatly benefited from the support of Katja Huutokari and Pekka Rötkönen, and we warmly thank them. We owe a special debt to Nikolas Coupland and Adam Jaworski, the series editors, for their critical eye and continuing support.

CONTRIBUTORS

Brigitta Busch, University of Vienna
Nikolas Coupland, Copenhagen University, University of Technology, Sydney, and Cardiff University
Monica Heller, University of Toronto
Alexandra Jaffe, California State University, Long Beach
Adam Jaworski, University of Hong Kong
Helen Kelly-Holmes, University of Limerick
Mireille McLaughlin, Université d'Ottawa
Cedric Oliva, California State University, Long Beach
Sari Pietikäinen, University of Jyväskylä
Joan Pujolar, Universitat Oberta de Catalunya
Crispin Thurlow, University of Washington, Bothell

Multilingualism and the Periphery

CHAPTER 1

Multilingualism and the Periphery

SARI PIETIKÄINEN AND HELEN KELLY-HOLMES

This book is an exploration of the ways in which centre–periphery dynamics shape multilingualism. This exploration focuses on peripheral sites, which are defined as such by a relationship (be it geographic, political, economic, etc.) to some perceived centre. Viewing multilingualism through the lens of centre–periphery dynamics helps to bring forth the language ideological tensions which are evident in issues of language boundary-making, language ownership, commodification, and authenticity. It also highlights the ways in which speakers seek novel solutions in adapting their linguistic resources to new situations and developing innovative and creative language practices.

The sites of concern to us in this volume involve complex multilingualism and minority languages—the minoritization of languages being part of peripheralization processes—and as such are subject to the dynamics of renegotiation and contestation characteristic of the centre–periphery relationship. In this volume, we explore multilingualism in minority language sites in order to examine how the dynamics of centre–periphery relations might shape language practices, and how these practices might, in turn, have wider resonance beyond the sites under investigation. We see these peripheral contexts as 'crucial sites' (Philips 2000) for understanding the current sociolinguistics of globalization (Coupland 2003, 2010; Blommaert 2010), although they are often neglected sites in sociolinguistic research, with the focus predominantly on urban spaces for understanding the linguistic dimension to contemporary globalization (cf. e.g. Block 2005; Harris 2006; Rampton 2006; Mac Giolla Chríost 2007; Pennycook 2010).

Centre–periphery dynamics—and how they are imagined—have a significant impact on the way that multilingualism in minority language contexts is conceptualized and practised. An unstable model of centre–periphery calls for a reassessment of what linguistic and cultural peripheries are, under globalization, and an exploration of how people evaluate and work discursively with these reconfigurations. Minority language sites are subject, by necessity, to various—and often conflicting—language ideologies, norms, and practices. These are spaces where tensions between various language ideologies are often made explicit, and their logics and borders are being tested (see e.g. da Silva, McLaughlin, and Richards 2006; Jaffe 2009; Pietikäinen 2010). Despite the fact that linguistic minority sites are often constructed from the centre as linguistically and culturally homogeneous, and while they may also be constructed internally in this way in order to pursue particular rights and economic benefits, the everyday language practices tend to be mixed, flexible, and diverse. What we want to explore in this book is the evolution of language practices which, on the one hand, challenge and disregard the centrist ideology and the normativity of parallel monolingualisms (cf. Heller 1999, 2003, 2006; Jaffe 2006), whilst, on the other hand, relying on it as a necessary resource (Moore, Pietikäinen, and Blommaert 2010; Pietikäinen and Kelly-Holmes 2011).

In consequence, this volume is concerned with processes of *peripheralization* and of *centralization*, since the centre–periphery relationship is never fixed, but instead constantly renegotiated and mutually constitutive. Key to this examination is the problematizing of two clashing perspectives on multilingualism in relation to minority languages: the standard language perspective, which is still largely informed by a view of languages and speech communities as bounded entities, so-called segregational linguistics (cf. Harris 1996); in contrast with the heteroglossic or polynomic perspective (e.g. Dufva 2004; Jaffe 2007; Zarate, Levy, and Kramsch 2008; Pennycook 2010), which emphasizes hybridity, fluidity, partial repertoires, and communities of practice. Given the complexity of contemporary multilingual processes, we see an inherent problem in adopting either of these approaches exclusively, and we see the peripheral perspective as a way of highlighting this and moving forward our thinking on multilingualism. Furthermore, the current globalizing processes call for examination of the different ways in which peripheralization and centralization happen, forcing us to ask how a particular kind of multilingualism in a particular kind of site becomes constructed as peripheral or as central, with what kind of consequences, driven by whom, and with effects for whom.

FRAMING PERIPHERAL MULTILINGUALISM

The current volume is embedded in and further develops a number of key interdisciplinary concepts and literatures. First of all, there is the concept of centre–periphery and the dynamics between centre and periphery; secondly, there is the concept of multilingualism, and the rethinking of multilingualism, particularly in relation to the sociolinguistics of globalization; thirdly, the notion of language ideologies, particularly in relation to a changing conceptualization of language as system to language as practice (cf. Rampton 2006; Pennycook 2010, Pietikäinen 2010; Kelly-Holmes and Milani 2011) and the implications of this for the concept of minority languages. We will now examine each of these to show how the volume both derives from and contributes to expanding these three areas.

Centre–Periphery

Centre–periphery is a common spatial metaphor used to describe and explain the unequal distribution of power in the economy, society, and polity. The centre–periphery is metaphorized, for example, in the division of the nation states of the world into First, Second, and Third worlds, and in emphasizing the difference between 'South' and 'North', or in describing 'West' or 'urban cities' as power bases (cf. Ang and Stratton 1996; Potter 2001; Vanolo 2010). Also communities and groups from the 'margins' of nations—or as Graburn (1976) describes it 'engulfed by the nations'—have employed this metaphor in constructing an alternative view of the centre–periphery relations, using concepts such as 'Fourth World' or 'First Nations'.

The centre is typically defined in terms of its advancement, metropolitanism, and political, economic, and trade power, while the periphery is characterized as marginal, the opposite of the centre, the boundary or outer part of it. Johnston et al. (2000: 48) conclude that 'the centre dominates whilst the periphery is dependent, and this dependence may be structured through the relations of exchange, production or evaluation between centre and periphery'. The use of the centre–periphery metaphor is common in political geography, political sociology, and studies of labour markets to explain both the concentration and the dispersion of mainly economic activity (Friedmann 1966; Centre–periphery model 1998; Andrew and Feiock 2010); but it is also used in history, cultural studies, and education to describe and explain disparities in uneven development (cf. e.g. Chakravorty 2003; Hayter 2003).

The centre–periphery model is also implicated in various types of world-system theories. Its first major articulation, and a classic example of this approach, is associated with Immanuel Wallerstein (1974, 1980, 2004). His world-systems theory provided a model for understanding both change in the global system and the relationship between its parts, referred to as centre, semi-periphery, and periphery. Wallerstein conceptualized a world system, comprised of centres and the periphery, which are tied together by a network of economic exchange processes (Goldfrank 2000). His work has had a major impact on sociological and historical thought and triggered numerous reactions, and inspired many to build on his ideas (cf. e.g. Blommaert 2010; Schubert and Sooryamoorthy 2010).

At the current moment of globalization, the fixed centre/periphery divide that was relatively clearly identifiable in the period of modernity, has become problematic. As, for example, Appadurai (1990: 6) points out, 'The global cultural economy has to be seen as a complex, overlapping, disjunctive order, which cannot any longer be understood in terms of existing centre-periphery models.' To capture this transition, concepts such as 'flow', 'networks', 'rhizome', and 'translocality' have been used to describe and explain movement and circulation (cf. Deleuze and Guattari 1987; Appadurai 1996; Pennycook 2007) of resources, including languages, in the contemporary era. Importantly, from this point of view 'centre' and 'periphery' (as well as locality, authenticity, tradition, and other key terms in this volume) are not given, but are instead understood as discursive constructs, products of social interaction, reflecting the circumstances and dynamics of their construction (see e.g. Pennycook 2010). The centre–periphery relationship is thus always constructed and subject to complex, socio-political and economic processes and practices. By no means a one-way relationship, it is both reciprocal and dynamic, and rarely stable or predictable in its nature or effects (Burke 2000; McCulloch and Lowe 2003).

However—and importantly from the point of view of this volume—these flows and shifts are not constituted randomly; mobility and circulation do not take place in empty space, but always in already constituted space. Moreover, space itself, as Lefebvre (1991/1974) tells us, is a complex and dynamic social construction, produced and experienced in human interaction (see also e.g. Scollon and Scollon 2004; Pennycook 2010; Thurlow and Jaworski 2010). This means that the historical and cultural situatedness of spaces crossed by these flows has a great impact on current processes and practices. Past structures and ideas remain powerful elements in the present-day trajectories of cultural flows and emerging practices. From this point of view, Ang and Stratton (1996: 28) argue that 'we should perhaps not so much replace the centre/periphery structure with that of flow, but rather articulate the two, to account for the ongoing, always shifting, multidimensional, heterogeneous and ambiguous relationalities which constitute our current global predicament'.

In this volume, we want to examine this theoretical transition from the notion of a fixed centre and periphery to notions of fluid, negotiated, and reconfigured ideas of centres and peripheries in relation to multilingualism. We suggest that this transition does not perhaps so much eliminate old bases of relations between centre and periphery, but rather situates them in a new, more complex configuration (cf. Ang and Stratton 1996). Consequently, the idea of the 'centre' and 'periphery' are still powerful; they are both the organizing factors in a system of global power relations and the organizing concept in a whole way of thinking and speaking (cf. Hall 1992). Peripheries could move to become part of the centre, and vice versa, as centre sites and locations became less dominant, they would move to the periphery of the system. As the cases in this volume show, some of the peripheral sites have already had their 'days of glory' while some sites are on the brink of being the centre themselves. There is an on-going dynamic between what is perceived as a periphery and what is perceived as a centre. Also in our understanding of peripherality, rather than changing over time, relative peripherality is changing constantly, so that one location, practice, or process can be at one and the same time both peripheral and central. Sites, areas, and processes which may be peripheral in one sense (e.g. distance from a national capital, large economic centre, or urban population centres or from established norms) may be central in others (e.g. in terms of their role and importance for national and international tourists, niche markets, and specialized industries, language and cultural politics and policies, etc.).

It is this simultaneous, shifting and ambiguous position between peripherality and centrality, and the tensions that arise from these transformations that make the examination of peripheral sites interesting and revealing. It is the contradictions and tensions between these two tendencies—on the one hand, the fact that centre/periphery relations are both multiplying and no longer fixed, and, on the other hand, the continuing discursive power of the 'centre' as the all-powerful centre—which have important implications for the sites, processes, and practices under study in this volume. We want to explore this further by focusing on regions, spaces, communities, and practices that are simultaneously perceived to be *peripheries for particular centres and centres for particular peripheries, or on the move from one to the other.*

Peripheries are, we argue, ambiguous and interesting spaces; they are spaces of transformation and negotiation, rendering them novel and revealing spaces to examine contemporary complexities in multilingualism. While the role of cities and urban centres in the globalized world system has been widely examined, as mentioned above, the peripheries are rarely examined in terms of their contribution to globalization; instead, they are often seen to follow rather than lead. We would like to examine the potential for peripheral sites to become centres of normativity rather than places to which norms are disseminated. In this way, we hope that the book provides an original perspective to the relationship between 'centre' and 'periphery' in general, and in relation to multilingualism in particular.

Multilingualism

In this volume, we start from the premise that changing centre–periphery relations play an important role in understanding and reconfiguring multilingualism in minority language spaces. A concern with centre–periphery relations is, of course, nothing new in sociolinguistics or in understanding multilingualism. For example, Kachru's (1996) model of the three circles of English involves an inner circle (a centre), which is both norm defining and controlling, and disseminates norms and practices to the outer circle of countries with English as a second language, and also to the expanding circle of countries with English as a foreign language. The three circles model has been challenged by increasing focus on hybridity and polycentric normativities (cf. Park and Wee 2009; Pennycook 2010) in both the outer and expanding circles, and the two-way flows between the three circles, which characterize the contemporary world. Another sociolinguistic thesis that uses the central–peripheral model to explain multilingualism is de Swaan's (2001) world language system, which also focuses on mobility and sees the more central languages as the more mobile. In his model, de Swaan categorizes languages across the globe as central, supercentral, or peripheral. Central languages are those which are the official languages of countries and which have the greatest communicative power in those countries, but less mobility between countries. Supercentral languages are modern-day lingua francas, with use and power beyond the borders of the countries in which they are located. English has special status as a hypercentral language, which holds the system together. At the other end of the scale are peripheral languages, which are the least mobile of the languages in the system and which generally have the least power and may not have a written form, and so on. Like Kachru's model, there are problems with de Swaan's system, since it is hard to classify many of the languages discussed in this volume in terms of this system. For example, where would regional minority languages which have official status (e.g. Welsh and Irish) be located? These are privileged, minoritized languages—peripheral and minoritized in some contexts and domains, and privileged and central in others. Furthermore, neither languages nor their speakers 'stay' in these categories but rather there is constant movement between and across categories: for example, regional minority languages may gain worldwide mobility through genres (hip-hop, advertisements) and practices (tourism, cultural production). The lived reality and actual everyday practices are far messier than these models suggest.

The current era of globalization has further challenged us to rethink multilingualism. For example, Dor (2004: 97) argues that

> most writers view today's linguistic world as a site of contestation between the *global* and the *local*: the spread of English as the lingua franca of the information age is viewed as the linguistic counterpart to the process of economic globalization; the causal factors working against the process of Englishization are thought of as locally bound and are equated with patterns of local resistance to economic (and cultural) globalization. This conception also determines the structure of the discourse on linguistic human rights: the need for *negotiated multilingualism* and the rights of speakers to resist global pressures and to use, maintain, and develop their local languages. (97)

This interest in global and local languages (echoing the centre–periphery distinction) has resulted in a wealth of studies on English as a lingua franca and linguistic imperialism, on the one hand, and an extensive literature on language endangerment, loss, and linguistic rights (e.g. Crystal 2002; Freeland and Patrick 2004; García, Skutnabb-Kangas, and Torres Guzmán 2006; Jenkins 2007; May 2007; Ostler 2010).

From the point of view of multilingualism, the current era of globalization can be seen as a new kind of order, impacting on how languages and their relations are constructed and are resulting in emerging ways of organizing and exploiting linguistic resources (Coupland 2010). Contemporary globalization also impacts, we argue, on what kind of multilingualism is perceived as 'central' (i.e. normal, desirable, and valuable) and what is considered 'peripheral' (i.e., marginal, devalued, and useless). With this view, the volume engages with the recent upsurge in language and globalization studies (see e.g. Coupland 2003; Heller 2003, 2011; Canagarajah 2005; Fairclough 2006; Heller and Duchene 2007; Blommaert 2010; Pennycook

2010). Further, contemporary globalization processes, particularly changing economic conditions and increased mobility, both open up new opportunities and create novel types of opportunities and restrictions for multilingualism and new multilingual spaces where individuals, communities, and institutions adapt to these changing conditions. One example of this, we argue in the volume, is the current valorization of certain types of bilingualism and the commodification of the periphery as a site of authenticity. In this context, the periphery has come to have a new value, perceived to offer experiences of authenticity, slow(er) lifestyle, solitude, and living with the challenges and opportunities afforded by the local environment. In this process, centres are constructed as predictable and unremarkable, whereas peripheries are seen as different, exotic, and other-worldly. The centre–periphery tension together with reconfigurations and mobilization of linguistic resources has led to novel types of diversity and tensions in peripheral sites under examination in this volume, with several contradictions and complexities which can then result in creative crossings. Further, the circulation and emergence of language practices show how fluidity and hybridity are part of language use and make it necessary to rethink and redefine many key concepts of language studies as these clearly acquire new meanings under new circumstances (cf. Canagarajah 2007; Makoni and Pennycook 2007). Indeed, the current conditions have put to the test the conceptualizations of languages as unified, bounded entities separate from the social world (cf. Bauman and Briggs 2003). These notions have been challenged both from the inside by the integrational linguistics of Harris (1981), and by studies of language ideologies (Blommaert 1999; Kroskrity 2002; Woolard 2004) and heteroglossia (Bakhtin 1981; Dufva 2010), which aim to understand how language and multilingualism may be understood differently in different contexts.

Language Ideologies

The reconfiguration of centre–periphery relations is, of course, a process taking place wherever people are mobilizing and reorganizing linguistic resources. It is for this reason, that the current volume examines centralizing and peripheralizing processes in changing and evolving multilingual minority language sites. Such a focus allows for the analysis and juxtaposition of sites where struggles, tensions, and innovations between various language ideologies are often made explicit, and their logics and the borders they attempt to create and maintain are being tested (see e.g. Jaffe 1999; Busch 2006; da Silva, McLaughlin, and Richards 2006; Pietikäinen 2010). Being named and categorized as a minority language is a result of centralizing and peripheralizing processes. To unpack these complexities, we draw on language ideological work on multilingual contexts (Blommaert 1999; Irvine and Gal 2000; Kroskrity 2000; Gal and Woolard 2001; Hill 2002; Gal 2006; Heller 2006; Jaffe 2007) and understand language ideologies as discursive constructs of the nature and meaning of language that are historically embedded and locally appropriated.

Language ideologies carry and convey articulations and beliefs about the nature, value, and functions of languages and are, at the same time, embedded in actual language practices of individuals and communities. This conception emphasizes the diachronic nature of any particular language ideology, its situational manifestation, and the impact it has on actual language practices.

The idea of a language ideological struggle implies the simultaneous existence of various language ideologies, particularly in contemporary evolving multilingual situations where language boundaries and norms are often dislocated, in flux, or renegotiated (cf. Nevins 2004; Meek 2007; Jaffe 2009; Pietikäinen 2010). This makes multilingual minority language sites a complex space for various ideological conflicts and contestations (cf. Lytra and Martin 2010), and consequently, important and revealing sites for examining the evolving notions of language, multilingualism, and other related concepts. As mentioned earlier, being considered and classified as a minority language is itself a result of language ideological processes and directly related to periphery/centre hierarchies. By their very existence, minority languages undermine the prevailing ideology of monolingualism and its message of 'one country, one language'. This language ideology is, of course, nurtured particularly within the context of the nation state and national identity (cf. Wright 2000), which involves creating a strong centre with its own norms and clearly defined peripheries. Minority language sites also provide evidence of what has been 'won' by minorities from the centre. This evidence typically consists of some central institutions that the centre has brought into the peripheries, and which function either fully or partly in minority languages and through the minority language community. This combination of economic, political, geographic, and ideological processes, as well as other factors, has meant that minority language sites 'have always had to invest in one form of multilingualism' (da Silva, McLaughlin, and Richards 2006: 185).

We can identify at least two language ideological formations that have structured our understanding of multilingualism and consequently have had an influence on how individuals experience 'languages' and talk about them. One powerful conceptualization, born and bred within the ideological framework of nation states and national languages, has been the idea that languages are autonomous and unified entities—often described as formal linguistic codes—with an 'essential' or natural relationship with a particular territory or the collective identity of a particular group, and essentially 'different' and 'separate' from each other (Heller 2006; Jaffe 2007). At the same time, we have also documented an alternative ideological formation—that manifests itself, for example, in discourses of plurilingual identities and competencies or 'polycentric' and 'polynomic' languages and language practices (Zarate, Levy, and Kramsch 2008; Jaffe 2009; Pietikäinen 2010). Also, as Bakhtin (1981) suggests, language can be imagined in terms of coexisting socio-ideological ways of speaking that, on one hand, emerge in a situated fashion, but, on the other, echo the past history. This heteroglossic perspective sees language as a practice, highlighting its expressive and communicative functions as opposed to linguistic form (cf. Dufva 2004; Heller 2006; Makoni and Pennycook 2007; Pennycook 2010). It can be argued that this perspective also captures the experiences of many multilingual speakers more appropriately by recognizing the inherent diversity and hybridity that characterizes multilingual living (Pietikäinen et al. 2008; Kramsch 2009). Further, this understanding of language seems to be in accord with—or perhaps even grow from—the various material and ideological shifts associated with processes of multilingualism under globalization.

The tensions between these two ideologies provide the dynamics of the centre–periphery relationship. While the centre has traditionally been seen as the source of norms to be adopted in peripheries, contributors to the volume explore how the dynamics of the centre–periphery relationship might instead lead to the deriva-tion of new and multiple normativities; and to various tensions which emerge from the dialectics between existing and emerging practices (cf. Heller 1999, 2006; Jaffe 2006; Kelly-Holmes, Moriarty, and Pietikäinen 2009; Pietikäinen and Kelly-Holmes 2011). Peripheral sites allow the examination of the shift from a centre-driven system of norms to fragmented and constantly changing systems of normativities. Norms were—and still are—generally the preserve and under the control of centres, with language policy being oriented towards, as well as formulated and implemented by, powerful centres (Wright 2004). The contemporary era has, however, witnessed a shift from these centrally controlled norms to polycentric normativities (Pennycook 2010; Pietikäinen 2010). In the 'practice turn' (Pennycook 2010; Kelly-Holmes and Milani 2011; cf. also Rampton 2006), normativities are now also seen as the outcome of various communities of practice and as such they are more fluid and situational than norms which were linked to fairly well-established and territorially bounded speech communities. Thus we see a shift from one centre which controls and decides norms, to multiple centres of normativity decided according to needs, situations, con-ditions, etc. Previously, it was—at least to a great extent—the centre with its large bureaucracy and complex network of institutions that decided, encoded, propagated, and policed norms. Even in areas where there was no explicit process, because of the dominance of the centre, what happened was invariably what was proper in a de facto, implicit (Schiffman 1996) or covert (Shohamy 2006) way. However, peripheral sites can themselves become the centres of new norms—deciding and showing what is and is not acceptable (Bourdieu 1991), at least within the local judgement of the com-munity of that particular site. These processes may lead to innovative combinations of global and local resources, which bring forth tensions that we would like to explore in the volume. The practices and normativities that emerge from centre–periphery relations can be seen as part of a wider process in sociolinguistics of rethinking mul-tilingualism (Heller 2006; Jaffe 2006; Rampton 2006; Makoni and Pennycook 2007; Blackledge and Creese 2009; Blommaert 2010; Coupland 2010; Pennycook 2010).

STRUCTURE OF THE BOOK

The contributions to the volume examine the variability and complexities of the processes and practices of peripheralizing and centralizing tendencies in multilingualism in a wide range of economic, cultural, political, and physical peripheral sites and spaces (tourism, education, minority language rights and politics, airports, gender relations, marketing, websites) in different geographic locations (Austria, Canada, Corsica, Catalonia, Finland, Ireland, Patagonia, Spain, Slovenia, United States, Wales). All contributions demonstrate how the constantly changing centre–periphery relationship plays an important role in understanding and reconfiguring multilingualism in current conditions of localized and lived aspects of globalization, particularly in relation to mobility, minority language spaces, and authenticity. The contributors draw on ethnographic, discursive, and sociolinguistic methods and share a common interest in 'big issues' (markets, mobility, economy, identity, etc.) as manifested in local language practices and experiences. The contributions to this volume show the impact of globalization, particularly in terms of (new) economic conditions, processes, and mobilities. By examining a range of cases of multilingualism in peripheral minority language sites in a variety of locations, the volume aims to provide a major insight into the various, emerging ways whereby centrality and peripherality are both created, maintained, and contested by the current flows and circulations, resulting in emerging ways of organizing and exploiting linguistic resources.

In Chapter 2, Monica Heller takes Francophone Canada as an example and examines the historical development of multilingual peripheries as a process of internal colonialism. She links this development to the rise of the nation state and its colonial expansion. With an ethnographic approach she examines some of the ways in which those peripheries now change position in a globalized new economy in which multilingualism is an asset rather than a problem to be controlled. The analysis shows how these changes and negotiations call into question common-sense ideas about language and identity, as well as notions of centres and peripheries.

Mireille McLaughlin also deals with Francophone Canada in Chapter 3, but she focuses on *Acadie*, the transnational Canadian and American linguistic minority, peripheral to many cultural and political centres. She adopts a concept of 'multilingual capital' and uses it to explore Acadian cultural production (in literature, comedy, music) in the globalizing economy. Her ethnographic analysis shows how Acadian artists mobilize local forms of multilingualism to index their peripheral cultural position, in order to present themselves as counter-cultural and to construct Acadian identity as cool for global niche markets.

In Chapter 4, Joan Pujolar examines the intersection of heritage, gender, and peripherality in the context of Welsh tourism. He argues that in this site, the concept of heritage is indexical of peripherality within the framework of modernity. By using a multi-sited ethnographic approach, he analyzes the different dimensions of peripherality constituted by dichotomies such as gender and nation, gender and tourism, and tourism and nation. He emphasizes how multilingual practices in such contexts reflect and contribute to constructing these articulations, in which ideologies of modernity play a key role.

The fifth chapter, by Sari Pietikäinen, focuses on indigenous Sámi heritage tourism in Finnish Lapland, a geographical periphery but simultaneously a cultural centre for the Sámi community. Using discourse analytical and ethnographic approaches, she examines what gets constructed as authentic in this context and what kind of tensions and creativity the economic capitalization of authenticity generates. Applying Bakhtinian concepts of centripetal and centrifugal forces, she shows how the dynamicity between standardized and flexible authentication practices creates a polycentric environment for multilingual and indigenous language practices and thus problematizes what is perceived as 'central' and what is perceived as 'peripheral'.

In Chapter 6, Alexandra Jaffe and Cedric Oliva examine how linguistic boundaries and statuses are negotiated through Corsican and other languages in commercial and tourist spaces in Corsica. Their ethnographic analysis shows how continuity with dominant, monolingual ideologies of language and identity is articulated within a historical, Corsican-French oppositional relationship. The findings suggest the ways in which Corsican may be repositioned as a form of 'added cultural value' in the tourist market, and the possibilities and tensions in terms of identity that this new market framework presents for speakers of the minority language. The findings also problematize the notions of 'centre' and 'periphery', showing them not so much as places, but as stance objects evoked in discourses and practices.

Chapter 7, by Helen Kelly-Holmes, is concerned with the tensions between centralizing and peripheralizing practices, policies, and ideologies of individual commercial actors in sites of peripheral multilingualism. The particular site is Dingle in the Corca Dhuibhne *Gaeltacht*, which is a minority language site and designated Irish-speaking/bilingual area, as well as a major tourist destination in South-West Ireland. Using the website of a local pottery workshop, she examines how individual actors in sites of peripheral multilingualism attempt to centralize or peripheralize Irish in their practices and whether individual commercial actors in sites of peripheral multilingualism adopt centre/centrist practices and ideologies (e.g. norm-driven, standards, parallel monolingualism, modernist concepts) or peripheral practices and ideologies.

In Chapter 8, Nikolas Coupland takes the trajectory of Welsh tea as an example of the mobility between variously perceived 'centres' and 'peripheries'. His analysis illustrates how shifting historical and geographical circumstances have variously positioned Wales and the Welsh language as more or less autonomous, and more or less peripheral, within particular cultural economies. The analysis demonstrates how centre–periphery relations are always relative and subject to radical transformation from one national or international configuration to another.

Chapter 9, by Adam Jaworski and Crispin Thurlow, examines airports as particular spaces of mobility and multilingualism. The semiotic landscapes of Cardiff Airport and Seattle-Tacoma International Airport are analysed in order to show how various discursive practices, including multilingual displays, are organized around different spatial norms and how they are shaped by the polycentricity of airports.

The analysis emphasizes how the mobility of languages, people, and objects reconfigure our understanding of centres and peripheries.

In Chapter 10, Brigitta Busch takes the region of Southern Carinthia in southernmost Austria as a site to examine how the seemingly static relationship between language and territory is dislocated. With an analysis of language practices, as well as discursive and spatial practices, she shows how changes at the economic and political macro level are translated into linguistic manifestations in the representational space at a micro level. The analysis also highlights how irony challenges the traditional bipolar and asymmetrical language regime and gives expression to growing linguistic diversification.

Finally, the concluding chapter reflects on the contributions to the volume and assesses the opportunities and challenges presented by adopting a peripheral multilingualism approach.

As all contributions to this volume show, the complex interactions between individual practices and institutional norms and ideologies, between language as system and language as everyday life, are seen as necessary and inherent to the novel practices that are emerging, and challenging us to rethink and re-image what language means. We are living in a time of transition in understanding and conceptualizing language: we are already witnessing a shift to a view of language as a heteroglossic resource (Busch 2006; Pietikäinen 2010) and as repertoire (Hymes 1974; Blommaert 2010); as a local practice (Pennycook 2010) and as the emotional and performative individual practices of subjects (Pavlenko 2005; Kramsch 2009; Blackledge and Creese 2010). Sites of peripheral multilingualism, we argue, provide important and revealing spaces to explore the processes, practices, and consequences of reinventing and reconfiguring the borders and values of linguistic and other semiotic resources, linked to the new economy of local resources and to the mobility and circulation of people and products.

REFERENCES

Andrew, Simon A., and Richard C. Feiock. 2010. Centre–peripheral structure and regional governance: Implications of Paul Krugman's new economic geography for public administration. *Public Administration Review* 70 (3): 494–499.

Ang, Ien, and Jon Stratton. 1996. Asianing Australia: Notes toward a critical transnationalism in cultural studies. *Cultural Studies* 10 (1): 16–36.

Appadurai, Arjun. 1990. Disjuncture and difference in the global cultural economy. *Theory, Culture and Society* 7: 295–310.

Appadurai, Arjun. 1996. *Modernity at large: Cultural dimensions of globalization*. Minneapolis: University of Minnesota Press.

Bakhtin, Mikhail. 1981. *The dialogic imagination: Four essays by M. M. Bakhtin*. Austin: University of Texas Press.

Bauman, Richard, and Charles L. Briggs. 2003. *Voices of modernity: Language ideologies and the politics of inequality*. Cambridge: Cambridge University Press.

Blackledge, Adrian, and Angela Creese. 2009. Meaning-making as dialogic process: Official and carnival lives in the language classroom. *Journal of Language, Identity, and Education* 8 (4): 236–253.

Blackledge, Adrian, and Angela Creese. 2010. *Multilingualism: A critical perspective.* London: Continuum.

Block, Andrew J. 2005. Language policy in the Basque Autonomous Community: Implications for nationalism. *Michigan Journal of Political Science* 2 (4): 5–65.

Blommaert, Jan, ed. 1999. *Language ideological debates.* Berlin: Mouton de Gruyter.

Blommaert, Jan. 2010. *The sociolinguistics of globalization.* Cambridge: Cambridge University press.

Bourdieu, Pierre. 1991. *Language and symbolic power.* Oxford: Polity Press.

Burke, Peter. 2000. *A social history of knowledge: From Gutenberg to Diderot.* Cambridge: Polity Press.

Busch, Brigitta. 2006. Changing media spaces: The transformative power of heteroglossic practices. In *Language ideologies, practices and policies,* ed. Clare Mar-Molinero and Patrick Stevenson, 206–219. Basingstoke and New York: Palgrave MacMillan.

Canagarajah, A. Suresh, ed. 2005. *Reclaiming the local in language policy and practice.* London: Routledge.

Canagarajah, A. Suresh. 2007. Lingua franca English, multilingual communities, and language acquisition. *The Modern Language Journal* 91 (5): 923–939.

Centre–periphery model. 1998. *A dictionary of sociology,* ed. Gordon Marshall. 2nd edn. Oxford: Oxford University Press.

Chakravorty, Sanjoy. 2003. Urban development in the global periphery: The consequences of economic and ideological globalization. *Annals of Regional Science* 37: 357–367.

Coupland, Nikolas. 2003. Introduction: Sociolinguistics and globalisation. *Journal of Sociolinguistics* 7 (4): 465–472.

Coupland, Nikolas, ed. 2010. *Handbook of language and globalization.* Cambridge, Mass.: Blackwell Publishers.

Da Silva, Emmanuel, Mireille McLaughlin, and Mary Richards. 2006. Bilingualism and the globalized new economy: The commodification of language and identity. In *Bilingualism: A social approach,* ed. Monica Heller, 183–206. Basingstoke and New York: Palgrave Macmillan.

Deleuze, Gilles, and Felix Guattari. 1987. *A thousand plateaus.* Minneapolis: University of Minnesota Press.

De Swaan, Abram. 2001. *Words of the world: The global language system.* Cambridge: Polity Press.

Dor, Daniel. 2004. From englishization to imposed multilingualism: Globalization, the internet, and the political economy of the linguistic code. *Public Culture* 16 (1): 97–118.

Dufva, Hannele. 2004. Language, thinking and embodiment. In *Bakhtinian perspectives on language and culture: Meaning in language, art and new media,* ed. Finn Bostad, Craig Brandist, Lars Sigfred Evensen, and Hege Charlotte Faber, 133–146. Basingstoke: Palgrave Macmillan.

Dufva, Hannele. 2010. Reclaiming the mind: Dialogism, language learning and the importance of considering cognition. In *Proceedings of the Second International Interdisciplinary Conference on Perspectives and Limits of Dialogism in Mikhail Bakhtin,* June 3–5, 2009, ed. K. Junefelt and P. Nordin. Stockholm: University of Stockholm.

Fairclough, Norman. 2006. *Language and globalization* London: Routledge.

Freeland, Jane, and Donna Patrick, eds. 2004. *Language rights and language survival: Sociolinguistic and sociocultural perspectives.* Encounters Volume 4. Manchester and Northampton: St. Jerome Publishing.

Friedmann, John. 1966. *Regional development policy: A case study of Venezuela*. Cambridge, Mass.: MIT Press.

Gal, Susan. 2006. Contradictions of standard language in Europe: Implications for the study of publics and practices. *Social Anthropology* 14 (2): 163–181.

Gal, Susan, and Kathryn Woolard, eds. 2001. *Languages and publics: The making of authority*. Manchester: St. Jerome's Press.

García, Ofelia, Tove Skutnabb-Kangas, and María Torres Guzmán, eds. 2006. *Imagining multilingual schools: Languages in education and glocalization*. Series Linguistic Diversity and Language Rights. Clevedon: Multilingual Matters.

Goldfrank, Walter L. 2000. Paradigm regained? The rules of Wallerstein's world-system method. *Journal of World-Systems Research* 6 (2): 150–195.

Graburn, Nelson H. H., ed. 1976. *Ethnic and tourist arts: Cultural expressions from the Fourth World*. Berkeley, Los Angeles, and London: University of California Press.

Hall, Stuart. 1992. New ethnicities. In *'Race', culture and difference*, ed. James Donald and Ali Rattanansi, 252–260. London: Sage.

Harris, Roxy M. 2006. *New ethnicities and language use*. Basingstoke and New York: Palgrave-MacMillan.

Harris, Roy. 1981. *The language myth*. London: Duckworth.

Harris, Roy. 1996. *Signs, language and communication*. London: Routledge.

Hayter, Roger. 2003. The war in the woods: Globalization, post-Fordist restructuring and the contested remapping of British Columbia's forest economy. *Annals of the Association of American Geographers* 96: 706–729.

Heller, Monica. 1999. *Linguistic minorities and modernity: A sociolinguistic ethnography*. London: Longman.

Heller, Monica. 2003. Globalization, the new economy and the commodification of language and identity. *Journal of Sociolinguistics* 7 (4): 473–492.

Heller, Monica, ed. 2006. *Bilingualism: A social approach*. Houndsmills: Palgrave Macmillan.

Heller, Monica. 2011. *Paths to Post-nationalism: A critical ethnography of language and identity*. New York: Oxford University Press.

Heller, Monica, and Alexandre Duchêne. 2007. Discourses of endangerment: Sociolinguistics, globalisation and social order. In *Discourses of endangerment*, ed. Alexandre Duchene and Monica Heller, 1–13. London: Continuum.

Hill, Jane. H. 2002. Expert rhetorics in advocacy for endangered languages: Who is listening, and what do they hear? *Journal of Linguistic Anthropology* 12: 119–133.

Hymes, Dell. 1974. *Foundations of sociolinguistics: An ethnographic approach*. Philadelphia: University of Pennsylvania Press.

Irvine, Judith T., and Susan Gal. 2000. Language ideology and linguistic differentiation. In *Regimes of language: Ideologies, polities, and identities*, ed. Paul V. Kroskrity, 35–83. Santa Fe, New Mexico: School of American Research Press.

Jaffe, Alexandra. 1999. *Ideologies in action: Language politics on Corsica*. Berlin and New York: Mouton de Gruyter.

Jaffe, Alexandra. 2006. Minority language movements. In *Bilingualism: A social approach*, ed. Monica Heller, 50–70. Houndsmills: Palgrave Macmillan.

Jaffe, Alexandra. 2007. Discourses of endangerment: Contexts and consequences of essentializing discourses. In *Discourses of endangerment*, ed. A. Duchene and M. Heller, 57–75. London: Continuum.

Jaffe, Alexandra. 2009. The production and reproduction of language ideologies in practice. In *The new sociolinguistics reader*, ed. N. Coupland and A. Jaworski, 390–404. New York: Palgrave.

Jaworski, Adam, and Crispin Thurlow. 2010. Introducing semiotic landscapes. In *Semiotic landscapes: Language, image, space*, ed. Adam Jaworski and Crispin Thurlow, 1–40. London: Continuum.

Jenkins, Jenifer. 2007. *English as a lingua franca: Attitudes and identity*. Oxford: Oxford University Press.

Johnston, R. J., Derek Gregory, Geraldine Pratt, and Michael Watts, eds. 2000. *The dictionary of human geography*. 4th edn. Oxford: Blackwell Publishing.

Kachru, Braj. 1996. World Englishes: Agony and ecstasy. *Journal of Aesthetic Education* 30 (2): 135–155.

Kelly-Holmes, Helen, and Tomasso Milani. 2011. Thematising multilingualism in the media. *Special issue of Journal of Language and Politics* 10 (4): 467–489.

Kelly-Holmes, Helen, Máiréad Moriarty, and Sari Pietikäinen. 2009. Convergence and divergence in Basque, Irish and Sámi media language policing. *Language & Policy* 8: 227–242.

Kramsch, Claire. 2009. *The multilingual subject: What language learners say about their experience and why it matters*. Oxford: Oxford University Press.

Kroskrity, Paul V. ed. 2000. *Regimes of language: Ideologies, polities, and identities*. Santa Fe, New Mexico: School of American Research Press.

Kroskrity, Paul V. 2002. Language renewal and technologies of literacy and postliteracy: Reflections from Western Mono. In *Making dictionaries: Preserving Indigenous languages of the Americas*, ed. William Frawley, Kenneth C. Hill, and Pamela Munro, 171–192. Berkeley: University of California Press.

Lefebvre, Henri. 1974. *La production de l'espace*. Paris: Anthropos.

Lefebvre, Henri. 1991. *The production of space*. Oxford: Blackwell.

Lytra, Vally, and Peter Martin. 2010. *Sites of multilingualism: Complementary schools in Britain today*. Stoke on Trent: Trentham.

Mac Giolla Chríost, Diarmait. 2007. *Language and the city*. Basingstoke and New York: Palgrave Macmillan.

Makoni, Sinfree, and Alastair Pennycook. 2007. Disinventing and reconstituting languages. In *Disinventing and reconstituting languages*, ed. Sinfree Makoni and Alastair Pennycook, 1–41. Clevedon: Multilingual Matters.

May, Stephen. 2007. *Language and minority rights*. London and New York: Taylor and Francis.

McCulloch, Gary, and Ron Lowe. 2003. Introduction: Centre and periphery: Networks, space, and geography in the history of education. *History of Education* 32 (5): 457–459.

Meek, Barbra A. 2007. Respecting the language of elders: Ideological shift and linguistic discontinuity in a Northern Athapascan community. *Journal of Linguistic Anthropology* 17 (1): 23–43.

Moore, Robert E., Sari Pietikäinen, and Jan Blommaert. 2010. Counting the losses: Numbers as the language of language endangerment. *Sociolinguistic Studies* 4 (1): 1–26.

Nevins, M. Eleanor. 2004. Learning to listen: Confronting two meanings of language loss in the contemporary White Mountain Apache speech community. *Journal of Linguistic Anthropology* 14 (2): 269–288.

Ostler, Nicholas. 2010. *The last lingua franca: English until the return to Babel*. London: Allen Lane.

Park, Joseph S., and Lionel Wee. 2009. The three circle redux: A market-theoretic perspective on World Englishes. *Applied Linguistics* 30 (3): 389–506.

Pavlenko, Aneta, ed. 2005. *Languages and emotions in multilingual speakers*. Clevedon: Multilingual Matters.

Pennycook, Alastair. 2007. *Global Englishes and transcultural flows*. London: Routledge.

Pennycook, Alastair. 2010. *Language as a local practice*. London: Routledge.

Philips, Susan U. 2000. Constructing a Tongan nation-state through language ideology in the courtroom. In *Regimes of language: Ideologies, polities and identities*, ed. Paul V. Kroskrity, 229–257. Santa Fe, New Mexico: SAR Press.

Pietikäinen, Sari. 2010. Sámi language mobility: Scales and discourses of multilingualism in a polycentric environment. *International Journal of the Sociology of Language* 202: 79–102.

Pietikäinen, Sari, and Helen Kelly-Holmes. 2011. Gifting, service, and performance: Three eras in minority-language media policy and practice. *International Journal of Applied Linguistics* 21 (1): 51–70.

Pietikäinen, Sari, Riikka Alanen, Hannele Dufva, Paula Kalaja, Sirpa Leppänen, and Anne Pitkänen-Huhta. 2008. Languaging in Ultima Thule: Multilingualism in the life of a Sámi boy. *International Journal of Multilingualism* 5 (2): 79–99.

Potter, Rob. 2001. Geography and development: 'Centre and periphery'? *Area* 33 (4): 422–427.

Rampton, Ben. 2006. *Language in late modernity: Interaction in an urban school.* Cambridge: Cambridge University Press.

Schiffman, Harold. 1996. *Linguistic culture and language policy: The politics of language.* London and New York: Routledge.

Schubert, Torben, and Radhamany Sooryamoorthy. 2010. Can the centre-periphery model explain patterns of international scientific collaboration among threshold and industrialised countries? The case of South Africa and Germany. *Scientometrics* 83 (1): 181–203.

Scollon, Ron, and Suzie Wong Scollon. 2004. *Nexus analysis: Discourse and the emerging internet.* London and New York: Routledge.

Shohamy, Elena. 2006. *Language policy: Hidden agendas and new approaches.* London: Routledge.

Thurlow, Crispin, and Adam Jaworski. 2010. *Tourism discourse: Language and global mobility.* Basingstoke and New York: Palgrave-MacMillan.

Vanolo, Alberto. 2010. The border between centre and periphery: Geographical representations of the world system. *Tijdschrift voor economische en sociale geografie* 101 (1): 26–36.

Wallerstein, Immanuel. 1974. *The modern world-system*, Vol. I: *Capitalist agriculture and the origins of the European world-economy in the sixteenth century.* New York and London: Academic Press.

Wallerstein, Immanuel. 1980. *The modern world-system*, Vol. II: *Mercantilism and the consolidation of the European world-economy, 1600–1750.* New York: Academic Press.

Wallerstein, Immanuel. 2004. *World-systems analysis: An introduction.* Durham, North Carolina: Duke University Press.

Woolard, Kathryn A. 2004. Codeswitching. In *A companion to linguistic anthropology*, ed. Alessandro Duranti, 73–94. Malden, Mass.: Blackwell Publishers.

Wright, Sue. 2000. *Community and communication: The role of language in nation state building and European integration.* Clevedon: Multilingual Matters.

Wright, Sue, ed. 2004. Multilingualism and the Internet. *International Journal of Multicultural Societies* 6 (1). pp. 183.

Zarate, Geneviève, Danielle Levy, and Claire Kramsch, eds. 2008. *Précis du plurilinguisme et du pluriculturalisme.* Paris: Editions des Archives Contemporaines.

CHAPTER 2

Repositioning the Multilingual Periphery

Class, Language, and Transnational Markets in Francophone Canada

MONICA HELLER

CENTRE, PERIPHERY, MULTILINGUALISM, AND GLOBAL CAPITALISM

The main goal of this chapter is to examine the underpinnings of a relationship between the 'periphery' and 'multilingualism' which we sometimes take for granted. I will argue that both terms are constitutive of each other and emerge out of the ways in which linguistic and cultural homogeneity ('monolingualism', 'monoculturalism') became building blocks of the nation-state capitalist centre in the eighteenth and nineteenth centuries. The centre–periphery (monolingual–multilingual) relationship, already always fragile, has been further destabilized by continuing capitalist expansion, in the form of what we often think of as the globalized new economy. Imperialism, nationalism, colonialism, linguistic minority movements, post-colonialism, all have had their role to play in these processes.

In the first part of the chapter, I will explain what views of global capitalism underlie this analysis of the relationship between centre–periphery relations and of the role of language in them. I will then provide an account of the particular case of peripheral multilingualism I am most familiar with, that of Francophone Canada. As is often the case, the sequence is the reverse of the analytical process; it was in trying to understand the historical and contemporary shifts in discourses and practices of language, culture and nation in a discursive space I agree, conventionally, to call 'Francophone Canada' that I came to the explanatory frame with which I begin.

Moving from language to political economy, it became necessary to engage with the work of scholars addressing the broad processes which take specific forms in specific places at specific times.

In the 1970s, scholars such as Wallerstein (1974) and Hechter (1975) examined the emergence and growth of capitalism as a process of expansion (punctuated by retractions) beginning in Europe in the sixteenth century, and eventually inscribing regions around the world in what Wallerstein (1974) called the 'world-system' (see also Braudel 1949, a precursor). Their point of departure was that capitalism creates a relationship of centre and periphery, because centres, in order to maintain their position, depend on relationships with zones of production and transformation of natural resources, and accessible sources of labour. The centre–periphery relationship takes a particular shape, then, in capitalism and is in many ways inherent in it.

In this chapter, I will build on this notion to explore how this centre–periphery relationship got connected to nationalist ideologies of language, nation, and state, and to the construction of multilingual peripheries with devalued linguistic repertoires (as against the élite multilingualisms of the centre). I will then examine how that assemblage is repositioned under contemporary political economic conditions, with a focus on the case of Francophone Canada.[1] While not a canonical case of European nation-state centre–periphery relations or of classic colonial ones, Francophone Canada shares many of their features.

Specifically, I will explore the ways in which Francophone Canada was constituted as a source of labour in the Canadian economy, becoming the first element in what the sociologist John Porter would later call the 'vertical mosaic' (1965), concentrated in zones of primary resource extraction and industrial transformation which became Francophone Canada's 'bastions traditionnels'. I will show how this ethno-class position was linked to specific ideologies of language, culture, and nation which helped reproduce it, and in particular to a concentration of English-French bilingualism among the Francophone élite and among working-age male members of the working class (Lieberson 1970). I will then show how current economic conditions reproduce this pattern to some extent, while adding to it the newer notion of bilingualism as a commodifiable resource in its own right, as well as a means of access to transnational globalized networks. The so-called language industries, globalized multilingual service industries, and the revaluing of the authentic through tourism and *terroir*, all constitute new areas in which linguistic and cultural resources are revalued and redeployed.

Creating Difference

In order to understand this and other cases of shifting multilingual peripheries, it helps to situate them as products of the kind of global expansion of capital discussed by Wallerstein, Braudel, and others (cf. e.g. Wolf 1982) in which the bourgeois, liberal democratic nation-state has played a key role. The nineteenth and twentieth centuries can be understood as the core moment of development of that political and economic formation: the nation-state was invented in the interests of construction of centralized national markets and their (internal and external) colonial peripheries (Hobsbawm 1990). This is the period of homogenization and standardization of language and culture as part of the process of making boundaries (Barth 1969) and making citizens. However, this process also involved the production of peripheries, both within newly constructed nation-states and with respect to Europe as a whole (Hechter 1975).

The legitimization of that process, Hechter argued, hinged on the production of social difference. While this process is familiar to students of empire, Hechter argues that a similar analysis applies to the Celtic fringe of Britain, and, by extension, to other similarly constituted peripheries. Constructing inhabitants of peripheries as (less competent) others helps justify the exploitation of their land and of their labour. Williams (1973) adds that the specific opposition of the country and the city, which contrasted the civilized but corrupt world of the national urban centre with the backward but pure and natural world of the rural periphery, helped bolster Romantic nationalist claims to territory and nationhood while legitimizing the marginalization of the areas (and social actors) at the heart of the nation-state's legitimizing authenticity.

In other words, the centralizing, standardizing, homogenizing nation-state actively (and necessarily) produces ethnolinguistic and ethnocultural difference as part of the legitimization of its core political economy. It draws not only on the dichotomies of Romantic nationalism described by Williams but also on their hierarchization within modernist models of linear progress, and scientific models of linear evolution, setting up the modern centre as more progressive and more developed. It draws also on Enlightenment theories about rationality, linking reason to liberal democracy and capitalism, and hence to citizenship and wealth.

However, as Bauman and Briggs (2003) show, despite the redistributive promises of the French Revolution, the masculine bourgeoisie resisted the full implications of 'égalité', using judgments of rationality to construct differential distribution and divisions of labour along gender, class, and ethno-racial lines. Women, the working class, subjects of internal and external colonialism, even the male bourgeois citizens of other nation-states, were constructed as flighty, emotional, weak-willed, corruptible, or otherwise incapable of the rational thought and behaviour required of modern citizens (see also Outram 1987). We can also think about this as a productive Foucauldian process, in which discursive processes of feminization, sexualization, and racialization are attached to categorization (difference-making) and stratification (inequality-making), and used to position specific bodies in specific ways.

Such differences and inequalities are made discursively on a variety of cultural terrains, involving a range of forms of semiosis: how you dress, where you live, what you eat, how you talk are all ways of making difference and distinction (Bourdieu 1979). Still, as we know, standardizing language in particular was a powerful way of making nation-states, given the way it combines both centralizing and uniformizing possibilities, and simultaneously allows for the masking of the privilege and power inherent in making decisions about what counts as a (proper) language, and what does not; it is possible to argue that language is learnable, and hence perfectly democratic (Higonnet 1980; Bauman and Briggs 2003). The rational procedures of science were applied to the project of linguistic standardization and boundary-making, in the process showing that some languages could be understood as more rational than others, and hence better adapted to the nation-building endeavours of capitalist democracy (Hutton 1999; Errington 2008).

The ideal model, then, was of a polity of speakers of uniformized, standardized languages; monolingualism became the norm and communication across language boundaries the exception to be managed by specialized actors (translators and interpreters) or a privileged élite capable of a multilingualism which remains our ideal today, consisting of multiple monolingualisms, that is, the ability to perform as a monolingual speaker in more than one language, with no traces of the boundary-crossing or multiple networks that multilingualism entails in practice (Heller 2007). Any other form of linguistic diversity was then constructible as irrational and contaminated (or contaminating) (Tabouret-Keller 1988).

Linguistic and cultural differences form resources for the construction of centre–periphery relations, whether understood as standard vs. vernacular, or dominant vs. dominated ethnolinguistic and ethnocultural groups. These hierarchized differences served in particular for the inscription of certain kinds of (speaking) bodies in certain kinds of economic activities. They also produced language and culture as terrains of struggle, notably over what counts as legitimate language and who counts as legitimate speakers (Bourdieu 1982). They construct bilingualism as a key mode of articulation not only among national élites (as discussed above) but also between centre and periphery. Typically, in this modern industrial regime, the burden of peripheral-vernacular vs. central-standard bilingualism falls to a class of bilingual brokers drawn from among the ranks of the marginalized or from another group altogether (Barth 1969).

In many ways, the very notion of multilingualism, and its specific forms of distribution and evaluation (who is understood to be multilingual and who is not, how one ends up being positioned as likely to become multilingual or not, who has an interest in multilingualism and who does not, what forms of multilingualism are considered of value and what forms are not) are a product of the political economy which produced centre–periphery relations, and indeed form a constitutive dimension of that process and its reproduction. Even the periphery's resistance to its peripheralization has followed the logic of nation-state markets, simply arguing that it can be understood in exactly the same terms as the centre and should constitute a new one (producing thereby its own, new, peripheries): the decolonizing and linguistic minority movements seeking emancipation from centralized states or empires have sought to establish themselves exactly in the image of their oppressors, standardizing their languages, establishing their territorial boundaries, and constructing their markets. We can think of any of the linguistic minority movements of Western Europe in these terms (Wales, Scotland, Brittany, Corsica), and the same is true, for example, of Quebec (Grillo 1989; McDonald 1989; Urla 1993; Heller 2011). Having been constituted as internal colonies in a centre–periphery relationship (Hechter 1975), such regions adopted and adapted the logic of the nation-state to establish themselves as new centres under regional control. The logic of the nation-state is simply reproduced, creating new standards and new variabilities, new legitimate languages and new stigmatized varieties.

MULTILINGUALISM IN LATE CAPITALISM

However, the continued expansion of capital, and the high modern emergence of the tertiary sector, or what we often think of as the globalized new economy, has shifted the position of multilingual peripheries in some ways, although not in others. Peripheries continue to occupy marginal territory in the globalized new economy, but the value of their marginality has changed. New minority elites mobilize the bilingualism that was once the hallmark of oppression in attempts to reposition the value of their cultural capital, in economic conditions which newly value it. Nonetheless, old tensions between standard and vernacular, and between elite and vernacular forms of bilingualism in particular, remain important grounds for the working out of attempts to reposition linguistic capital and its holders in contemporary transnational markets. In this section, I will briefly review one analysis of the role of language in late capitalism which is based on a number of studies of the nature of globalization itself; this analysis holds that language has become more salient in economic processes in the globalized new economy (see Heller and Duchêne 2011 for an extended version of this argument). Regarding globalization I draw notably on Harvey (1989), Giddens (1990), Castells (2000), and Inda and Rosaldo (2008); regarding the role of language in general and multilingualism in particular in the globalized new economy, I draw on recent ethnographies of the shifting multilingualisms of the periphery (see e.g. contributions to Tan and Rubdy 2008 and to Duchêne and Heller 2011, or studies reviewed in Heller 2010).

The argument rests on the premise that our contemporary era is characterized more by continuity than by rupture, albeit in ways which destabilize our taken-for-granted assumptions about language, identity, culture, nation, and state. The expansion of capital set in motion around the sixteenth century is still the central feature of our political economy; however, the late twentieth century and early twenty-first constitute a moment of reorganization of the relationship between capital and governance, between the economic and the political. National markets and industrial products are insufficient to allow for continued expansion, and for the increasing saturation of markets. The result has been a re-positioning of the state, from what we have known as the welfare state to what we call the neoliberal one, that is, one in which the state is clearer about its role in the support of global expansion of capital, and in which, as a result, political discourses are subordinated to economic ones (Fairclough 2006).

Language, in general, and multilingualism, in particular, become more salient for a number of reasons.

- The saturation of markets leads to an increased emphasis on niche markets and on niche products or products with added value. One way of developing added value is through symbolic means, such as discursive ones. Among the semiotic material available for making distinctions, we are able to mobilize the existing distinctions of the nation-state among recognized varieties or identities, and the value accorded to their authenticity. We see this process at work clearly in industries like tourism (see Coupland, this volume; Pietikäinen, this volume; Pujolar, this volume), but also in the global circulation of 'authentic' goods, and even in their hybridization in forms of popular culture such as hip-hop (Pennycook 2003).
- The management of globalized chains of production and consumption, including of the circulation of niche products and consumers, requires increased reliance on communication and mobilization of diverse linguistic resources, both for reaching the social actors involved and for branding the products from label to service.
- Increased competition is also linked to an emphasis on flexibility, whether for sourcing material resources, human resources, or new markets, with a concomitant value placed on the ability to mobilize diverse linguistic resources. In addition, older sources of primary resources and labour among internal colonies are replaced by economic neo-colonies, which also increasingly ensure management services; simultaneously, the centre relies increasingly on intensified circulation of human resources.

These processes destabilize the existing nation-state linguistic regime without destroying it. Peripheries find themselves in need of economic restructuring, since the primary and secondary sectors on which their reproduction relied have been relocated. Their populations can then either try to find new frontiers of primary resource extraction in which to exercise their skills or reinvent themselves within the context of the tertiary sector. As zones of both authenticity and multilingualism, former peripheries have much to offer in the new circumstances, both in terms of cultural and linguistic goods, and in terms of useful communicative resources. They may also find themselves repositioned with respect to old centres and peripheries more interested in (or required to) participate in global networks and processes than national ones. The linguistic resources of the periphery are reframed in the new linguistic markets and their value called into question. Indeed, the close relationship between nation-state and empire peripheralness and peripheral and élite multilingualism comes under scrutiny.

In the next section, I will take a closer look at how those processes are unfolding in a social space I will refer to as 'Francophone Canada', a space whose discursive and political economic development I have been following for some time, and which usefully blends a variety of positions as periphery and centre in its history and its contemporary transformations.

FRANCOPHONE CANADA: REPOSITIONING A MULTILINGUAL PERIPHERY

From Colonizer to Colonized

Francophone Canada has a complicated history connected to both forms of colonialism, empire and nation-state. It was initially established as New France, a clear form of European imperialism in which the colony was set up through the differentiation, exploitation, and erasure of the indigenous population, whom the French either harnessed to the production of the primary sources the metropole sought (furs in this instance) or removed to allow for unrestricted appropriation of territory (Wolf 1982). It also served as a place to send France's own surplus population.

The colonial construction of the indigenous Other has been well-documented (Irvine and Gal 2000; Errington 2008; Hanks 2010) and does not seem to have taken a radically different form in New France. Missionaries were charged with civilizing the 'savages' through conversion, which entailed the usual complex relationship between European acquisition of indigenous languages as a means to bring the word of God to the 'Indians', and the teaching of French to them as a means of bringing them the language of civilization. The fur trade also had its bilingual brokers, sometimes drawn from the aboriginal population, but also often from the fringes of the settlers, who acted as brokers between the indigenous suppliers of furs and their European managers and buyers. These became mythic figures, the *coureurs des bois* (literally, runners of the woods), close to nature, and, in the popular imagination, freer from British (or clerical) domination than those who lived more settled lives.

This relationship was complicated by the loss of New France to Britain in two stages, in 1713 and 1763, as a result of treaties ending two of the many wars among imperial powers which marked the eighteenth century. The French became both colonizer and colonized, their expertise useful in brokering fur production with the indigenous population, their settlement of the land problematic when desired for British uses, but useful as a stand-in claim to territory. Their political allegiance was always suspect, especially given the strong anchoring of the rivalry between Britain and France in struggles over their own territories, and subsequently in struggles for power in Europe and in imperial expansion. The difference, indeed the oppositional categorization, was part of the discursive landscape. And yet, coexistence on the northern fringes of North America was also an option, given initial lack of investment in British colonization, and the relatively larger numbers of Francophones, with useful knowledge and potentially useful bodies, who stayed behind when their leaders went back to France.

The resulting ambivalent relationship led to a variety of strategies over the years. The most dramatic example is the expulsion of the (originally French) Acadians of the Annapolis Valley (in what is now the Atlantic province of Nova Scotia) in 1755, after Acadians refused to swear allegiance to the British Crown, and British settlers began to eye their land. At the other extreme, we find the later declaration of the colonial governor, who published a report in 1838 arguing for the assimilation of Francophones into the civilized British population. In between, we find Francophones participating in brokering with the aboriginal population, in settling their land, and increasingly providing labour in new areas of primary resource extraction (especially lumber, fish, and minerals) and their industrial transformation, as well as, by the end of the nineteenth century, in the growing manufacturing industry.

Despite the fact that Francophones have historically been concentrated in the St. Lawrence River valley, the heart of New France, Francophone settlements have had a more complicated relationship to space, and particularly to that form of boundable space which is amenable to being produced as a national place. To begin with, Canada's nationability was in any case subordinated to its status as British colony. Second, it was a colony with a frontier, which Francophones helped to exploit as labour and to settle, albeit from the late nineteenth century onwards as only one of many racialized or ethnicized groups, along with immigrants (though people, including aboriginals, tended to become white Anglophones if they passed into a more central social position). Third, the Francophone professional and clerical elite worked to produce a Francophone nationalism constructed in opposition to the capitalist values of the British rulers; complicit in the Williamsian dichotomization of country and city, they produced a discourse of spiritual nationalism, tied to nature, and more specifically to the North, understood as a frontier in which autarky would be possible (Morissonneau 1978). Francophones moved west and north, as Canada's economic reach extended, both in the search for new sources of wealth and for the means to extract, transport, and secure access to it by building infrastructure and occupying the territory. At the same time, with this development, the dream of rural autarky stood in starker and starker contrast to the involvement of Francophone labour in resource extraction and processing industries, infrastructure building, and, eventually, in urban factories.

The peripheralization of Francophone Canada thus began in stages, embedded first in a complex colonial relationship which set up Francophones as peripheral participants in British-controlled exploitation of natural resources, and pawns in imperial and post-imperial struggles over the control of North America (first with France, then with what became the United States), then largely as labour in primary resource extraction and industry. This position was achieved in part through the organization of relations of power between Anglophone rulers (and owners) and Francophone labour through the Francophone elite, drawn from the ranks of the clergy and the liberal professions (which were in any case constituted via Church-run education). When Francophone Canada was not actually constituted in geographically peripheral spaces, it was constituted in socially peripheral ones.

Multilingualism is, obviously, one key to understanding the dynamics of the articulation between centre and periphery, an articulation, I hope to have shown, constitutive of the interdependence of centre–periphery relations. There are many different ways in which linguistic difference can be used to dominate or resist domination; in this case, the British dominated (and Anglophones in Canada still dominate) by remaining largely monolingual. If you want to speak to them, you have to learn their language, and since they control both the political and economic realms, speaking to them is difficult to avoid. Just as *coureurs des bois* were useful for their knowledge of indigenous languages, the work of learning English, the burden of bilingualism, fell largely to their Francophone descendants (along, of course, with Canada's other minorities). Of course, there are exceptions to this pattern, with some knowledge of (European) French among the English-speaking élite, and some managerial tasks involving some version of Canadian French. And, in fact, most Francophones were not individually bilingual, leaving the work of brokerage, or articulation, up to their own élite. However, in fact, we possess little knowledge of the patterns of bi- or multilingualism in the eighteenth and early nineteenth century, in part because categorization was largely understood as primarily an issue of race, secondarily of religion, and only partly of language (Heller and Labrie 2003). Our interest in language is more recent (for reasons I will explore further below) and dominated by contemporary or future-oriented concerns (although some work on the Austro-Hungarian Empire, the French Revolution, and on the work of missionaries in colonial Africa and America provides helpful models of how we might better attend to history; cf. e.g. Higonnet 1980; Fabian 1986; Branca-Rosoff 1994; Rindler-Schjerve 2003; Errington 2008; Gal 2011).

Still, it seems clear that industrialization and urbanization created a new boundary of articulation within worksites, between Francophone labour, labour recruited from other (immigrant) groups, and Anglophone management and ownership. This is a different form of peripheralization that accompanies a growing sense of Canada as less of a colony and more of a country, and ties Francophones in a different way to the world economy.

From Colonized Race to Peripheral Citizen

Through the course of the nineteenth century, the Canadian economy focused less and less on furs (although they still figure marginally in the Canadian economy to this day), and more and more on other forms of primary resource extraction, the transformation of those resources, and other forms of manufacturing. In some cases, these activities took place in the rural areas long imagined as the redoubt of Frenchness, as Francophones became increasingly involved in the lumber industry and in mining. The mythical figures of the *coureur des bois* and the *habitant* (peasant), or the fisherman on the high seas, were joined by the *bûcheron* (lumberjack) and the *draveur* (responsible for getting the logs down rivers to the mills), although not, it must be said, by the equally present mill worker, fish plant worker, or their eventual colleague, the miner. (The mythical female figure was, predictably, a bearer of children or a celibate devoted to the people, cf. Pujolar, this volume.)

But even with a diversifying economy, the particular functioning of agriculture in rural areas produced surplus labour (Ramirez 1991), and developing urban industrialization needed workers. The late nineteenth and early twentieth centuries saw a major population movement not only from east to west and north but also from rural to urban areas, both in Canada and in the United States. In both countries, ethnolinguistic difference was used as an organizing principle to legitimize the restriction of Francophone and immigrant groups to the ranks of the working class, and simultaneously to prevent the development of class consciousness and solidarity.

This period is also the period of the consolidation of the United States and of Canadian independence (1867), although Canada continued to act as part of the British Empire (more specifically, a 'Dominion' thereof). Politically and economically, Canada began to organize itself as a central producer, not a colonial provider of raw materials to the metropole, although its economy remained (and in many ways today still remains) based on primary resources. The economy was dependent on capital investment and control by Anglophone owners, who recruited workers first from the available Francophone population, and then, increasingly, through immigration.

Typically, Anglophone (and usually Protestant) owners and managers were residentially segregated from the (usually Catholic) workers, living to the west (and upwind) of their factories, or on higher ground. The workers lived closer to their workplaces, often in neighbourhoods organized around their places of worship (usually Catholic), and ethnolinguistically separated from each other, if not in separate towns altogether. (Welland, Ontario, for example, still bears the traces of French Canadian, Italian, Hungarian, Polish, and Croatian working-class neighbourhoods, while Woonsocket, Rhode Island, is largely populated by the descendants of French Canadians, who replaced more expensive Americans in the textile mill.)

Lieberson (1970) points to the actual workers as sites of bilingualism in post-war Montreal; my own work in a Montreal factory in the late 1970s identified a small group of bilingual Irish-origin superintendents as the sites of articulation between Francophone labour (whom they oversaw) and Anglophone management (Heller 2011). Laid-off male workers in Welland, Ontario, in the 1990s, however, described to us how they made friends with their Italian or Polish co-workers, joshing with them in English, or trading a few words in each other's languages, though they sat at separate tables in the cafeteria, went home to different neighbourhoods, and belonged to different sections of the Catholic service organization the Knights of Columbus, attached to different churches. Still today, construction workers on oil sands sites in Northern Alberta describe how they are forced to learn English 'on the fly' when they start to work under Anglophone foremen and with Anglophone co-workers, but how workers wear Acadian, Newfoundland, or Nova Scotia flags on their hard hats and congregate in homogeneous groups in the eating and sleeping areas of the camps. Nonetheless, it is the ones who learn English the best (or the fastest), who are granted supervisory capacity over their more monolingual fellow workers, or who simply emerge as leaders of their group when it comes time for talking to Anglophone others. In no case is it the monolingual Anglophones who need to learn French (or any other language, for that matter).

This is one dimension of the constitution and reproduction of the vertical mosaic described by Porter (1965), and more specifically of the economic peripheralization of Francophones in Canadian and American industrial capitalism. Language is still not the most salient characteristic of the social categorization in operation (people understand themselves still to some extent in racial terms, or at least in ethnocultural ones), but it remains an important element. More importantly for our purposes here, however, it is the distribution of multilingualism among the population (restricted to active workers, sometimes to specific ranks responsible for relations between workers and managers), and in the lives of individual bilinguals (restricted to their lives as workers), which helps explain both how multilingualism worked and works in the constitution and reproduction of the periphery, and why it is there that we find it, under conditions of industrial modernity.

From Periphery to Centre

Those same conditions underlie the modes of resistance to peripheralization which have been discursively available. The constitution of the idea of the homogeneous nation as normal and normative, and of the national as the principle of social organization, rendered the idea of the 'nation' available as a means to dominate, and therefore also as a means to resist. As I noted earlier, initially the idea of 'nation' was mobilized by the Francophone élite to resist British domination, not in the form of a liberal democratic nation-state, but rather as a spiritual, organic body, a nation in the Herderian sense. Nonetheless, the mobilization of this concept in order to justify a nation-state became quickly available; while not dominant during the nineteenth and much of the twentieth centuries (for reasons having to do with the suppression of state-building liberal democratic movements in the early nineteenth-century British colony, the hegemony of Anglophone interests in the emerging Canadian state in the late nineteenth century, and the conservative politics of the Catholic Church), it did circulate.

It was not, however, until the mid-twentieth century that the idea was able to gain some purchase. There are a number of reasons for this, largely having to do with the growth of wealth in the post-war period, Cold War interest in the far North, and economic expansion in the North and West, all of which drew the Anglophone élite away from the centre of traditional Francophone bastions and produced greater access to wealth for Francophones themselves. There was room for some movement, and resources to accomplish it.

The idea of the nation was available as a means for leveraging such social mobility, in Canada as elsewhere. What needed undoing was the idea of pan-Canadian solidarity among Francophones, while the more general movement of decolonization and nation-building of the 1960s provided an alternative model. The linguistic minorities of First World states proclaimed solidarity with European colonies seeking freedom and used the template of the nation-state to argue for the legitimacy of new ones, distinct and liberated from their former centres (think of Brittany, Corsica, Catalunya, Wales, Scotland, Friesland). In the specific case of Francophone Canada, as is well-known, the proposal has been to constitute Quebec as a Francophone state, independent from Canada, as a means to attend better to Francophones whose linguistic difference has been used to justify their exploitation and marginalization, and to safeguard the nation understood to constitute the foundation of that difference. Francophones elsewhere in Canada (indeed, in North America) are invited to join the Québécois nation, or, possibly, attempt to follow the Quebec model and constitute a nation-state of their own.

The mobilization of this model, of course, reproduces all of its effects. Far from destabilizing the centre–periphery relationship, it merely displaces it. Francophone Quebec becomes a new centre, with its own periphery, albeit one shared uncomfortably with the Canadian state to which Quebec remains tied. Quebec's construction of itself as a centre is seen in its economic relations, for example, in its exploitation of the natural resources of the indigenous-inhabited North (notably in hydroelectricity; for example, one of the first acts of the nationalist government of the 1960s was the nationalization of that industry); in its political relations (e.g. increased control over immigration, the gaining of representation on key international bodies such as la Francophonie, the establishment of a foreign policy and overseas Délégations du Quebec, internal legislation on language and citizenship); and in its cultural and linguistic ones (the establishment of language planning agencies, national media, education policies)—in short, all the usual strategies of nation-building. The periphery is thus not only the resource-rich North but also the rest of Francophone North America, and populations and practices whose difference makes them available as Other, and as marginalizable in social, economic and political terms. Indeed, this effect has been deeply problematic for Quebec, as it tries to legitimize the Québécois centre as a liberal, democratic state attentive to difference and marginalization because of its own history.

For the issue that concerns us here, we can see how centrification changes the value placed on multilingualism. Quebec has been explicitly constituted as a monolingual state, insofar as the 1977 Charter of the French Language proclaimed French the only official language of the province and defined measures to make it the dominant, and in some cases only required, language of key domains. Multilingualism is valuable in so far as it does not destabilize monolingual domains or individuals and reproduces the dominant ideology of whole bounded systems in contained contact one with the other. The vernacular which serves as an emblem of the marginalized and oppressed status of Francophones is devalued and understood to require correction (although, of course, it also legitimizes the authenticity of the nation, landing Quebec in the same contradiction between authenticity and authority which has long dogged nation-states). Particularly problematic, of course, is the way in which that vernacular bears traces of contact with English. And of particular concern has been the effort to shift what has been understood as the burden of bilingualism, asking non-Francophones to learn French, and freeing Francophones from the obligation to learn English.

However, it is not only the contradictions of the modern nation-state which make it difficult for Quebec to claim its legitimacy. The political economic shifts of the last part of the twentieth century, and the early part of this one, have made it difficult to sustain the work of making homogeneity out of diversity and of keeping peripheries in their place. In the next section, I will consider some of the ways in which these shifts call into question what the centre–periphery relationship is about, where it lies, and what the role of linguistic diversity is in producing and reproducing it.

Repositioning the Periphery: Late Capitalism and the Globalized New Economy

The restructurings of late capitalism have repositioned centre and periphery in some interesting ways. Off-shoring production has left former centres in search of new economic bases, for the most part anchored in the tertiary (symbolic) sector. At the same time, the management of global capital itself shifts, leaving former centres sometimes managed, or at least serviced, from afar (think of the complex ways in which Indian call centres relate to clients in Britain and the United States; cf. Sonntag 2006; Cowie 2007). The saturation of markets places an emphasis on the development of niche markets and products with added value, both of which are constructed largely through capital of distinction (Bourdieu 1979).

Multilingualism becomes important as a means of articulating global chains of consumption and production, and as a source of production and management of capital of distinction. In particular, both the old standardized variety and the messier vernacular variety are called into play; the first facilitates the (sometimes desperate) attempts to Taylorize the globalized new economy (whose communicative activities are somewhat less amenable to Taylorization than manual or mechanical labour), while the second harnesses the vernacular indexing of authenticity as a source of added value (as against industrially produced goods and services).

The monolingualizing constructions of the centre and periphery in Francophone Canada encounter these tensions in particular ways. First, the objective of centrification was always to allow Francophones full access to modernity, but as Francophones (that is, without having to pass as Anglophones). While the Canadian economy was always dependent on international, and in particular English-speaking, markets, Francophone Canada attempted to develop international Francophone relations based on old relations of empire. It has become, however, increasingly difficult to avoid English, not only because of older economic networks and relations but also because English has become the major lingua franca of late capitalism (Melchers and Shaw 2003; Rubdy and Saraceni 2006; Pennycook 2007). English thus now indexes both older relations of colonialist inequality and new forms of access to the global economy.

This has triggered fierce debate within Quebec regarding access to English, notably through schooling and post-secondary education: on one side, we find the proponents of construction and maintenance of Francophone monolingual institutions of socialization (linked to a modernist nationalist view of education as an institution for producing citizens), who argue that learning English is at best a private affair and not the responsibility of the state; and on the other, we find the proponents of increasing English instruction in school or easing access to English-language educational institutions (linked to a neoliberal view of education as an institution for facilitating individual success). Recently, Quebec has seen both attempts to require certain segments of the population to attend not only elementary and secondary school in French but also post-secondary colleges should they continue their education (not universities, however). At the same time, the provincial government has promoted the introduction of intensive ('immersion'-type) English instruction in Grade 6 in French-language schools (that is, for students who are typically 11 to 12 years old). In addition, in Quebec as elsewhere, there has been a rise in interest in other languages, notably Spanish, understood as a gateway to Latin America.

In other parts of Francophone Canada, the French-English bilingualism which was a hallmark of peripheralness (and inferiority) has now become a distinct advantage, facilitating access to both Anglophone and Francophone global networks. The lack of ability to claim territorial boundaries or rootedness has turned into the possibility for claiming mobile, global citizenship. This is most striking in the case of 'Acadie'. The 1755 Deportation of Acadians from what became Nova Scotia to various parts of North America, the Caribbean, and Europe was long constructed as the tragic fragmentation of a beautiful, bucolic national dream (and used as such to politically mobilize Acadians in laying claims to national, including territorial, rights). Not being able to lay claim to a heartland or bastion was a problem to be overcome. The diaspora has now also laid the basis for the construction of a sense of global *acadianité*, facilitating the mobility of people and of cultural products, and legitimizing new Acadian claims to being authentic global citizens, that is, true citizens of the world.

The arrival of Francophones from outside Canada, which has been part of the global circulation of skilled labour, has also been experienced in two, contradictory ways. On the one hand, it is understood as a potential threat to the reproduction of the authentic nation, while on the other, it is seen as a passport to globalization. By incorporating immigrants into Francophone institutions and social networks, Francophone Canadians can appropriate the global ties those immigrants bring with them.

It is important to emphasize that the older idea of the authentic nation remains potent not only because of existing investments in that particular discursive formation and its attendant markets but also because of the new conditions which retain and recast its value. As capital of distinction it is mobilized in many of the new economic sectors which both former centres and former peripheries can (indeed, must) develop. Notable among these are tourism and the development of *produits du terroir* (Le Menestrel 1999; Barham 2007), marketable commodities whose difference is based on the authenticity of local production (bearing the characteristics of the particular corner of the earth from which they sprang, and which by definition is unique; for obvious reasons, this is often used for branding food products). One of the ways in which products can be authentified is through the use of the very vernaculars which were long associated with the organic nation, while also stigmatized as indices of the backwardness of the nation's pre-modern wanderings in the dark (see e.g. Le Menestrel 1999; Coupland, Garrett, and Bishop 2005; Bunten 2008; Comaroff and Comaroff 2009). That tension too remains, as Taylorizable sectors such as call centres (see Cameron 2001; Sonntag 2006; Cowie 2007; Boutet 2008; Duchêne 2009), or even the management of multiple clients and providers in sectors such as tourism, exert pressure to conform to modernist modes of multilingualism (each variety in the repertoire understood to be a separate standard), while authentification depends on the vernacular. We see this tension, for example, in negotiations over linguistic choices in the production or delivery of tourist products in the context of heritage tourism (French and English? French only? Which French? See Heller 2011: 136–138.).

Perhaps most importantly, the periphery becomes a source of added value, albeit as a kind of commodified periphery. It even becomes transportable as such, whether through Acadian-type diasporic claims to global citizenship, travel, and tourism or through the circulation of cultural goods on world circuits (e.g. of music, art, crafts, or food: see McLaughlin, this volume). Centres equally become mobile, attached less to territory than to capital.

For Francophone Canada, the moment of centrification seems to have been lost. Instead, late capitalism commodifies its identity, potentially reshaping the subjectivity of its members and its relationship to language and culture. The formerly hegemonic linkages among uniformized languages, cultures, spaces, and identities, with their legitimizing historical narratives, have not disappeared, but it has become more difficult to experience them as hegemonic, and therefore natural. Partly this is because of their commodification, but it is also due to the increasing mobility and dispersion of the centre–periphery relations of industrial capitalism.

CONCLUSION

This may be the most salient thing about the changes underway: they ask us to think again about what it means to invest (even believe) in the social categories which we have long used to organize ourselves and our relation to the world, notably to the resources we value and to the ways we regulate their production and distribution. I will not be so bold as to try to predict how things will unfold; rather, my aim here has been to sketch out the importance of understanding how what we think of as 'multilingualism' is inextricably tied to the specific political economic conditions of our times, and those times are stretching our imagination to its limits.

We certainly need to stop understanding multilingualism as an observable fact, and see it instead as a construct produced by specific ideologies linking ideas about language to ideas about how to make differences harnessable to producing unequal positions in relations of power (Irvine and Gal 2000). Its shapes and their value are tied to the position of social actors in particular regimes of production, that is, in particular markets, spatialized in what are now increasingly fragmented relations of centre and periphery.

It is usually the case that relations of power are seen most clearly from a position of relative disadvantage; as Bourdieu pointed out, the dominant have a vested interest in not seeing how they dominate (Bourdieu 1982), although I would add that that may be particularly true in liberal democracies legitimized by ideologies of equality and meritocracy. The periphery thus affords us a privileged vantage point on processes that affect us all.

NOTES

1. The research on which this chapter is based was funded by the Social Sciences and Humanities Research Council of Canada and the Wenner-Gren Foundation for Anthropological Research. I am grateful for their support, and for the many things I have learned from both project participants (who must remain nameless here) and the other members of the research team: Gabriel Asselin, Maurice Beaudin, Lindsay Bell, Michelle Daveluy, Mireille McLaughlin, and Hubert Noël. I am, of course, solely responsible for errors.

REFERENCES

Barham, Elizabeth. 2007. The lamb that roared: Origin-labelled products and place-making strategy in Charlevoix, Quebec. In *Remaking the North American food system: Strategies for sustainability*, ed. C. Clare Hinrichs and Thomas Lyson, 277–297. Lincoln: University of Nebraska Press.

Barth, Fredrik, ed. 1969. *Ethnic groups and boundaries*. Boston: Little, Brown.

Bauman, Richard, and Charles Briggs. 2003. *Voices of modernity*. Cambridge: Cambridge University Press.

Bourdieu, Pierre. 1979. *La Distinction: Critique sociale du jugement*. Paris: Minuit.

Bourdieu, Pierre. 1982. *Ce que parler veut dire*. Paris: Fayard.

Boutet, Josiane. 2008. *La Vie verbale au travail: Des manufactures aux centres d'appels*. Toulouse: Octares.

Branca-Rosoff, Sonia. 1994. *L'Écriture des citoyens: Une analyse linguistique de l'écriture des peu-lettrés pendant la période révolutionnaire*. Paris: Klincksieck.

Braudel, Fernand. 1949. *La Méditerrannée et le monde méditerrannéen à l'époque de Philippe II*. Paris: Colin.

Bunten, Alexis Celeste. 2008. Sharing culture or selling out? Developing the commodified persona in the heritage industry. *American Ethnologist* 35 (3): 380–395.

Cameron, Deborah. 2001. *Good to talk?* London: Sage.

Castells, Miguel. 2000. *The Information Age: Economy, society and culture*. Oxford: Blackwell.

Comaroff, John, and Jean Comaroff. 2009. *Ethnicity Inc*. Chicago: University of Chicago Press.

Coupland, Nik, Peter Garrett, and Hywel Bishop. 2005. Wales underground: Discursive frames and authenticities in Welsh mining heritage tourism events. In *Discourse, communication and tourism*, ed. Adam Jaworski and Annette Pritchard, 199–222. Clevedon: Channel View Publications.

Cowie, Claire. 2007. The accents of outsourcing: The meanings of 'neutral' in the Indian call centre industry. *World Englishes* 26 (3): 316–330.

Duchêne, Alexandre. 2009. Marketing, management and performance: Multilingualism as commodity in a tourism call center. *Language Policy* 8 (1): 27–50.

Duchêne, Alexandre, and Monica Heller, eds. 2011. *Language in late capitalism: Pride and profit*. London: Routledge.

Errington, Joseph. 2008. *Linguistics in a colonial world: A story of language, meaning and power*. Oxford: Blackwell.

Fabian, Johannes. 1986. *Language and colonial power*. Berkeley, Los Angeles: University of California Press.

Fairclough, Norman. 2006. *Language and globalization*. London: Routledge.

Gal, Susan. 2011. Polyglot nationalism: Alternative perspectives on language in 19th Century Hungary. *Langage et Société* 136: 31–54.

Giddens, Anthony. 1990. *The consequences of modernity*. Stanford, Calif.: Stanford University Press.

Grillo, Ralph. 1989. *Dominant languages*. Cambridge: Cambridge University Press.

Hanks, William. 2010. *Converting words: Maya in the Age of the Cross*. Berkeley, Los Angeles: University of California Press.

Harvey, David. 1989. *The condition of postmodernity*. Oxford: Blackwell.

Hechter, Michael. 1975. *Internal colonialism: The Celtic fringe in British national development, 1536–1966*. Berkeley, Los Angeles: University of California Press.

Heller, Monica, ed. 2007. *Bilingualism: A social approach*. London: Palgrave.

Heller, Monica. 2010. The commodification of language. *Annual Review of Anthropology* 39: 101–114.

Heller, Monica. 2011. *Paths to postnationalism: A critical ethnography of language and identity*. Oxford: Oxford University Press.

Heller, Monica, and Alexandre Duchêne. 2011. Pride and profit: Changing discourses of language, capital and nation-state. In *Language in late capitalism: Pride and profit*, ed. Alexandre Duchêne and Monica Heller, 1–21. London: Routledge,

Heller, Monica, and Normand Labrie. 2003. Langue, pouvoir et identité: Une etude de cas, une approche *théorique*, une *méthodologie*. In *Discours et identities: La francité canadienne entre modernité et mondialisation*, ed. Monica Heller and Normand Labrie, 9–40. Fernelmont, Belgium: E.M.E.

Higonnet, Pierre. 1980. The politics of linguistic terrorism and grammatical hegemony during the French Revolution. *Social Theory* 5: 41–69.

Hobsbawm, Eric. 1990. *Nations and nationalism since 1760*. Cambridge: Cambridge University Press.

Hutton, Christopher. 1999. *Linguistics and the Third Reich*. London: Routledge.

Inda, Jonathan, and Renato Rosaldo, eds. 2008. *The anthropology of globalization*. Oxford: Blackwell.

Irvine, Judith, and Susan Gal. 2000. Language ideology and linguistic differentiation. In *Regimes of language: Ideologies, polities and identities*, ed. Paul Kroskrity, 35–81. Santa Fe, N. Mex.: School of American Research Press.

Le Menestrel, Sara. 1999. *La Voie des Cadiens*. Paris: Belin.

Lieberson, Stanley. 1970. *Language and ethnic relations in Canada*. New York: Wiley and Sons.

McDonald, Maryon. 1989. *We are not French*. London: Routledge.

Melchers, Gunnel, and Philip Shaw. 2003. *World Englishes: An introduction*. London: Arnold.

Morissonneau, Christian. 1978. *La Terre promise: Le Mythe du Nord québécois*. Montréal: HMH Hurtubise.

Outram, Dorinda. 1987. Le Langage mâle de la vertu: Women and the discourse of the French Revolution. In *The social history of language*, ed. Peter Burke and Roy Porter, 120–135. Cambridge: Cambridge University Press.

Pennycook, Alastair. 2003. Global Englishes, Rip Slyme and performativity. *Journal of Sociolinguistics* 7 (4): 513–515.

Pennycook, Alastair. 2007. *Global Englishes and transcultural flows*. London: Routledge.

Porter, John. 1965. *The vertical mosaic: An analysis of social class and power*. Toronto: University of Toronto Press.

Ramirez, Bruno. 1991. *On the move: French-Canadian and Italian migrants in the North Atlantic economy, 1860–1914*. Toronto: McClelland and Stewart.

Rindler-Schjerve, Rosita, ed. 2003. *Diglossia and power: Language policies and practice in the 19th Century Habsburg Empire*. Berlin: Mouton de Gruyter.

Rubdy, Rani, and Mario Saraceni. 2006. *English in the world: Global rules, global roles*. London: Continuum.

Sonntag, Selma. 2006. Appropriating identity or cultivating capital? Global English in offshoring industries. *Anthropology of Work Review* 26 (1): 13–19.

Tabouret-Keller, Andrée. 1988. *La Nocivité mentale du bilinguisme: Cent ans d'errance. Euskara Biltzarra 155–169*. Vitoria-Gasteiz: Eusko-Jaurlaritzaren Argitalpen-Zerbitzu Nagusia.

Tan, Peter, and Rani Rubdy, eds. 2008. *Language as commodity: Global structures, local marketplaces*. London: Continuum.

Urla, Jacqueline. 1993. Contesting modernities: Language standardization and the production of an ancient/modern Basque culture. *Critique of Anthropology* 13 (2): 101–118.

Wallerstein, Immanuel. 1974. *The modern world-system: Capitalist agriculture and the origins of the European world economy in the sixteenth century*. New York, London: Academic Press.

Williams, Raymond. 1973. *The country and the city*. London: Chatto and Windus.

Wolf, Eric. 1982. *Europe and the people without history*. Berkeley, Los Angeles: University of California Press.

CHAPTER 3

What Makes Art Acadian?

MIREILLE MCLAUGHLIN

COMMODIFYING THE MARGINS IN A GLOBAL ECONOMY

In this chapter, I show that multilingual capital, like any form of capital, participates in the reproduction of unequal post-colonial and post-national power relations (Bourdieu 1982; Heller 2002, 2010). This is particularly evident in the case of the peripheral multilingual space of *l'Acadie*, a space traversed by globalizing processes and ideologies. Acadie is a transnational Canadian and American linguistic minority, peripheral to cultural centres, be those centres defined as Canadian, international Francophone, Québécois, North American, or even global (see Heller, this volume; Savoie 2000). Acadian elites have invested heavily in political activism seeking representation and partnerships with the Canadian state, at a time when welfarism and industrialism were in their heyday (Heller and Labrie 2003). In this modernizing shift, prescriptive ideologies of language (Kroch and Small 1978) were used to argue for control of school boards, for access to publicly funded media, and for public services in French. These negotiations inscribed Acadians in territorialized power-relations at the community level, in relationships with the English-speaking majorities and with *Québécois* cultural elites. It is in a context of nation-building, reliant on ideologies linking the 'quality' of languages to the survival of cultures, that the multilingualism characteristic of Acadians' lived experiences was erased in favour of ideologies of monolingualism (Heller 1999). Today, however, Acadian peripheral multilingualism is proving to be marketable in a global economy of niche markets centred on the consumption of cool, authentic and counter-cultural products (Da Silva et al. 2007 Kelly-Holmes and Atkinson 2007).

The marketing of Acadian cultural production for a globalizing economy has rippling effects on Acadie, its practices, its ideological discourses, and the valued linguistic capital within its space. This globalization of Acadian cultural production is currently presented by the state as mandatory: minorities, in this context, have to be competitive on a global economic terrain if they are to subsist in a global economy. In ethnographic fieldwork carried out from 2006 to 2010, I followed the effects of globalization and a repositioning of state policies, from welfare to neoliberal, on Acadian identity through the field of cultural production. Acadian artists mobilize local forms of multilingualism to index their peripheral cultural position, to present themselves as counter-cultural, and to construct Acadian identity as cool for global niche markets (McLaughlin 2010; Heller 2003). It is peripheral multilingualism itself, traditionally perceived by Acadian nationalist elites as problematic, which becomes a resource within the global mediascape (Appadurai 1996; Kelly-Holmes and Atkinson 2007; Kelly-Holmes 2010; Leppänen and Pietikäinen 2010). This peripheral multilingual cool, however, participates in the reproduction of ideologies linking authenticating linguistic practices to nationalism, race, and ethnicity (Coupland 2003; Jaworski and Thurlow 2004, 2010; Coupland, Garrett, and Bishop 2005; Kelly-Holmes and Mautner 2010). In this way, it is a source of contradiction for local artists and community actors as they mobilize cosmopolitan ideologies to redefine Acadian identity as civically inclusive, all while having to rely on stereotypical understandings of identity to render their products legible and successful on global markets.

This chapter follows the ways in which peripheral multilingualism is gaining value as linguistic capital and is therefore participating in the restructuration of ethnic categories. First, I will discuss theories of cosmopolitanism and link them to contemporary sociolinguistic theories of multilingualism as a potential terrain for challenging neo-imperialist power relations. I will then analyse how Acadian artists orient both towards and against nationalist language ideologies to construct a post-colonial critique of prescriptive language ideologies. In a global landscape where cultural hybridity is deemed emancipatory, artists mobilize peripheral multilingualism to construct a cosmopolitan stance. This cosmopolitan stance relies, however, on the reification of ethnic boundaries and ethnic stereotypes which can be understood and marketed in the global context. As such, I argue that it is important to consider multilingual practices as social capital and to track how they reify or reorganize ethnic categories.

GLOBALIZATION AND THE NEW COSMOPOLITAN SUBJECTIVITIES

In political philosophy, debates around cosmopolitanism usually centre on the tensions between cultural differences and political liberalism (Kymlicka 1995) and upon questions of the recognition of difference and the politics of redistribution of resources in order to augment the status of minorities (Habermas 2000; Fraser and Honneth 2003). Today, cosmopolitanism is taken up by political philosophers as a way to critique the West's implicit naturalization of its own cultural beliefs as 'reason' in core institutions such as the nation-state. Iris Marion Young (1990), for instance, draws on cultural and gender differences as the political positions that can balance the ways in which Western 'reason' continues to produce social inequalities. In short, cosmopolitanism is a political ideology that reflects upon the conditions for an equitable dialogue across cultural, religious, and ethnic differences.

If cosmopolitanism is a site of discussion in social theory, it is often taken up as an ideological stance by social actors who wish to argue against localized and nationalized forms of power. Social actors invested in global networks tend to adopt cosmopolitan standpoints as a way to legitimate their own transnational and/or hybrid cultural capital (Davidson 2005; O'Reilly 2005). Sociolinguists and linguistic anthropologists note that constructions of self as cosmopolitan are often prevalent amongst youths who are, much like the participants of this study, a part of an upwardly mobile fraction of a previously marginalized category (Smith-Hefner 2007). Cosmopolitan youths often define themselves in opposition to prescriptive national projects, on the one hand, and localized marginal populations, on the other. They do this by participating in the construction of global networks where their multilingual and 'exotic' linguistic practices are valued through various forms of linguistic commodification. The affinities between economic globalization and cosmopolitanism lead political economist David Harvey to a scathing critique of contemporary uses of cosmopolitanism: 'If this is what contemporary cosmopolitanism is about, then it is nothing other than an ethical and humanitarian mask for hegemonic neoliberal practices of class domination and financial and militaristic imperialism' (Harvey 2009: 84). Cosmopolitanism is, therefore, at present problematically embedded in neoliberal agendas and the different values attached to transnational cultural capital (be this transnationalism acquired through personal travels or mediated through involvement in niched media products).

Cosmopolitanism can serve, however, as a counter-discourse to nationalism and its contingent discourses of languages as bounded systems (Heller 2009). Cosmopolitanism as a political ideology capable of deconstructing or reconstructing nationalism was indeed the mark of my research participants. The group of twenty-three artists and community workers who participated in my study, and/or whose press clippings I followed as documentation, were generally active in the independent global music scene, in their respective genres (from rap to world-beats to acid jazz to folk-rock). The participants were well-travelled, most having sojourned, studied, and worked in other parts of Canada and the world, some born and raised elsewhere. Many split their time between projects in major urban centres (Montreal, Toronto, New York, New Orleans, Paris) and geographically and economically peripheral but far-from-culturally-isolated rural communities. They were invested in a cosmopolitan, hybridizing view of cultural identities, some claiming Metis status, others their Acadian-African origins. Most strove to access alter-globalizing networks (aka, networks which were felt to be an alternative to mainstream cultural production and its purported homogenizing effects) and all were invested in creating contemporary, urban, cosmopolitan, and multicultural images of *Acadianité*. These Acadian artists were not the exception: they shared a similar lifestyle to the majority of contemporary Acadian artists. Their multidimensional symbolic capital (Lahire 2011) had the most value in globalizing, multi-ethnic, networks. These were where authenticating non-prescriptive (read non-nationalist) linguistic practices came to be an important marker of Acadian global hip. Peripheral multilingualism granted access to and success in these spaces, most of which, such as a Celtic music festival or the global rap scene, relied on authenticating but anti-nationalistic performances of ethnicity, as was the case for Radio Radio, discussed below.

PERIPHERAL MULTILINGUALISM AS LINGUISTIC CAPITAL IN THE GLOBAL ART SCENE

Modern cultural production has expanded on a logic of authenticity and originality which promotes the commodification of counter-cultural products (Harvey 1990; Heath and Potter 2005). From the expansion of world music to the spread of global hip-hop, marginality is a popular trope of the contemporary global music and art scenes (Leppänen and Pietikäinen 2010). It is therefore no surprise that Acadian cultural producers mobilize the peripheral position of Acadian identity to access global markets. Artists mobilize the notion of the periphery and peripheral multi-lingualism to construct their position as speaking against local and global systems of oppression. It is, paradoxically, neoliberal public policies and a global public in search of distinction that allows for the current emergence of Acadian 'hip' on the global scene. Here, as elsewhere, the lines between political cosmopolitanism and the commodification of subjectivities are often blurred.

Sociolinguistics is well positioned to understand the tensions of cosmopolitanism and commodification (and the paradoxical commodification of cosmopolitanism). The field has often contested nationalist ideologies of monolingualism that legitimated (and continue to legitimate) the social exclusion of non-dominant speakers (Bourdieu 1982). Critical sociolinguistics has tackled the ideologies that rendered monolingual nationalist ideologies operational: the belief that languages are bounded systems, linked to one specific culture, organized within neat territorialized and often racialized boundaries (Pietikäinen 2008; Heller 2010). Sociolinguistics critiqued these views, arguing for the recognition of language as a situated resource (Blommaert 2003; Pietikäinen 2008) and of multilingualism as central to the daily experiences of speakers (Heller 2009).

Nationalism has been critiqued for reproducing social inequalities through bounded and prescriptive understandings of languages (Hobsbawm 1990). Linguistic nationalism participates in the definition of citizenship or group belonging and reproduces inequalities in the job market and in access to the public space by qualifying and disqualifying individuals on the basis of the construction of linguistic competence. Because of nationalism's focus on prescriptivism and linguistic homogeneity, contemporary sociolinguistics often critiques nationalism by focusing, instead, on the emancipatory power of the recognition of hybrid, multilingual linguistic practices. Multilingualism is, here, presented as the counter-discourse capable of keeping nationalist inequalities in check. In the field of language and cultural production, Pennycook, studying the 'mixing, borrowing, shifting and sampling of language, lyrics and ideas' (2010: 599) typical of hip-hop, comments that:

> The mixed codes of the street, and the hypermixes of hip-hop, pose a threat to the linguistic, cultural, and political stability urged by national language policies and wished into place by frameworks of linguistic analysis that posit separate and enumerable languages. Hip-hop language use can therefore be read as resistant and oppositional not merely in terms of lyrics, but also in terms of the language choice. Keeping it linguistically real (adopting the code of local authenticity) is often a threat to those who would prefer to keep it linguistically pure. (ibid. 602)

I contribute to the reflection on multilingualism and its capacity to undo social inequalities by focusing on globalization and the uses of multilingualism in cultural production. Opposition and resistance are not outside of the discourses that give them salience. I argue that it is because globalization reentextualizes stereotypes inherited from colonization, such as nation, race, and gender that linguistic hybridity and multilingualism are gaining value in the global cultural scene. As such, I question multilingualism's capacity to undo social inequalities and wonder at the global art scene's attachment to essentialist understandings of cultural and ethnic differences. A longitudinal ethnography of Acadian cultural production reveals that the mixing and borrowing typical of global cultural production are not without constraints or consequences. While it allows for emancipatory practices in regard to territorialized and local nationalist ideologies reliant on linguistic prescriptivism, it also relies on cultural authentication that informs the circulation of cultural products, as well as the trajectories of cultural producers. In a call to deepen our understanding of language practices and power relations in a globalized world, I trace how ideologies and practices of multilingualism and language hybridity are themselves becoming capital in the global art scene, with consequences for what counts as Acadian art and who can produce it.

THE ERASURE AND RE-EMERGENCE OF ACADIAN MULTILINGUALISM

While there is certainly debate as to how to define the Acadian community (see McLaughlin and Leblanc 2009), the Canadian state predominantly conceptualizes the community as a French-speaking linguistic minority residing in Atlantic Canada. There are also Acadians along the East Coast of the United States and links to Cajun identity in Louisiana, but as I document a Canadian shift in policy, I will focus on Acadians residing in Canada and their institutional discourses. In Canada, statistics usually link Acadian identity to the predominant use of French both as a first learned official language and a language still spoken at home. When taking these linguistic criteria as elements to define the group, Acadians (including different types of ethnic and racial categories but excluding individuals who have English as a first language but who may consider themselves to be Acadian) represent approximately 12 per cent of the population of Atlantic Canada. Again, when focused solely on linguistic criteria (a move the Canadian state is wont to use to manage its official bilingualism), Acadians share the territory of the Atlantic Provinces with 85 per cent of people whose first language is English and 3 per cent of the population whose first language is neither French nor English (Statistic Canada 2006). Other types of counting, along indigenous, ethnic, or racial lines, produce a more varied but not dissimilar portrait: Acadians (this time as a white-settler ethnic category and not as a multiracial French-speaking one) are demographically the most important linguistic and/or cultural minority in Atlantic Canada, alongside an English-speaking white-settler majority.

Acadian linguistic practices have long been a site of moral panics and exoticism in Canada. Many studies have shown, for instance, that Acadians show important levels of linguistic insecurity all while valuing the authenticity of their practices (Boudreau and Dubois 1993; LeBlanc 2010). The majority of Acadians (90%) are French-English bilingual (Statistic Canada 2006). While Acadians speak a variety of linguistic registers in French, they are stereotypically represented as having a specific phonetic 'accent' when speaking French, one that differs from Québécois French. Linguists explain this difference in terms of regions of origin and subsequent political isolation (Péronnet 1989; Poirier 1994). Acadians originally migrated from Poitou Charente, whereas most Quebec migration originated from Normandy. Acadians were politically isolated from exchanges with France and Nouvelle-France (Québec) when the colony was traded to the British Crown in 1713, some sixty years prior to France's cession of Nouvelle France. Throughout most of Canadian history, Acadians were subjected to (mostly) assimilationist imperial politics (Griffiths 2005). These politics kept them at the margin of the economy and eventually fostered an Acadian nationalist movement. While this movement allowed for the emergence of a French-speaking Acadian elite, the majority of Acadians survived through a subsistence economy coupled with contractual employment as working-class employees in English-run businesses (Johnson 1999; see also previous chapter in which Monica Heller gives an overview of these historical processes).

Outside of Atlantic Canada, Acadians are often assumed to all speak Chiac, a linguistic variety typical of South Eastern New Brunswick, characterized by the use of words considered archaic in standard French and the inclusion of English morphemes and syntax. English proximity, its prevalence in social life, as well as its central position as the language of economic modernization, meant that many Acadians living in contact regions started incorporating English phonemes, morphemes, and syntax when speaking French (Perrot 2006). A portion of the population also practised (and continues to practise) in-group code-switching (Acadians might switch from French to English and French again within the same conversation, if not the same sentence). The presence of code-mixing and code-switching in the linguistic repertoires of some Acadians has long been indexed by French Canadian and Acadian nationalist elites as the effects of oppression, if not the marker of the Acadian working class's acculturation to English values. It would index, in other words, participation in the English-speaking world, be it through employment, marriage, or media consumption. Code-mixing and code-switching were therefore also perceived by Acadian and French Canadian elites as gateway practices leading to linguistic assimilation. As such, nationalists put a lot of emphasis on speaking and learning 'proper French', often presenting the inability to do so as a mark of a lack of education, national sentiment, and even, perhaps, laziness on the part of the deviant speakers.

As a result of nationalist ideologies, the quality of the French language (in terms of closeness to or deviation from a prescribed/perceived norm) and the capacity to speak French without English interferences soon became a central site of interventionism for French Canadian and Acadian elites (Heller 2002). The contrast between linguistic purism and mixed practices also served to legitimate unequal access to positions of power within the Acadian community itself. Acadian multilingualism, a product of uneven economic conditions, was problematic for community leaders, who wished to erase it (Irvine and Gal 2001). And yet, contemporary economic conditions, combined with the democratization of access to media production, have rendered multilingualism impossible to ignore. What is more, in a knowledge economy, Acadians now fare economically better in regions where they can mobilize their multilingualism. Is it any wonder that this multilingualism, born out of marginalization, policed by nationalist prescriptivism, is now mobilized to construct the type of counter-cultural claims valued in the globalized media-scape and cultural markets?

The inscription of Acadian cultural products in global networks has brought about an observable ideological change as to the value of peripheral multilingual practices. Artists now mobilize peripheral multilingualism to position themselves as speaking for the traditionally excluded. But, where, in past representation, this bilingualism was a symbol of oppression, it is now touted as a symbol of peripheral cool (Pennycook 2010; Pietikäinen 2010). That is to say, multilingualism and multilingual capital are gaining value as symbolic capital in global markets. To document the ideological transformation at work, I mobilize data from two studies. In 2000–2002, I carried out a series of interviews with Acadian writers. The focus of the study was on their representation of the field of literature and the value of multilingual practices in it. In 2006–2010, I focused on the emergence of niche markets for Acadian artists and how it changed state investment in the production of Acadian cultural production. In this part of the chapter, I investigate how ideologies of prescriptivism are being superseded by ideologies of multilingual cosmopolitanism. I then follow how peripheral cool is constructed and its consequences for local artists. Efforts to inscribe Acadian identity in the global market raise the stakes on linguistic and cultural grounds. Ethnic, national, and cultural stereotypes have capital on global markets (Piller 2003; Kelly-Holmes 2010). Language plays a central role in the production of these marketable stereotypes, especially for linguistic minorities. In most instances, its communicative value is erased while its symbolic value is fetishized (Kelly-Holmes 2000). What matters most in the fetishization of language is its 'authenticity'. Authenticity is itself socially negotiated (Coupland 2003; Pietikäinen, this volume), and generally based on the perceived moral-economic value of a practice. The definition of what counts as authentic and legitimate Acadian linguistic practices is a fertile ground for local debates.

Global markets are avid consumers of cultural authenticity, one that is linked to nationalist understanding of the links between language and culture. Here is where Acadian peripheral multilingualism, be it local varieties such as Chiac, Acadjonne, or code-alternations between these varieties, standard French and English, gains value. Whether in Canada, Québec, or Europe, the public apparently buys into ideologies which link Acadian artists' use of Chiac or Acadjonne to an exotic but authentic performance of identity. This, however, is a source of tension among Acadians who, first of all, do not all speak Chiac or Acadjonne and who, second of all, have undergone close to two centuries of language prescriptivism. In the next sections, I explore how the emergence of a global market has undone ideologies of prescriptivism in favour of ideologies where authenticating peripheral multilingualism is valued. I focus on the discourse and trajectories of two Acadian artists and one rap group: Mila, a writer in her thirties; Dano, a multidisciplinary artist best known for producing an animated teleseries called *Acadieman*; and Radio Radio, a rap band who are topping the Québécois music charts and getting noticed in some Anglophone networks. I show that the value of multilingualism on global markets is linked to questions of counter-cultural authenticity. Finally, I argue that this reliance on authenticity reproduces racial hierarchies inherited from colonization.

MULTILINGUAL AND COSMOPOLITAN

Multilingual Authenticity

Language prescriptivism has been a central tenet of the ways in which the category of 'Acadian' has been institutionalized (Heller 2002). The discourses surrounding the valorization of peripheral multilingualism in the art field evolved through the 2000s in the Acadian context. For some artists, such as Mila, the use of multilingualism was originally felt as authentic but potentially isolating. At an important Acadian cultural celebration, the *Congrès Mondial Acadien* 2004, Mila was asked to speak about her experiences as an Acadian writer. The audience was composed of Acadian social activists and academics, a crowd usually associated with prescriptive ideologies of language. She was presenting with two other writers who both argued that the defence of French was an important part of their work as a way to help the community fight against English domination. Born in a rural area and then living and studying in Louisiana, Mila, on the other hand, took the podium to argue for linguistic hybridity as authentically Acadian. She presented an argument in favour of the recognition of multilingualism and linguistic hybridity as the authentic languages of her upbringing in the rural Acadian area:

> *mes personnages reflètent aussi toutes les langues qui m'habitent depuis mon enfance icitte à la Baie / euh il y a de l'anglais du français des accents peut-être difficiles à comprendre / pour les autres / euh mais pourquoi réduire ce réseau complexe / euh quatre groupes culturels / en un seul / en un seul monde / je trouve que: l'hybridité (rires) l'éclatement / des rencontres / culturelles et linguistiques sont plus intéressantes et et honnêtes (que les contraintes linguistiques du monolinguisme)*

> my characters also reflect all the languages that have inhabited me since my childhood here at la Baie / ah there is some English some French some accents perhaps hard to understand / for others / but why simplify that complex network / ah four cultural groups / in one alone / in one world / I think that: hybridity (laughter) / fragmentation / of encounters / cultural and linguistic are more interesting and and honest (than monolingual linguistic constraints) (my translation)

Mila's valorization of linguistic hybridity in and of itself is not surprising in the current context of literary production, where post-colonial approaches to culture are a leading paradigm (Bhabha 1994). But she goes on to present her multilingual stance as deviant in terms of the dominant ideologies of the Francophone and Canadian cultural markets. In her view, her propensity for multilingualism constrained her trajectory in the contemporary institutionalization of funding for the arts in Canada. As a budding writer, she felt the Acadian milieu was definitely pushing her to choose French. Indeed, the legitimating discourses of the scene (and the funding it received) mandated that writers and artists work to save the language and save the culture (through French).

> *certains artistes en tout cas ils m'encourageaient de / de choisir le français euh / il y avait un certain monsieur qui / il aimait ça de m'encourager / il faut vraiment Mila il faut que tu choisisses le français arrêtes d'écrire en anglais arrêtes euh / de de t'obstiner avec ça (rires Mila et membres de la foule) parce qu'il fallait absolument sauver la culture acadienne il fallait absolument préserver notre langue euh bla bla bla (rires de membres de la foule) et puis écrire des poèmes en anglais c'était point / c'était point intéressant / ça menait / ça menait pas à grand-chose (ibid.)*

> some artists in any case were encouraging me to / to choose French ah / there was one man who / he liked to encourage me / you really must Mila you must choose French / stop writing in English stop ah / persisting with that (laughter Mila and members of the public) because we absolutely had to save Acadian culture we had to save our language ah bla bla bla (laughter from members of the public) and then writing poems in English wasn't / wasn't interesting at all / it didn't lead / it didn't lead anywhere (my translation)

In Mila's narrative, the community perceives the purpose of artistic production to be one of 'saving' the culture through the use of one linguistic system (French and its varieties). Only in this way can writing in English be perceived as 'not leading anywhere'. Mila, however, reports that she could never limit herself to choosing 'one' of the three languages that were, according to her, part of her everyday life. She could never restrain her writing within a linguistic conceptual framework and this, she revealed later in the speech, is part of the reason why she decided to continue her work in Louisiana. She felt that the linguistic considerations that were constraining her in Canada were not quite as present in the Cajun art scene. She mobilizes the idea of artistic integrity to justify her multilingual stance. She opposes multilingual linguistic authenticity as a defence against language prescriptivism and monolingualism put forward by language activists (see Heller 1999 for a discussion of how ideologies of monolingualism structure language activism in Francophone Canada).

euh / j'accepte / pis je comprends ça / euh / ça va / euh // s : / je trouve c'est important moi je veux m'exprimer en français mais / euh / je trouve que comme artiste / euh / c'est comme impossible de choisir une langue au dépend d'une autre / euh // j'ai essayé / de choisir le français de de comme partir d'un cadre conceptuel linguistique puis de me mettre là pis me dire ok ben je vais écrire de même là / pis / j'ai pas trouvé cet exercice intellectuel-là vraiment euh intéressant / euh si je suis artiste c'est parce que je suis libre / selon moi / si je suis artiste / euh je me censure pas / je laisse passer ce qui doit passer euh de mon expérience jusqu'à la page / pis euh je comprends pas comment écrire / comment créer quelque chose de vrai et d'honnête euh en m'imposant des / des contraintes linguistiques / euh moi je suis point activiste / (rires) / j'ai décidé (rires Mila et de la foule) je comprends qu'il faut parler de (xxx) euh pis il faut que les programmes d'école les subventions puis tout ça ça continue mais moi comme comme artiste / euh je désire simplement être honnête / euh et de de m'exprimer / d'exprimer toute la gamme / euh de possibilités et de mondes qui m'habitent / la langue dans le fond selon moi ce ce n'est que un outil / euh c'est un chemin à suivre qui aide à raconter / j'adore les mots je les trouve fascinant / euh je je trouve ça fascinant de voir les images se créer sur la page en utilisant les mots (ibid.)

Ah / I accept / and I understand that / ah / it's okay / ah // s/ I find it's important I want to be able to express myself in French but / ah / I find that as an artist / ah / it's like impossible to choose one language at the expense of another / ah // I tried / to choose French to to like start from a linguistic conceptual framework and to sit myself down and tell myself all right well I'm going to write like this / and / I didn't find that intellectual exercise that interesting / ah if I am an artists it's because I am free / according to me / if I am an artist / I don't censor myself / I let flow what must flow from my experience to the page / and ah I don't understand how to write / how to create something real and honest ah by imposing some / some linguistic constraints on myself / ah I am not an activist / (laughter) / I've decided (laughter from Mila and the crowd) I understand that we have to speak of (xxx) ah and that school curriculum and grants and all that has to keep going but for me as as an artist / ah I simply want to be honest / ah and to express myself /

express myself in the whole array / ah of possibilities and worlds that inhabit me / language in the end is nothing but a tool / it's a road one follows which helps to tell a story / I love words I find them fascinating / ah I I find it fascinating seeing images created on the page by using words (my translation)

This brings Mila to advocate for authenticity, cultural hybridity, and multilingualism, a wager that she feels is somewhat dangerous: who is the public for her particular kind of multilingualism? Will Franco-Canadian activists, the very ones who share her linguistic and cultural upbringing, follow her lead and want to read pieces in the multilingualism they have been trying to contain for decades? Is there a global public for multilingual literary pieces?

In 2004, the global market for Acadian peripheral multilingualism was only beginning to expand. Mila's speech was striking, because it was still fairly defiant to argue for multilingualism as an integral part of Acadian's everyday lives and sense of personhood. While there had been many writers, such as Antonine Maillet Herménégilde Chiasson, Gérald LeBlanc, or Guy Arseneau LeBlanc who mobilized multilingualism in their work, these writers usually did so in the framework of cultural homogeneity. In *Mourrir à Scoudouc* (1974), for instance, Chiasson's use of English was meant to represent the social domination of English in everyday life in Southern New Brunswick. Guy Arseneau's *AcadieRock* (1973), for its part, framed 'Chiac' as the language of the growing Acadian urban working class (in Moncton New-Brunswick) while Antonine Maillet's *Sagouine* (1971) represented the local dialect of a rural Acadian working-class community. Gérald LeBlanc would glorify this variety in later years as the emblem of the emergence of an urban Acadian art scene (LeBlanc 2004). With the exception of LeBlanc, these writers maintained that English was somehow the language of the other, and framed Chiac as being 'French' and therefore part of Acadian identity. This all served to maintain an idea of Acadian cultural homogeneity. Mila's argument brings her elsewhere (literally and figuratively): she mobilizes English, Acadjonne, and French as integral parts of her identity. Her use of peripheral multilingualism serves, in this case, the function of revealing actual linguistic practices: it is not only lower-class uneducated Acadians who are multilingual, but most Acadians living in regions where they are a minority.

Multilingual and Counter-Cultural

As Acadian peripheral multilingualism serves to index an authentic stance, it also constructs the works where it is showcased as counter-cultural. In 2005, multimedia artist Dano LeBlanc[1] found himself at the centre of a media blitz and intense public debates when Rogers Communication, the leading private telecommunications company in Canada, produced and aired the animated television show *Acadieman*. *Acadieman*, 'the first Acadian superhero', is LeBlanc's homage to an Acadian 'regular

Figure 3.1:
Acadieman, the first Acadian superhero, a creation by Dano LeBlanc

guy', who works in call centres by day, attends community college, hangs out on the couch with his buddies, and is called upon to save Acadians from the threat of a second deportation during the Congrès Mondial Acadien 2009 (Figure 3.1).

At the centre of the debate was not LeBlanc's critique of the commodification of Acadian culture, his humorous take on the pomposity of the local art scene, or even his characters' propensity to get themselves into trouble (by, say, having unprotected sex). As would be expected in a space where a specific language is called upon to save the community, it was LeBlanc's use of multiple local varieties (Chiac, Brayon, Québécois, etc.) and English code switching which caught the public's attention. The naysayers centred their critiques on two main claims: (1) *Acadieman* put all Acadians to shame because he represented them as poor speakers of French and (2) *Acadieman* was a dangerous icon for Acadian youths because he glamorized linguistic hybridity and code-mixing.

And yet, in an interview, LeBlanc touted: '*C'est comme politically correct astheure de parler chiac.*' (It's like politically correct now to speak Chiac.) LeBlanc, after all, had created the character to contest what he perceived to be the linguistic prescriptivism of local elites. For him this prescriptivism served the gate-keeping strategies of the elite. To his surprise, *Acadieman* was hailed as an Acadian Icon by the media and, more importantly, a fraction of the local intellectual elite. Indeed, led by a group of sociolinguists (myself included) who had been arguing, from a Bourdieusian framework, for the valorization of Chiac as one of the languages of the community, part of the local intellectual elite had taken the multilingual stance: *Acadieman* was popular among youth because it portrayed their language. *Acadieman*, in other words, was perceived as an authentic representation of youth's linguistic practices. From there, it was a small hop, skip, and jump to conclude that *Acadieman* helped foster young people's pride in their Acadian identity and thereby served the goals of political activists: to retain and convert souls to the identity.

This sudden Chiac political correctness came as a surprise to LeBlanc, who had produced the character as a way to contest the prescriptive ideologies that had governed the institutionalization of Acadian identity for years. He reported that his work had never been appreciated by the public-sector funded institutions because of its multilingualism. In fact, the only way he could get his work recognized was by turning away from the local community sector and by producing in the emergent private sector. There he was able to make free use of multilingualism. He also felt the private sector allowed him to openly take a counter-cultural anti-elitist stance:

DANO: *ben moi au début [le projet] c'était vraiment c'était une joke right / c'était kind of comme / pis c'était pas une joke c'était kind of une joke pis un fuck you en même temps parce que / j'étais tellement tanné de // comme d'être forcé d'écrire dans une langue ou un autre quand-ce que je faisais de la création tu sais là / j'ai juste dit fuck it / tu sais là / je va faire cecitte pis / ça me donne la liberté de faire whatever que je veux / j'écrirai en anglais si je veux j'écrirai en français si je veux / pis j'écrirai en chiac si je veux so*

MIREILLE: *Parce que, quoi c'est qui te forçais à choisir l'une ou l'autre langue ?*

DANO: *Ben / je veux dire / si t'appliques pour des bourses ou n'importe quoi il faut / ça ça a beaucoup à faire avec pourquoi j'ai tombé dans le privé aussi tu sais là / parce que moi ce que je fais ça tombe un petit peu plus comme dans it's not considered high art tu sais là c'est de l'art populaire pis c'est pas évident / (…) moi je suis tombé dans le privé à cause que je pouvais pas j'aurais pas pu créer ça si j'avais cherché des bourses du gouvernement parce que*

MIREILLE: *ça fittait pas dans leur cadre là*

DANO: *non ça fit pas dans le cadre à la fois pour parce que c'était nouveau média pis c'était de l'animation à la fois parce que la langue c'est-y du français c'est-y anglais c'est-y c'était nébuleux.*

DANO: Well in my case at first Acadieman was really like a joke right / it was kind of like / and it was a joke and a fuck you at the same time because / I was so fed up with / with being forced to write in either one language or the other when I was doing creation you know / I just said fuck it / you know / I'm going to do this / it gives me the freedom to do whatever I want / I'll write in English if I want and I'll write in French if I want / and I'll write in Chiac if I want so

MIREILLE: because what forced you to choose one language or the other?

DANO: well / I mean / if you apply for scholarship or stuff like that you have / that has a lot to do with why I fell into the private sector too you know / because what I do it falls a bit more like it's not considered high art you know it's popular art and it's not obvious / (…) I fell in the private sector because I couldn't have I wouldn't have been able to create if I had looked for scholarship because

MIREILLE: it didn't fit in their framework

DANO: no it didn't it fit in the framework simultaneously because it was new media and it was animation and also because of the language is it French is it English it was nebulous.

LeBlanc sees his work not only as countering the linguistic ideologies of the modern Acadian art scene; he also argues that he is speaking from a working-class position for the traditionally excluded Acadians. It is precisely because of a history of language prescriptivism that LeBlanc's product is innovative. It is precisely because the product counters a dominant prescriptive language ideology that it is consumed as counter-cultural by youths, media, and academics alike. It is this acceptance that leaves LeBlanc perplexed. As Pietikäinen notes for language ideologies in Sámiland, the ideology of prescriptivism is, here, slowly being displaced by an ideology which favours multilingualism and linguistic authenticity (2010).

Peripheral Hip

While Dano LeBlanc uses peripheral multilingualism to construct a product that contests prescriptive ideologies of language, Radio Radio rappers squarely use peripheral multilingualism to construct a cosmopolitan stance. Gabriel Malenfant, Alexandre Bilodeau, and Jacques Doucet have broken into the global rap market with their use of Chiac, Acadjonne, and English (Figure 3.2). Their band, Radio Radio, goes beyond a contestation of local language debates about French varieties to package Acadian as part of the new 'global hip', precisely because of its peripheral position. Three of their latest releases have topped the music charts in the province of Québec, a contemporary music market which has been a fervent consumer of linguistically hybrid songs. The Québec market, in fact, is the ideal fit for Radio Radio: on the one hand, the rappers' peripheral multilingualism situates them favourably in the hip, multilingual, and culturally hybrid, Montreal-based hip-hop scene (Sarkar 2009). On the other, their recognizable accent (which makes them identifiable as Acadians, and so—peripheral to Québec politics) situates them as an exotic yet non-threatening band for the larger Québec market. As audible Acadians, Radio Radio is simultaneously part of French Canadian identity while being outside of Québec identity. The band raps about a postmodern French Canadian identity, one that is playfully accepting of cultural differences. Indeed, they mobilize their peripheral stance as a way to construct themselves as cosmopolitan, outside of the nationalist politics that govern language debates in Canada. They do this by aligning themselves with other forms of peripheral cultural identities, for example, collaborating with First Nation rappers, neo-Canadian musicians, or showcasing indigenous cultural practices in their videos.

They mobilize the myth of marginality and oppression to showcase their upward social mobility and their new position of power in a globalized world. In their songs and videos, the rappers play with traditional images of oppression and sell Acadian rural coastal regions as an integral part of global 'hip'. They are hip precisely because they are peripheral. As such, they participate in redefining Acadian identity outside the usual tropes of oppression (whether economic or linguistic) and suffering. They playfully thank the British Crown for 'the free cruise' (e.g., the deportation of

Figure 3.2:
Rap band Radio Radio, © 2012 Mamoru Kobayakawa

approximately 9,000 Acadians in 1755) while constructing contemporary Acadian lifestyles as simultaneously urban-yet-rural, hip and postmodern. *'Pas un cent à mon nom à cause de Louis Vuitton (...) Je dirais pas je suis pauvre, je dirais plutôt que je suis broke'* (not a cent to my name, because of Louis Vuitton (...) I wouldn't say I'm poor, I would say I'm broke[2]), they quip in a song, distinguishing between the devalued habitus of poverty and the cosmopolitan capital of global travel and hyper-consumption.

The rappers represent themselves as happy navigators of global cities, broke because of recent purchases of high-fashion commodities, but easily able to hitch a ride to the (Acadian) shores of Nova Scotia, where a sumptuous lifestyle of access to pristine beaches, family seafood dinners, grand parties, car racing, and outdoor Jacuzzis awaits them. In fact, it is through their link to Atlantic Canada (the Maritimes in the following excerpt) and their use of code-mixed slang that they come to embody *joie de vivre* to a non-Acadian public (in this part of the excerpt, it is the Québec public, but in the text, the charm of the Maritimes will also take the American, Canadian, and European publics by storm).

> In 2008, the quartet formed by Jacobus, LX, TX and Timo signs onto **Bonsound Records** and *Cliché Hot*, their first album, sees the light of day in May of 2008. The charm of the Maritimes instantly takes over the province of Québec and the expression 'cliché hot' becomes common slang within the local indie scene, as the song *Jacuzzi* becomes a real ode to joy. (Laradioradio.com)

While they have entered a playful upwardly mobile Acadie, they still lay claim to a unique identity because of the peripheral location, one that grants privileged access to valued resources in the global economy: nature, friends, easy living and, more importantly, a unique cosmopolitan and counter-cultural identity.

Nowhere is this more apparent than in their video for *Cargué dans ma chaise*. Here, the rappers link multilingual practices to a cosmopolitan stance. While the lyrics to the song are about time spent talking from one's own relaxed position (*cargué dans sa chaise*), the video explores what subjectivity means in the post-industrial landscape. The video, shot at the Kukulkan pyramid in southern Mexico, starts with a voiceover featuring Tiburcio, a Mayan shaman, announcing that he will do an interpretative dance showcasing the nine stages of the evolution of the universe. He speaks in a Mayan language while French subtitles allow the intended Francophone Canadian public to understand. Radio Radio then invites the listeners to 'sit back, relax', an utterance made in English—but which could be understood as typical Acadian code-switching (at least by Chiac-speaking Acadians). The video then proceeds to show the rappers ascending the pyramid, with the help of a youth which one is to understand is also Mayan, as the shaman takes them through the nine stages. These stages are introduced, every time, with a written presentation: *le big bang, les premiers animaux, les premiers singes, les premiers humains, langages* (note the plural), *civilisations, le règne industriel, le galactique*, and finally, 'le oneness field' (the big bang, the first animals, the first apes, the first humans, languages (note the plural), civilizations, the industrial era, the galactic, and the oneness field). The act of speaking is revered, in the lyrics, for its capacity to be 'All inclusive, non-intrusive'. In between the industrial era and the *galactique*, the lyrics of the songs invite the listener to join the conversation (sit on the couch), adopting the relaxed stance advocated at the beginning of the song. One of the rappers then asks: '*Yeah pis là quoi?*' (Yeah and then what?) at which point the Mayan youth chants the Latin phrase: '*Magnus ab integro seclorum nascitur ordo*', (a new order begins again). This order, we are to understand, will be multilingual, led by taking part in intercultural dialogues with indigenous cultures. In short, it will be cosmopolitan.

Radio Radio embodies one of the leading paradoxes of the global art scene and its cosmopolitanization. Radio Radio frequently collaborates with First-Nations and neo-Canadian musicians and rappers on stage, and, in the video for another song, *Deckshoo*, cast themselves as jury for an Inuk high jump competition (a symbolic move that was surprisingly well-received in the Inuit community). In their chart-topping video, Guess What, they play with gender and sexual orientation stereotypes, showcasing themselves as toy boys (alongside bikini-clad but allegedly powerful women), while rapping about the fact that they are contemporary metrosexual, sensitive men, whose sexual orientation is up for debate. Radio Radio's use of humour to contest and play with stereotypes relies on globalizing practices: rap, the valorization of lifestyle commodities, access to travel, and even the capacity to sit back and relax to discuss a new world order which depends on a life of leisure. Stereotypes, however, remain central in articulating an image of previously peripheral identities (be they Acadian, Inuit, or Mayan) as hip and cosmopolitan. What marks them as apt representatives of the new global in the rap scene is their allegiance to a formerly stigmatized community. The rappers reverse the image of Acadians as poor and passive by flipping the script on images of the stigmatized use of multilingualism. Acadian peripheral multilingualism is used, in their production, as a way to authenticate their position and participate in the construction of a cosmopolitan Acadian identity. Radio Radio's use of peripheral multilingualism grants them global legitimacy. Access to peripheral registers, in other words, is capital in the global art scene—but is still understood in ethnicizing terms. This is far from being the case for all Acadian artists. Artists who, for instance, are racialized (black or Asian) or artists who do not mobilize peripheral multilingualism have to either compete in the broader Francophone or Anglophone markets or otherwise participate as representatives of Canada's multiculturalism policies. At the global level, this reifies l'Acadie not as a cosmopolitan category, but as one that is caught up in the re-essentializing trends of globalization.

CONCLUSION

There are tensions between nationalist and global constructions of Acadianité. Multilingualism, particularly the authenticating kind, is a resource in the globalized economy, one that relies on stereotype to reproduce or subvert ethnic subject positions, to give cachet to products, and to access global markets. Acadian nationalism was premised on prescriptivism: this renders multilingualism available as a way to contest domination. Social actors contest Acadian nationalism by constructing linguistic authenticity on the terrain of multilingualism. Peripheral multilingualism becomes a resource to contest national Acadian elites and to represent the upwardly mobile Acadian working-to-middle-class. That opposition allows this upwardly mobile group to participate in the construction of a 'cosmopolitan globalization' which is hip, cool, networked, and multi-ethnic. Participation, however, is still premised on stereotypes. As such, authenticity and the value of peripheral multilingualism create two streams for Acadian artists: those who can legitimately participate in the global scene as Acadians (those who have access to the right kind of Acadian peripheral multilingualism from the market's perspective) and those who are recognized as Acadians at the local/Acadian national level but who participate in the global market as representative of Canada's multiculturalism (thereby reproducing a white ethnic image of Acadian identity that is problematic at the local level).

Sociolinguistics is equipped to understand the ways in which peripheral multilingualism participates in contesting or reproducing power relations in the global economy, as discourses of globalization are reshaping the value of linguistic practices within linguistic minorities (Jaffe 2007; Pietikäinen 2010). In the global art scene, peripheral multilingualism becomes a resource, a symbolic capital capable of authenticating products as emanating from an increasingly valued counter-cultural periphery. Peripheral multilingualism functions as capital precisely because such practices are the counterpart to long-dominant nationalist monolingual prescriptive language ideologies. And yet, the global market's reliance on authenticating linguistic practices ensures the reproduction of ethnic, linguistic, and racial stereotypes. This structure of the market is a source of tension for artists as they navigate the global art scene, as well as for language communities, as they strive to redefine themselves from ethnically defined to civic and inclusive minorities.

NOTES

1. Translated by the author.
2. Participant identified with his authorization.

REFERENCES

Appadurai, Arjun. 1996. *Modernity at large: Cultural dimensions of globalization.* Minneapolis: University of Minnesota Press.

Arseneau, Guy. 1973. *Acadie rock.* Moncton: Les Éditions d'Acadie.

Bhabha, Homi K. 1994. *The location of culture.* New York: Routledge.

Blommaert, Jan. 2003. Commentary: A sociolinguistics of globalization, *Journal of Sociolinguistics* 7 (4): 607–623.

Boudreau, Annette, and Lise Dubois. 1993. 'J'parle pas comme les Français de France, ben c'est du français pareil; j'ai ma *own* p'tite langue. In *L'Insécurité linguistique dans les communautés francophones périphériques,* Actes du colloque de Louvain-la-Neuve, Cahiers de l'Institut linguistique de Louvain, ed. Michel Francard, vol. 1 : 147–168.

Bourdieu, Pierre. 1982. *Ce que parler veut dire.* Paris: Fayard.

Chiasson, Herménégilde. 1974. *Mourir à Scoudouc.* Moncton: LesÉditions d'Acadie.

Coupland, Nikolas. 2003. Sociolinguistics and authenticity: An elephant in the room. *Journal of Sociolinguistics* 7 (3): 417–431.

Coupland, Nikolas, Peter Garrett, and Hywel Bishop. 2005. Wales underground: Discursive frames and authenticities in Welsh heritage tourism events. In *Discourses, communication and tourism,* ed. Adam Jaworski and Annette Pritchard, 199–221. Clevedon: Channel View Publications.

Da Silva, Emanuel, Mireille McLaughlin, and Mary Richards. 2007. Bilingualism and the globalized new economy: The commodification of language and identity. In *Bilingualism: A social approach,* ed. Monica Heller. Basingstoke: Palgrave MacMillan, 183–206.

Davidson, Kelly. 2005. Alternative India: Transgressive spaces. In *Discourses, communication and tourism,* ed. Adam Jaworski and Annette Pritchard, 150–169. Clevedon: Channel View Publications.

Fraser, Nancy, and Axel Honneth. 2003. *Redistribution or recognition? A political- philosophical exchange.* London and New York: Verso.

Griffiths, Naomi Elizabeth Sandaus. 2005. *From migrant to Acadian: A North American border people 1604–1755.* McGill: Queen's University Press.

Habermas, Jurgen. 2000. *Aprés l'état-nation: Une nouvelle constellation politique.* Paris: Fayard.

Harvey, David. 1990. *The condition of postmodernity.* Cambridge: Blackwell.

Harvey, David. 2009. *Cosmopolitanism and the geographies of freedom*. New York: Columbia University Press.

Heath, Joseph, and Andrew Potter. 2005. *The rebel sell: Why the culture can't be jammed*. Toronto: Harper Collins Publishers.

Heller, Monica. 1999. *Linguistic minorities and modernity*. London and New York: Longman.

Heller, Monica. 2002. *Éléments d'une sociolinguistique critique*. Paris: Didier éditeur.

Heller, Monica. 2003. Globalization, the new economy, and the commodification of language and identity. *Journal of Sociolinguistics* 7 (4): 473–492.

Heller, Monica. 2009. *Bilingualism: A social approach*. Basingstoke: Palgrave Macmillan.

Heller, Monica. 2010. *Paths to post-nationalism*. New York: Oxford University Press.

Heller, Monica, and Normand Labrie. 2003. *Discours et identités: La francité canadienne entre modernité et mondialisation*. Bruxelles: Éditions modulaires européennes.

Hobsbawm, Eric. 1990. *Nations and nationalism since 1780*. Cambridge: Cambridge University Press.

Jaffe, Alexandra. 2007. Minority language movements. In *Bilingualism: A social approach*, ed. Monica Heller. Basingstoke: Palgrave MacMillan, 50–70.

Jaworski, Adam, and Crispin Thurlow. 2004. Language, tourism and globalization: Mapping new international identities. In *Language matters: Communication, identity, and culture*, ed. Sik Hung Ng, Christopher N. Candlin, and Chi Yue Chiu, 297–321. Hong Kong: City University of Hong Kong Press.

Jaworski, Adam, and Crispin Thurlow. 2010. Language and the globalizing habitus of tourism: A sociolinguistics of fleeting relationships. In *The handbook of language and globalisation*, ed. Nikolas Coupland, 256–286. Oxford: Wiley-Blackwell.

Johnson, Derek. 1999. Merchants, the state and the household: Continuity and change in a 20th-century Acadian fishing village. *Acadiensis* 29 (1): 57–75.

Kelly-Holmes, Helen. 2000. Bier, parfum, kaas: Language fetish in European advertising. *European Journal of Cultural Studies* 3 (1): 67–82.

Kelly-Holmes, Helen. 2010. Rethinking the macro-micro relationship: Some insights from the marketing domain. *International Journal of the Sociology of Language* 202: 25–40.

Kelly-Holmes, Helen, and David Atkinson. 2007. Minority language advertising: A profile of two Irish language newspapers. *Journal of Multilingual and Multicultural Development* 28 (1): 34–50.

Kelly-Holmes, Helen, and Gerlinde Mautner. 2010. *Language and the market*. Basingstoke: Palgrave MacMillan.

Kroch, Anthony, and Cathy Small. 1978. Grammatical Ideology and its effects on speech. In *Linguistic variation: Models and methods*, ed. David Sankoff. New York: Academic Press, 45–55.

Kymlicka, Will. 1995. *Multicultural citizenship*. New York: Oxford University Press.

Lahire, Bernard. 2011. *The plural actor*. Cambridge: Polity Press.

Laradioradio.com. Official website of Radio Radio, viewed on 30 June 2011.

LeBlanc, Gérald. 2004. *Techgnose*. Moncton: Éditions Perce-Neige.

LeBlanc, Matthieu. 2010. Le Français, langue minoritaire, en milieu de travail: Des représentations linguistiques à l'insécurité linguistique. *Nouvelles perspectives en sciences sociales: Revue internationale de systémique complexe et d'études relationnelles* 6 (1): 17–63.

Leppänen, Sirpa, and Sari Pietikäinen. 2010. Urban rap goes to Arctic Lapland: Breaking through and saving endangered Inari Sámi language. In *Language and the market*, ed. Helen Kelly-Holmes and Gerlinde Mautner, 148–160. Basingstoke: Palgrave Macmillan.

Maillet, Antonine. 1971. *La Sagouine*. Montréal: Leméac.

Marion Young, Iris. 1990. *Justice and the politics of difference*. Princeton: Princeton University Press.

McLaughlin, Mireille. 2010. 'L'Acadie post-nationale: Producing Franco-Canadian Identity in the Global Economy', Doctoral Thesis, University of Toronto.

McLaughlin, Mireille, and Mélanie LeBlanc. 2009. Identité et marchés dans la balance: Le Tourisme mondial et les enjeux de l'acadianité. *Francophonies d'Amérique* 27: 21–51.

O'Reilly, Camille. 2005. Tourist or traveller: Narrating backpacker identity. In *Discourses, communication and tourism*, ed. Adam Jaworski and Annette Pritchard, 150–169. Clevedon: Channel View Publications.

Pennycook, Alistair. 2010. Popular cultures, popular languages and global identities. In *The handbook of language and globalisation*, ed. Nikolas Coupland, 256–286. Oxford: Wiley-Blackwell.

Péronnet, Louise. 1989. *Atlas linguistique du vocabulaire maritime*. Québec: Les Presses de l'Université Laval.

Perrot, Marie-Ève. 2006. Statut et fonction symbolique du chiac: Analyse de discours épilinguistiques. *Francophonies d'Amérique* 22: 141–152.

Pietikäinen, Sari. 2008. Sámi in the media: Questions of language vitality and cultural hybridisation. *Journal of Multicultural Discourses* 3 (1): 22–35.

Pietikäinen, Sari. 2010. Sámi language mobility: Scales and discourses of multilingualism in a polycentric environment. *International Journal of the Sociology of Language* 202: 79–101.

Piller, Ingrid. 2003. Advertising as a site of language contact. *Annual Review of Applied Linguistics* 23: 170–183.

Poirier, Claude. 1994. *Langues, espaces, société: Les Variétés du français en Amérique du Nord*. Québec: Les Presses de l'Université Laval.

Sarkar, Mela. 2009. Still reppin por mi gente: The transformative power of language mixing in Quebec hip hop. *Global linguistic flows: Hip hop cultures, youth identities, and the politics of language*, ed. H. Samy Alim, Awad Ibrahim, and Alastair Pennycook, 139–157. New York and Abingdon: Routledge.

Savoie, Donald. 2000. *Community economic development in Atlantic Canada: False hope or Panacea?* Moncton: Institut canadien de recherche sur le développement régional.

Smith-Hefner, Nancy. 2007. Youth language, Gaul Sociability, and the new Indonesian middle class. *Journal of Linguistic Anthropology* 17 (2): 184–203.

Statistic Canada. 2006. Census Data. Government of Canada.

CHAPTER 4

Tourism and Gender in Linguistic Minority Communities

JOAN PUJOLAR

In this chapter,[1] I argue that peripheral positions allow in some circumstances for social actors to carry out innovations and transformative social practices that challenge dominant ideologies and power relations. I explore how different intersecting dimensions of peripherality play out in the small town of Glanporth in Wales in the context of a comparative project about language, tourism, and identity in Wales, Catalonia, and Francophone Canada. By looking into various tourist sites in these linguistic minority communities, I argue that heritage discourses present inbuilt contradictions in terms of gender and ethnicity as they reproduce the classic ideological divisions of modernity and thus construct specific hierarchies and centre–periphery relations. Heritage, I contend, is constituted in the geographical, economic, and social peripheries of modernity. As such, it points at the marginality of both women and minorities from its core processes. However, as women and linguistic minorities increasingly participate in tourism development in their communities, contradictions emerge. In places such as Glanporth, local actors react by developing cosmopolitan representations of minority identities.

Specific forms of multilingual practices, as I will show, are intimately bound up with these ideological struggles. Linguistic minority tourism confronts local actors with the global marketplace in which local languages can suffer new forms of displacement, either because of the communicative currency of transnational languages in tourist contexts or because local languages can be recruited in the commoditization of local cultures in ways that present them (again) as remnants of pre-modern lifestyles and economies (Phillips 2000; Pujolar 2006; Heller 2011). In Glanporth, local Welsh speakers carefully crafted initiatives which used the resources of tourism to carve out spaces for the Welsh language without investing in its commoditization as heritage.

Heritage tourism is constituted through the production of modernist narratives about identities and cultural practices largely located in peripheries and in the past. In terms of gender, this involves the appropriation of discourses about history that have been traditionally male-centred (Edensor and Kothari 1994; Edensor 1997), together with a focus on ways of life in which patriarchy was eminently normalized (Aitchison 1999). In terms of national identities, it involves constructing regional minorities as cultural remains, very much what nation-states have always sought to do as agents of homogenization and peripheralization and what minorities have sought to resist. Although narratives of history and memory have always been essential to the articulation of resistance on the part of minority nationalism, heritage discourses invite tensions as they involve, on the one hand, processes of Othering or exoticizing and, on the other hand, the appropriation of narratives in which idealizations of the national past typically mobilize contentious gendered representations.

In this chapter, I show how linguistic minorities develop different articulations of gender and national identity in tourism depending on how much they invest in heritage discourses or, alternatively, more cosmopolitan representations. I shall also discuss how multilingual practices in such contexts reflect and contribute to constructing these articulations, in which ideologies of modernity play a key role. To do so, I shall pay attention not only to the representations of national identity and gender that emerge in the sites but also to the ways in which women participate in the tourist process more generally (i.e. both as producers of nationalist discourses and as workers and entrepreneurs in the tourist industry). As the analysis focuses on how communities develop their own forms of representation, the perceptions of tourists or visitors shall not be addressed centrally.

I draw on data from a research project on the marketization of linguistic minority identities in tourism that included fieldwork in various Catalan-speaking sites, French-speaking minorities in Canada, and, finally, Welsh-speaking areas of Wales, which is the main case drawn on in this chapter. The research project focused on what Pitchford calls 'identity tourism': 'attractions in which collective identities are represented, interpreted, and potentially constructed through the use of history and culture' (2008: 3). The study was devised as a collection of cases to be used for comparison and to gain a general view of how linguistic minorities were getting gradually involved in new areas of activity in which identity was turned into a commodity. It is a multi-sited ethnography in which fieldwork consisted less of extended residence than of short visits to the sites, explorations of the landscape, informal contacts with the locals, formal interviews with participants (tourist workers, tourist policy officers, cultural activists), and documentation gathering (through websites, the press, and policy reports). All proper names from the Welsh site, 'Glanporth' included, are pseudonyms, and non-essential details of the description have been slightly changed to prevent traceability as much as possible.

The chapter is organized as follows: first, I argue that the concept of heritage is indexical of peripherality within the framework of modernity; secondly, I map out the different dimensions of peripherality that are constituted through dichotomies such as gender and nation, gender and tourism, and tourism and nation. After this, I will show how these different dimensions of peripherality become integrated and are resisted in complex ways in Glanporth.

HERITAGE AS PERIPHERY

Peripherality is a productive concept when it comes to characterizing how heritage products are produced and consumed basically because heritage constitutes a meeting point for the artefacts and practices that get *centrifuged* from modernity (i.e. that become obsolete or pushed to the margins of social life). As such, heritage is a site of articulation of multiple peripheralities. I shall expound here on how modern capitalism produces heritage as a continuous process, and how this mobilizes gender and nationalist ideologies in complex intersectionalities (see also Heller, this volume).

Feminist thought has long established how modernity was constituted in ways that endowed European male, white, upper-class elites with the cultural values of rationality that legitimized control over the colonies, women, minorities, and the lower classes. Bauman and Briggs (2003) have provided a cogent account of how this modern thought developed the diverse strands of antiquarianism and (Herderian) linguistic nationalism from the eighteenth century. Antiquarianism sought to document past, obsolete, forms of life and social practice often associated with women, while linguistic nationalism constructed the legitimacy of national identities as primordial and inherited from the 'fathers' to their children (2003: 176). Both lines of thought constituted responses to the profound cultural break that positioned modernity as in opposition to a past connected with superstition, obscurantism, and underdevelopment (i.e. in opposition to tradition). However, some aspects of tradition were recruited, reconstructed, and mobilized in the production of national identities, as Hobsbawm and Ranger (1983) have documented; and the selection was often encoded in terms of gender. Herderian nationalism was successfully adopted to legitimize the modern nation-state through a primordialist conception of the national community that was eminently male-centred.

Important forms of aestheticization and idealization of the past developed in the nineteenth century as the industrial revolution dislocated previous forms of production and social organization. Harvey has documented how changes in technologies and transport brought about new representations and forms of control over territories, dislocated existing geographies, accelerated urbanization, and changed cultural perceptions of place: 'transformations in spatial and temporal practices implied a loss of identity with place and repeated radical breaks with any sense of historical continuity... historical preservation and the museum culture experienced strong bursts of life' (Harvey 1989: 272).

It is also important to bear in mind that not only space but time was important in the equation in the sense that places often achieved their significance in terms of their value in (national) history and memory. Urbanization effectively turned rural areas into an economic and cultural periphery such that, as R. Williams (1975) showed, the countryside was transformed into a commodity for urban dwellers. Here it is also important to recall Pratt's (2002) argument that modernity has a constitutively diffusionist character, a logic that constructs centres as modern and peripheries as pre- or not-yet-fully modern (as discussed by Pietikäinen and Kelly-Holmes, in the introduction to this volume). According to Edensor (2002), such developments are often used to (re)deploy nationalist discourses, typically of a conservative character, as the artificial, technological, and culturally diverse city is set in contrast with a natural and racially unpolluted countryside. Linguistic minorities thus can also mobilize the countryside as a site where the national past is somehow still available, peripheral to the urban present, and often embodied in outdated cultural and economic lifestyles. Tourism is the typical space where these images are produced, distributed, and consumed.

Thus, heritage is by definition the periphery of modernity, as it gathers the social and cultural material outdated by social and productive transformations. It follows from this that discourses and practices about heritage are bound to reproduce the ideological processes and social divisions of modernity which construct specific forms of gender, class, and ethnicity as anachronisms. And it also implies that it has an important geographical component that inscribes the past eminently to rural areas (although it can naturally be found in urban settings too). This clearly places heritage in potential tension with both feminism and minority nationalism, that is, with the principles of gender and ethno-cultural emancipation that they pursue. To understand these tensions, it is necessary to specify some of the ways in which women and ethnolinguistic minorities have been positioned as peripheral to modernity and capitalism, as well as how nationalism has historically constructed gender relations.

GENDER, MINORITY NATIONALISM, AND TOURISM

Gender relations in general can also be constructed in terms of cores and peripheries. As Connell (2005) argued, they can be characterized as featuring a 'hegemonic masculinity' that defines the terms upon or against which other forms of gender and sexuality position and define themselves. Thus, most men or key men in powerful positions invest in this hegemonic masculinity that produces the dominant gender regime and places other models of gender and sexuality as closer or further to normality, as more or less peripheral (see also Walby 1997; Chen 1999).

Linguistic minorities in Europe also respond to a general pattern of geographical, political, and economic peripherality (with some exceptions, such as the Catalans or the Flemish). They normally occupy a region under the jurisdiction of a nation-state and where the national capital city, the main nodes of communication and the traditional industrial and economic centres lie outside of it, comparably distant.

State institutions operate in the language of a dominant majority that typically controls both access to economic resources and public institutions, and thereby has the power to define the 'normal' linguistic and cultural practices in the public sphere which give access to social mobility. This is why processes of language shift have characteristically presented an urban-rural profile, with the dominant state language increasingly occupying territories and social spaces closer to political and economic centres and pushing minority languages further to the peripheries. This is also why linguistic minorities have often been portrayed as anachronisms, particularly by nation-state institutions and their intellectual élites.

A common response from these communities has been the adoption of a nationalist ideology that explicitly aimed at the modernization of their language and culture through processes of linguistic standardization, control over public institutions, and the creation of a cultural market (Grillo 1989; Hobsbawm 1992). This is the case of Wales as a British internal colony from the Middle Ages. Welsh language and culture have historically been pushed to the margins of the Anglicized and industrialized areas of South Wales, which generally enjoy better road and rail connections with England and London than the North of the Country, where speakers of Welsh are still comparatively numerous (National Statistics Office 2004). Important groups of mainly Welsh speakers have developed their own forms of nationalism that rely on modernizing discourses about language, culture, and tradition, as we find amongst most linguistic minorities in Europe (Hobsbawm 1992; C. H. Williams 1994; Heller 1999; Heller 2011).

Minority nationalism, however, by drawing on modern ideologies also reproduces their ideological divisions. Feminist analyses of nationalism have documented its overwhelmingly masculinist character. The exclusion of women from public spaces has been extensively documented and takes specific forms from the French Revolution (Outram 1987; Landes 1988). Such developments went hand in hand with the discursive articulation of the French nation as a political subject, where exclusion of women was accompanied by the exclusion of regional minorities and languages, as well as members of particular social classes. Classical studies of nationalism represented by Anderson (1991), Hobsbawm (1992), or Gellner (1983) are eminently gender-blind; but feminist critiques of nationalism have examined how gender has been articulated through dichotomies such as state and nation or the public and the private. Women, according to Nagel (2001) get assigned various roles in the latter categories, particularly connected to the tasks of biological and cultural reproduction of the national group taking place at home and associated spaces such as schools. Beyond this, representations of women may also be mobilized to signify ethnic/national differences. Finally, they can also be recruited as participants in national, economic, political, and military struggles; though always in low capacities (i.e. in positions peripheral to those occupied by men) (Yuval-Davis, Anthias and Campling 1989; Yuval-Davis 1997; Nagel 2001; Puri 2004). Thus, nationalism has historically played a key role in the articulation of patriarchal gender roles and in marginalizing women and alternative sexualities in terms of the definition of national communities and participation in public life (Anthias, Yuval-Davis, and Cain 1993; Edensor 2002).

Following their expansion in the late twentieth century, tourism and the heritage industry (Hewison 1987; Urry 1995) have become important sites for the production and dissemination of national identities both for nation-states and minority communities (Picard and Wood 1997; Kapferer 1998; Pritchard and Morgan 2001; Heller 2003; Hallett and Kaplan-Weinger 2004; Takashi Wilkerson and Wilkerson 2004; Pujolar 2006; Pitchford 2008). However, the ways in which different communities relate to tourism are very much historically contingent. Acadians, for instance, have developed cultural tourism since the 1960s as a form of economic development (see McLaughlin, this volume). Catalans have historically exploited the Sun, Sex, and Sand mass tourism model and have had little interest in cultural tourism until recently. In contrast, Wales—especially Welsh-speaking Wales—has had a problematic relationship with tourism historically. The seaside resorts along the South and South-West coasts became early foci of Anglicization (particularly as a result of the advent of the railway during the mid-nineteenth century); indeed, Welsh-speaking populations in these areas were gradually displaced and generally did not participate in the entrepreneurial initiatives from which important profits could be made (Jones 2000; Phillips 2000). Thus, tourism in Wales has characteristically been largely based on English-speaking entrepreneurs relying on local bilingual or English-speaking workforce. This is why Welsh cultural sectors and the population in general developed mistrust for tourism, given that Welsh speakers rarely controlled the businesses and received the benefits of this economic sector (e.g. Phillips 2000).

In view of this, the *Bwrdd Croeso Cymru* (Welsh Tourist Board), in collaboration with the *Bwrdd Yr Iaith Gymraeg* (Welsh Language Board), developed in the early 2000s a series of policies and specific campaigns to prop up the role of Welsh identity and of Welsh-speaking communities in tourism (Pitchford 2008): the 'Homecoming 2000-Hiraeth 2000' initiative, the *Croesawiaith* (language welcome) scheme, *Ennill Tamaid* (Table Talk), *Naws am Le* (Sense of Place), and *Croeso Cynnes Cymreig* (A Warm Welsh Welcome) have aimed to provide training, resources, and grants to Welsh-speaking tourist sector businesses in particular (Pujolar 2006; Pitchford 2008) These concepts pointed at the connection between Welshness, language, and territory as a specific added value that Welsh-speaking communities could bring into tourism, arguably in a bid to commoditize Welsh as heritage (see also Coupland, this volume). The effects of and responses to these policies were visible in the case of Glanporth, which I analyse below.

So far, there is no evidence that minority nationalisms have been different from state-sponsored hegemonic nationalism with respect to their gender politics. At least, the few studies that touch on this aspect suggest that the trajectories of these social movements are also eminently male-centred with regard to the actors involved and the discursive trajectories (Aaron 1997; Vilalta 2006). This does not preclude the fact that the ethnocultural hierarchies that minorities have had to confront have often been constructed or expressed in gender terms, which means that minorities can often get desexualized, feminized or, alternatively, hypersexualized by majorities (Browne and Misra 2003; Fernàndez 2008). In any case, the peripherality experienced by these minorities does not seem to have made their societies more sensitive to gender peripherality. Instead the trajectories of women in these contexts suggest that a specific form of 'double' peripherality takes place that is comparable with the classic case of black women that gave rise to the literature on intersectionality (Collins 1990).

Tourism is an area of activity that also has important implications for gender relations. In the literature on gender and tourism, there is a general consensus to apply a basic distinction between everything having to do with tourists (and the consumption perspective) and the workers (from the perspective of production). The first aspect affects the experiences and services offered to tourists, which are often segmented according to sex or gender. Sex tourism is the classical example (Enloe 2000); but there are many other aspects that incorporate gendered components, such as the offer of events or entertainment (night life, festivals, concerts, and sports), representations of local communities and particular patterns of host-tourist interaction. The second aspect has to do with the fact that tourism, for the host society, is embedded in political and economic activities where actors have different forms of access to symbolic and material resources.

The gender divisions of the tourist workforce are an important aspect (Hennessy 1994; Purcell 1997; Sinclair 1997; Enloe 2000). Purcell (1997) clearly showed that, in the case of the United Kingdom in 1995, women made up the majority of the workforce (62 per cent) in 'accommodation and catering activities'; but that almost three quarters of them (72.4 per cent) were employed in low-paid, part-time positions. Further evidence showed that women had only exceptional access to stable employments with career prospects in the sector, which were overwhelmingly occupied by men. As Enloe (2000) points out, employers in the sector have historically sought to minimize employment costs by defining most jobs as 'unskilled' or 'low-skilled', particularly those that women workers are assumed to do 'naturally', such as household maintenance. Of particular interest are what Purcell terms 'patriarchally prescribed occupations', typically in small businesses, where 'husband and wife teams work together, with the woman frequently employed as "unpaid family worker"' (1997: 49). Thus, when it comes to tourism employment, women are the numerical majority but are nevertheless peripheral in relation to those in a position to control and profit most from tourism. At the intersection of tourism, heritage, and nationalism, we also find a characteristic gender profiling in female voluntary work: women volunteers were found to be essential in an Ontario Francophone pageant (Malaborza and McLaughlin 2006; Heller and Pujolar 2010), in the development of some Catalan literary heritage sites (Pujolar and Jones 2011), and, near Glanporth itself, in a project of a British Heritage Foundation where 80 per cent of volunteers where women.

It follows from this that identity tourism potentially provides a site for the reproduction of (and resistance to) the gender inequalities fostered by nationalist movements. So far, existing literature has identified sites where national identities are constructed 'by drawing almost exclusively upon male experience and male activity' (Edensor and Kothari 1994: 183; Aitchison 1999; Knox and Hannam 2007), particularly where the remembrance of heroes and battles clearly draws from historical narratives where women are eminently absent. However, heritage tourism provides a much wider range of themes, some of which do provide roles for women. One example is the sites devoted to the representation of past forms of everyday life, which have been well documented in the Welsh context by Pitchford (2008), though not from a gender perspective. Such sites, as I will show, are also amenable to a critique of their investments in specific gender relations (Aitchison 1999: 61–62). Additionally, representations of national communities can also be accomplished more subtly in tourist services such as hotels, bed & breakfasts, restaurants, cafeterias, and other sites that constitute the scenarios, props, and landscapes for tourists. Davidson (2006), for instance, argues that hotel space has characteristically acted as a liminal space between the local and the global and, in places like early twentieth-century Barcelona, was mobilized to overcome Catalan cultural and economic peripherality. My examples will draw mainly on these liminal spaces, although a nod to conventional heritage representations needs to be made also to attend to the wider picture. In fact, Acadian heritage tourism and Welsh ethnological museums constitute good examples of this conventional heritage based on the 'antiquarian' perspective and its nationalist and gender correlates.

In New Brunswick (Canada), sites such as the *Village Historique Acadien* in Caraquet or *Le Pays de la Sagouine* in Bouctouche rely on impressive reproductions of farm households, workshops, or village life in the old days. They include actors styling themselves as the old residents, perfectly trained to explain and discuss any relevant details to visitors. Women—again more numerous—can be found mainly in the farms, the men working as printers, innkeepers, or carpenters: they are all, so to speak, in their places, including their involvement in activities and skills they can explain and enact for visitors (for women: cooking, baking, weaving, cloth-making, child-rearing, care of small animals). (See also Boudreau and White (2006) for a similar heritage site in the province of Nova Scotia.) These representations largely subscribe to the conventional formulae of reproductions of past forms of life, work, and artistic performance where the family and the domestic sphere take precedence. This entails an adoption of traditional forms of feminine performance and hence the uncritical reproduction of a historical patriarchal order. It also involves, however, an active participation of women in the tourist industry as skilled and semi-skilled professionals and hence a significant degree of control by women over the representations of identity that are kept in circulation.

The development of a Welsh perspective on tourism has recently triggered debates about how Welsh identity is represented, what the emblematic sites are, and how these should be presented and interpreted. Pitchford (2008) mentions the castle-trail, its most popular sites having been built by the English kings to ensure the military control of the territory in the face of strong local opposition. These castles can both be presented as a symbol of English domination and of Welsh staunch resistance. On the other hand, there are the numerous sites devoted to characterizations of Welsh culture and ways of life: mining and slate museums and heritage sites, museums about Welsh crafts, traditions, and religions. These genres of tourist narrative have also been criticized for: (a) romanticizing the past and erasing the suffering of workers; (b) emphasizing the rural over the urban dimension of Welsh experience; (c) presenting Welshness as something connected with the past rather than the present; and (d) constructing Welsh art as folklore rather than art as such (Lord 1993). Neither Pitchford (2008) nor Lord (1993) raises the issue of gender. However, John (1991) and Aaron (1997) argue that representations of Wales and the Welsh have historically been made from a masculine point of view that marginalizes women's perspectives. Aaron (1997) observes that the disappearance of the mining industry has left a void in received representations of Welsh identity.

These tensions over heritage tourism point to the more general issue of whether Welsh identity should be associated with tradition or modernity (i.e. to peripheries or cores). When representations about Welshness get saturated by heritage discourses and practices, there appears a danger that Welshness gets linked with the past, the folklore, and dated forms of socialization and economic production, including the old patriarchal regimes and nationalist histories. In short, it may be constructed, or interpreted, as being an identity that is peripheral to contemporary forms of modernity.

TOURISM AND WELSH IDENTITY IN GLANPORTH

There are other options to present Welshness in tourism beyond the heritage paradigm, and the case of Glanporth shows one of them. In this town, a group of entrepreneurial women promoted the social and economic development of the town in ways that appeared compatible with a contemporary cosmopolitan community and a business-oriented Welsh identity. As such it presented an atypical profile of participation by Welsh speakers and women both in tourism and in the construction of national identity. In this context, the use of Welsh played an important role, one that stressed its value as a public language rather than as an exclusively cultural product. This means that Welsh appeared as a functional language in public communications orientated towards practical needs of information and signalling and not just as an aesthetic addition to texts mainly written or spoken in English. Thus, this group of actors was mobilizing in the periphery with peripheral resources and identities; but they were at the same time discarding the appropriation of the typical symbolic devices through which peripherality is commonly constructed, namely to present language and identity as heritage.

Glanporth is a small-sized town of about 1,500 inhabitants sited in an area where Welsh is reported as spoken by more than two thirds of the population (National Statistics Office 2004), although English has long dominated in the town itself. According to one interviewee, Welsh speakers perceived the town centre as an English-speaking space where the possibility to use the language in shops and services needed to be asserted or signalled. Glanporth had never had an important industry or mines in the vicinity; but it had reportedly thrived in the early twentieth century thanks to its port until the railway had rendered it redundant. Agriculture had also remained relatively strong until the 1990s, after which local farmers could no longer rely on the London market to take up their dairy produce at reasonable prices. Although the touristic information reported on the existence of some old industries and workshops (a woollen mill, a forge, a tannery, a wood turner, and a wheelwright), no manufacturing existed anymore. A number of offices of the county authority were sited there, which also provided skilled employment for Welsh speakers. Otherwise, the sponsor list for the 2006's town jubilee attested to the touristic orientation of the local economy: apart from two web and video design companies, one translator, eight sports or social clubs, and forty-one local suppliers and services (shops, solicitors, public, offices), there were sixty-three tourist establishments (hotels, restaurants), nine crafts makers, and twenty-seven building-related businesses. As the town had not grown significantly during the previous century, the urban landscape had remained agreeable and one fourth of the houses were listed as being of architectural interest. There was a beach and a port and opportunities for hiking or dolphin sighting. The main touristic asset of the place was in the consumption of the quiet natural, sea and urban landscape.[2] There were none of the more spectacular tourist resources, such as big castles or famous sites.

The significance of a visit to Glanporth needed to be worked upon. This was done to a great extent through the initiative of a network of locals in which women played key roles. As local authorities have very limited resources in Britain, this network concentrated on fund raising and mobilizing local actors such as social clubs and cultural associations, in the organization of public events that were reported in the press and that positioned the town as a place worth visiting. Other initiatives predominantly run by men consisted of the organization of an agricultural fair and engaging a British Heritage Foundation to restore and put up visitors in an old nobleman's house. The women's group worked primarily on the organization of the 2006 Jubilee, a city walking trail, and other regular yearly celebrations that involved activities in the streets (at Christmas, Halloween, Carnival, etc.). In this process, an important role was played by three women who, together with their husbands, were investing in new business initiatives that sought to promote a revitalization of the town's life while catering for tourists at the same time. These were one restaurant-pub (established 2002), one textile shop (established 2003), and one hotel (established 2005).

I identified a total of five women who seemed to constitute a core network that was however not formally constituted. In the interviews we conducted with four or them, I have reconstructed an account based on my observations whereby participation in many city committees, associations, the city council, and various initiatives (involving, of course, many other women and men) appeared to have this group as a common denominator. They themselves did not explain the situation in the way I do, although most other interviewees kept mentioning their names as the people to talk to. Not only this: although the three businesses mentioned were run by married couples, most locals (men included) also identified the women as at least an equal partner or as the main driving force behind the initiative. At least in one case, it was clear from the interview that the female partner had developed the idea, done the investment, and most of the work. On the website, one could read the following about the establishment of the business:

Extract 1: excerpt from the textile shop's web presentation.
Welsh version
—gan Aeron Gwyther a Dyl Edwards, gŵr a gwraig sydd bellach yn byw yn y dref ac sydd wedi eu geni a'u magu yng Ngwyradd

English version
—by Aeron Gwyther and her husband Dylan Edwards who live in the town and were born and bred in the county of Gwyradd

This unusual collocation of a married couple, with the woman first and the husband's position defined according to his marital status, expresses a reversal of the conventional forms of naming that have traditionally been denounced as sexist and thus dispels the reading that the wife could play only a secondary role in such joint ventures, as usually happens according to the literature on employment. It must be noted however that the Welsh version includes the expression 'husband and wife' in this order, which is less stylistically marked.

Most of the interviewees presented life trajectories characterized by a confrontation with economic and cultural peripherality. They had been born in Glanporth or very near; but they had also lived and worked in other parts of Wales. One of them was retired and had just returned after working and raising a family in an English city. Another one had also migrated but recently returned and remarried. Most of the younger women had gone away to college, had worked for a few years in the media or other occupations rare for Welsh speakers of former generations, and had sought employment or directly set up a business in Glanporth. The three women entrepreneurs had also been connected in their previous professional life. Thus, they had all experienced the difficulties of an attachment to a place that offered little economic prospects. Their strategy was not just about earning a living but also about developing Glanporth and developing it as a Welsh space.

Aeron, the owner and manager of the textile shop, expressed this approach very clearly. She got the idea for the shop while walking in the street and realizing how old and simple the town's commercial landscape was. Locals had to drive to larger towns to find nice shops. So the idea was to create a situation whereby it made sense for both locals and tourists to go shopping in Glanporth (i.e. to confront its peripherality). After many years of participation in local cultural and youth clubs, she was in close touch with the local community and aware of the need to stimulate it. So, the shop offered not just a space for retailing but also a café room for socializing, as has become common in some bookstores (Aeron actually said that it was a good idea for men to have somewhere to sit and spend time while their partners were in the shop). The opening reportedly attracted a large number of friends and relations as local people felt involved in the success of the venture and that the shop brought something new to the town. Aeron acknowledged that it was made viable both by tourists and also by the locals who shopped less intensively but more constantly throughout the year. Thus, this venture was partly motivated by a will to stimulate (Welsh) community life, and it needed this same community dynamism to survive.

The combination of community life and tourist activities was also promoted by the hotel, particularly through the intensive use of a blog, where constantly updated information told about local events, outings and hikes by locals, and small celebrations around gastronomic topics (most of which were open to hotel guests, so that these could potentially participate in local life during their stay). The restaurant had also achieved a fine balance through the use of two different spaces: one offered the service of a conventional restaurant with pricy and elaborate cuisine and another basically functioned as a local pub, always quite full of customers even on week days.

The balance between an orientation to (a largely Welsh) local community and a (largely Anglophone) transnational tourist constituency was articulated in various ways: first, through bilingualism; secondly, through the promotion of local produce; thirdly, through the incorporation of cosmopolitan design and aesthetics. Thus, these were entrepreneurial initiatives led by women (or partnerships in which women were equal) who used their local networking resources (in one case, local women as potential consumers) to push the town into recovering its role as a commercial centre and by using Welsh as the main medium of communication. Gender, economic, and ethnolinguistic peripheralities were being overturned in one stroke.

Welsh Bilingualism in Glanporth

Reports by interviewees, particularly older ones, bear witness to times in which speakers of Welsh were in even higher proportions than today but the use of the language was exclusively restricted to the private domain, and limited to farmers and fishermen, in contrast with the contemporary experience of Welsh being used in schools and in the public sphere and also in new neighbourhoods inhabited by middle-class mobile sectors. The establishment of a Welsh Assembly and the official enforcement of bilingual signage throughout the country had recently turned Welsh-English bilingualism into a normal feature of the scriptorial landscape (Gade 2005). All signs from public institutions were systematically bilingual. Not so consistent were, however, the language choices of private establishments (cf. Kelly-Holmes, this volume). Shop signs and their commercial information were mostly in English only, with Welsh restricted to the generic description and in second position or smaller font (Pharmacy/*Fferyllfa*). Some shops had a Welsh name more visible but accompanied by a translation or, in any case, all practical information in English. In one of the cafés, for instance, the name of the establishment was Welsh; but a board on the wall and another in the pavement displayed the products on offer in English.

The interviewees had very different levels of competence in Welsh and acknowledged the existence of tensions over language use within the community. One member of one of the three couples could not speak it fluently; two other interviewees were basically monolingual English speakers; one of the more active participants could speak it and write it with difficulty.

Language choice was often a delicate issue: council meetings could not be held in Welsh because not all members could follow, some local actors demanded communications from the council in Welsh, some jobs and roles in local committees required Welsh speakers, translation could be arranged for some events and not for others, business owners worried when they could not find Welsh-speaking workers, as this might make some clients uncomfortable. Although there were no local offices of Cymdeithas yr Iaith or other language activist groups, all interviewees avowed their commitment with the Welsh language. The question was how this commitment was brought into practice, and two interviewees argued that Welsh could not be 'forced down people's throats' and hoped that the extension of Welsh could be made gradually.

The three establishments analysed, in any case, had a policy of linguistic equality that in some aspects reversed the logic of the private commercial sector and its tokenistic, emblematic, non-communicational use of Welsh. Two of them had an English name, such as 'The Traveller's Inn' or 'The Railway Hotel', with the Welsh translation not always visible and in secondary position. The other's name did not mean anything in any recognizable language. But otherwise Welsh was present throughout the premises and often in first position: in fixed signs (e.g. about toilets, private rooms), in more-or-less carefully printed more variable messages, on printed menus and blackboards, in the room plaques that remind visitors of the extension number and service hours, on the key rings, on cards and leaflets, in a text explaining the meaning of the room's name and the history of Glanporth, in the '*Llonyd plis* / Do not disturb signs' hanging off door knobs, in signs indicating how to use the toiletries, in welcome messages and instructions about hotel/restaurant services (such as telephone calls) and sale of merchandizing, in the quality appraisal forms, in the list of town services, safety instructions, recommendations about behaviour in common spaces (control of pets or children), price tags and offers, warnings to thieves or smokers, directions, and so on. English-only texts appeared exceptionally in items that might be difficult to obtain in bilingual versions, such as some safety equipment, beer pump signs, soft drinks bottles, and so on.

When asked for the reasons for the use of Welsh, interviewees focused primarily on the rights of Welsh speakers to use Welsh and circulate in Welsh scriptorial landscapes. When asked if the use of Welsh might be appreciated by tourists as a sign of local character (which was the argument of various campaigns by the official Welsh language and tourism authorities), their responses were non-committal or treated the question as an 'interesting idea'. One of the interviewees actually asked for advice about what to do with Welsh in events attended by tourists. Another, however, recalled that some time ago tourists used to steal the menus of her parents' restaurant to keep them as souvenirs, because the presence of Welsh was then so rare. In any case, my exploration of Internet tourist forums in July 2010 did not give evidence of specific linguistic awareness by tourists. Out of forty finds about the Glanporth establishments, all in English, clients concentrated overwhelmingly on the comfort of the rooms and the quality of the food, and sometimes the landscape. The adjective 'Welsh' almost invariably referred to food, except for a positive remark about the restaurant exuding 'a certain Welshness' and the ability of the staff that 'adjusted between the Welsh and English speakers in the restaurant well'.

Thus, the bilingualism of the establishments was one more way of reconciling the division between the local Welsh and the foreign tourists, although local English speakers were also important and interviewees also talked about an increasing number of Welsh-speaking tourists, many of them from Cardiff, the capital, and South Wales, which attests again to the ongoing change in the social and geographical profiles of Welsh speakers. In the hotel blog, for instance, most announcements were made bilingually; but many news items and most comments by blog visitors were in English, including one complaining about a Welsh company that commercialized sauces and did not label its products in Welsh. The blog, in any case, reflected well the ambivalence of the business as it addressed both locals and tourists and used the two languages.

From this perspective, the Welsh-English equality choice was a specific form of positioning that needed constant attention by the owners of the establishments as to how the two languages should be used. Thus, the choice made by the three entrepreneurs to use Welsh to the maximum extent possible was primarily a statement about Welsh identity as deserving a place in modern public life rather than as a heritage display (see Pietikäinen and Kelly-Holmes 2011). If they considered that the use of Welsh lent some ethno-cultural flavour to the sites or products—as Piller (2001) and Kelly-Holmes (2000) documented in relation to non-English multilingual advertising in Europe—they did not own up to this potential reading. Their linguistic policy was rather presented as one intended to cater for the need to address specific market segments, both local and global, characterized by differing linguistic profiles (see Kelly-Holmes 2005); where no hint of a hierarchical difference between the two markets and languages was projected.

Local Food, Colour, Fabric, and Capital

According to one town councillor, the recent development of Glanporth in terms of tourism and Welsh identity had to be understood against the backdrop of economic change. The demise of industry and the fall in agricultural prices had forced farmers to focus on locality and authenticity, which had made wide sectors of the population especially sensitive to issues of identity. Although this is a view that, however interesting, cannot be contrasted in terms of the causal connections it suggests (at least with the data I have), it is indicative of the local political economic mood, as is reflected in the following excerpt.

Extract 2: excerpt from interview.
Local councillor: More money comes into this county through tourism than anything else · and that even goes as far as farmers (...) they've had to diversify farmers have had to look at how they operate (...) and they've done it I think very successfully (...) changing needs of the visitor (...) who likes to go to the farm (...) and is interested in · food · local food

This commitment to local food was clearly visible in the menus and products in cafes, pubs, hotels, and restaurants. It was a nationwide trend, often symbolized by the mention of the Ty Nant mineral water. One of the entrepreneurs explained that she had increased her supplies of this type of Welsh product, which often came from firms run by Welsh speakers who also used the language both in transactions and in the marketing of the products. This was held to signify that Welsh speakers were crossing the old line that had allegedly kept them away from the world of business initiatives.

The focus on food did not lead, however, to an investment in traditional Welsh cuisine. As one press reviewer (rightly) expressed, cuisine showed 'a serious effort to combine the best local ingredients with global influences'. Thus, the products on offer referred predominantly to Italian, French, and other transnational products: tapas, lasagne, baguette, and espresso coffee. A typical example would be 'Bruchetta ai pepperoni—Toasted slice of bread topped with warm Abergavenny goats cheese and slices or roast peppers.' This is contemporary menu style, combining multilingualism with a short descriptive line. Interestingly enough, it is Italian that is used here to provide some distinct ethnocultural flavour, not Welsh.

This distance from what would constitute a traditional portrayal of Welsh identity was, I would argue, a distinctive feature of the business models analysed and arguably of the presentation of Glanporth to outsiders more generally. In Wales, sites devoted to the marketization of Welshness usually gather a number of elements; typically signs in Welsh and/or Welsh Celtic fonts, flags, and merchandizing in the flag's colours, particular filigree designs. No such semiotic repertoire was present in these businesses, and it was also much lower key in Glanporth as a whole as compared with other Welsh touristic towns. Here the reflections of one hotel owner show the extent to which this was a reflected choice:

Extract 3: excerpt from interview.
Nick: [...] we got a chef · we (did) the restaurant out ·· we (x) a chef we advertise (x) it's very good does italian so- mediterranean sort-of food [...] well we got italian menus

you can't really put italian into welsh we can't put spanish into welsh it's a [...] and we had a welsh designer to do the place · in welsh · the bedrooms are done in welsh tapes-tries · · the who- the whole idea is to be we- [...] our idea was not to be like raffles in singapore or some bar in you know ours is trying to be everything [...] but we didn't want to be just stick a welsh bar because it is blood- is boring as hell • you know if we had a proper welsh pub • then you'd had as that as that a (saunas) and that's it • • you know • people don't bother- we've been trying to make it women friendly • women have got say in the last thirty years • far more identity in pubs and businesses than they did before • • before it was all the men sitting around all evening (xxx) playing dominoes or playing games in front of everyone • and now it is women who come out • you know they want to sit in a bar • • women go into a pub • • not like before with old men looking at

Joan: how do you make it women friendly[?]

Nick: eee • • you make it clean you get away with what is a what is identified as a man • e • you sell lot more wine you advertise wine • • saying trying to be more continental as opposed to • continental bars are far more (xxx) to women than say the old british pub you know?

Here Nick voices in everyday language how the aesthetic balance should be negoti-ated between providing local flavour and catering to the expectations of contempo-rary customers who—as he was explaining earlier—could be Welsh or English; but also German, French, or Spanish. As with the food, the result was that Welsh raw materials were incorporated in a more contemporary eclectic design. Rooms had a lot of natural light without dark corners, all tables high over the knees, the furniture looking relatively new (not antique) in the hotel (with a Mediterranean flavour) and the Café (more Starbuck's style) and heavy real-wood square-shaped walnut-coloured in the restaurant (suggesting natural material but not traditional style). Reviews and client feedback provide further evidence of how this style was con-sumed: 'A cobalt blue boutique restaurant that's modern yet perfectly in tune with this stylish little town', 'It was decorated in a contemporary style, but using fabric from a tradition welsh woollen mill in a pattern used from 1859', 'terrific 'gastropub' food', 'Cosy but cool', 'Seaside chic', 'hip', 'beautifully styled and totally without pre-tence', 'it could be in London or Paris'.

Extract 4: excerpt from interview.
Kathryn: we've had to reinvent ourselves · I mean you can (xx) this place I mean (this place) you could be anywhere couldn't you the [Restaurant] it could be in a city it could be anywhere · it's great

To summarize, Glanporth presented an interesting profile where economic initia-tives were developed through relatively separate (though compatible) networks with either male or female predominance. In the female network, a key role was played by three couples who developed their own businesses as a way to stay or move back to the town. These businesses had an ambivalent agenda of economic sustainability and promotion of Welsh-speaking social life. As such, they were public meeting places for largely English-speaking tourist clients on the move in the periphery and as centres for the construction of Welshness for locals. This Welshness was both cultural and business orientated, transgressed traditional delimitations in the access of Welsh-speaking women to business and nation building and inscribed itself in contemporary gender-neutral ideologies that seek to position local identities in the global marketplace. This was achieved by performing hybridity at various levels: through bilingualism, through using local ingredients to make a globalized cuisine and through Welsh styles subtly contained in a postmodern patchwork. Conventional, tradition-bound, male-centred representations of Welsh identities were set aside in spaces that, like in the early Catalan hotels mentioned earlier, lay claim to both local identity and global orientation (Davidson 2006).

CONCLUDING REMARKS

Identity tourism is inscribed in a wider context of economic restructuring in which primary- and secondary-sector economies have receded and left peripheral areas dependent on tourism and few other options (cf. Heller, this volume). Policies of economic development in these areas have targeted heritage resources as a way to create unique selling points in the global marketplace (Urry 1995). Linguistic minority identities have become open to commoditization in the process, which raises new questions as to who has the right to represent local culture and how, including what the legitimate linguistic resources are (Le Menestrel 1999; Pritchard and Morgan 2001; Heller 2003; Boudreau and White 2006; Malaborza and McLaughlin 2006; da Silva and Heller 2007; Pitchford 2008; Pietikäinen and Kelly-Holmes 2011). The case of Glanporth provides an interesting window on the tensions that arise as linguistic minorities vie to participate in the tourist market. Different forms of representing national identity and different patterns of multilingualism emerged as new actors—women and/or Welsh speakers—staked their claim as participants in business initiatives and local economic development.

The Glanporth example provides evidence that representations of national identities in tourism can be produced in distinctly different ways, namely by investing or not in a conception of identity as heritage. An analysis of the gendered aspects of these contrasting representations interrogates the genealogy of heritage discourses and their deep investments in ideologies of modernity. Amongst linguistic minorities, heritage discourses mobilize historical and national narratives that are intrinsically gendered as they reproduce the hierarchical divisions and the diffusionist logic of modernity. Heritage is embedded in the complex web of discursive trajectories of modernity that elaborate ideologies of national identity and gender on the basis of dichotomies between tradition and modernity, the public and the private, the past and the present, the rational and the emotional, the civilized and the savage, the male and the female, the white and the coloured. These dichotomies, as has been widely contended, constitute established hierarchies that structure fundamental divisions such as marked/unmarked, high/low, normal/deviant, and, last but not least, core/periphery. Heritage, by commodifying the 'Other', provides space for assigning value to the ideological peripheries of modernity. As such, a critique of heritage requires an intersectional perspective that looks at the production of the various dimensions of social categorization and social difference.

Peripherality is mobilized as a resource in tourism, particularly with the marketization of local landscapes and local produce that draw their value from their scarcity in urban centres. In linguistic minority heritage more specifically, cultural representations of ethnicity and language can also be marshalled as products that retain a value as enduring relics of state-building, industrialization, and modernization more generally: thus, ethnicity as periphery, is often signalled or iconized through the tokenistic use of local languages. There are however some potential tensions in these processes, namely, in the fact that nationalist discourses characteristically pursue cultural and linguistic modernization as opposed to folklorization, and also in the fact that both nationalist politics and tourist development involve processes of internal hierarchization, the marginalization of women being one of their features. In the context of tourism, where women occupy characteristically inferior positions in terms of employment patterns and in terms of participation in decision-making processes, heritage sites can easily resort to either male-only heroic-military renderings of national history or depictions of national life of a characteristically patriarchal profile. So far these tensions have caused debates in nationalist and feminist constituencies.

Women and linguistic minorities participating in tourism development must therefore make choices as to whether they subscribe to these discursive trajectories and social histories. In the Acadian case referred to above, women are very present—actually numerically predominant—at all levels of the structure, even in leading positions, and subscribe to classical versions of heritage in a context where feminine figures were traditionally prominent as national signifiers. In Glanporth, a group of women who dominated local politics and new economic initiatives chose to mobilize some aspects of peripherality as a resource and discard other aspects of it. Thus, Welsh was adopted as a fully functional communicative language and not only as a token for display at the same time that other traditional resources for displaying Welsh identity were discarded in favour of local agricultural produce and the adoption of a hybrid aesthetic that combined the local with the global. These female entrepreneurs designed their initiatives so that the symbolic and economic capital acquired through tourism could also be channelled to provide space for Welsh language and culture in their communities. Their preoccupation with Welshness showed an orientation to the present and the future rather than the past. Thus, these Glanporth women, together with their husbands, were overcoming the typical peripheral position of both women and Welsh speakers in politics, business, and tourism and were doing so by both mobilizing Welsh peripherality as a marketable commodity at the same time as challenging the construction of Welshness as a peripheral ethnicity.

NOTES

1. This chapter is based on the research Project 'Language, culture and tourism: Identity discourses and the commoditization of languages in global markets' funded by the Dirección General de Investigación of the Ministerio de Educación y Ciencia in Spain: Ref. HUM2006–13621-C04–04/FILO. It is also inscribed in the activities of the Linguamón-UOC Chair in Multilingualism. Monica Heller (University of Toronto) and Kathryn Jones (IAITH: Welsh Centre for Language Planning) contributed to the fieldwork. I am also indebted to Maite Puigdevall (Universitat Oberta de Catalunya) for her help with materials written or spoken in Welsh, and to Monica Heller and Maria Sabaté for their comments on earlier drafts of the text.
2. Through careful web searches, I found some markedly different forms of tourism and leisure in the area. Some hotels or private individuals organized, normally off season, boxing matches, special disco nights, or car-crash gatherings. These activities did not appear in the conventional materials for tourism promotion and were not mentioned by any of the interviewees. The fact that these activities were not mentioned—not even for criticism— suggest that they were comparably marginal, both symbolically (in the local imaginary) and economically (in terms of visitor numbers and revenue). It is interesting, however, that some of them point to the construction of the tough masculinities that are declining in legitimacy.

REFERENCES

Aaron, Jane. 1997. Women in search of a Welsh identity. *Scottish Affairs* 18: 69–81.
Aitchison, Cara. 1999. Heritage and nationalism: Gender and the performance of power. In *Leisure/tourism geographies: Practices and geographical knowledge*, ed. David Crouch, 59–73. London: Routledge.
Anderson, Benedict. 1991. *Imagined communities: Reflections on the origin and spread of nationalism.* London: Verso.
Anthias, Floya, Nira Yuval-Davis, and Harriet Cain. 1993. *Racialized boundaries: Race, nation, gender, colour and class and the anti-racist struggle.* Oxon: Routledge.
Bauman, Richard, and Charles S. Briggs. 2003. *Voices of modernity: Language ideologies and the politics of inequality.* Cambridge: Cambridge University Press.
Boudreau, Annette, and Chantal White. 2006. Turning the tide in Acadian Nova Scotia: How heritage tourism is changing language practices and representations of language. *The Canadian Journal of Linguistics/La revue canadienne de linguistique* 49 (3): 327–351.
Browne, Irene, and Joya Misra. 2003. The intersection of gender and race in the labor market. *Annual Review of Sociology* 29 (1): 487–513. doi:10.1146/annurev. soc.29.010202.100016.
Chen, Anthony S. 1999. Lives at the center of the periphery, lives at the periphery of the center. *Gender & Society* 13 (5): 584–607.
Collins, Patricia Hill. 1990. *Black feminist thought: Knowledge, consciousness, and the politics of empowerment.* New York: Routledge.

Connell, R. W. 2005. *Masculinities*. Berkeley and Los Angeles: University of California Press.

Da Silva, Emanuel, and Monica Heller. 2007. *From protector to producer: The role of the state in the discursive shift from minority rights to economic development*. The American Ethnological Association (AES) and the Canadian Anthropology Society (CASCA).

Davidson, Robert A. 2006. A periphery with a view: Hotel space and the Catalan modern experience. *Romance Quarterly* 53 (3): 169–183.

Edensor, Tim. 1997. National identity and the politics of memory: Remembering Bruce and Wallace in symbolic space. *Environment and Planning D: Society and Space* 15 (2): 175–194. doi:10.1068/d150175.

Edensor, Tim. 2002. *National identity, popular culture and everyday life*. Oxford: Berg.

Edensor, Tim, and Uma Kothari. 1994. The masculinisation of Stirling's heritage. In *Tourism: A gender analysis*, ed. Vivian Kinnaird and Derek R. Hall, 164–187. Chichester: Wiley.

Enloe, Cynthia H. 2000. *Bananas, beaches and bases: Making feminist sense of international politics*. Los Angeles: University of California Press.

Fernàndez, Josep-Anton. 2008. *El malestar en la cultura catalana*. Barcelona: Empúries.

Gade, D. W. 2005. Language, identity, and the scriptorial landscape in Québec and Catalonia. *Geographical Review* 93 (4): 429–448.

Gellner, Ernest. 1983. *Nation and nationalism*. Oxford: Blackwell.

Grillo, Ralph D. 1989. *Dominant languages: Language and hierarchy in Britain and France*. Cambridge: Cambridge University Press.

Hallett, Richard W., and Judith Kaplan-Weinger. 2004. The construction of independence: A multimodal discourse analysis of Lithuanian tourism websites. In *La Communication touristique: Approches discursives de l'identiteet de l'alterite/Tourist communication: Discursive approaches to identity and otherness*, ed. Fabienne Baider, Marcel Burger, and Dionysis Goutsos, 215–234. Paris: L'Harmattan.

Harvey, David. 1989. *The condition of postmodernity: An enquiry into the origins of cultural change*. Oxford: Wiley-Blackwell.

Heller, Monica. 1999. *Linguistic minorities and modernity: A sociolinguistic ethnography*. London: Longman.

Heller, Monica. 2003. Globalization, the new economy and the commodification of language and identity. *Journal of Sociolinguistics* 7 (4): 473–492.

Heller, Monica. 2011. *Paths to post-nationalism: A critical ethnography of language and identity*. New York: Oxford University Press.

Heller, Monica, and Joan Pujolar. 2010. The political economy of texts: A case study in the structuration of tourism. *Sociolinguistic Studies* 3 (2): 177–201.

Hennessy, Sinead. 1994. Female employment in tourism development in South-West England. In *Tourism: A gender analysis*, ed. Vivian Kinnaird and Derek Hall, 35–51. Chichester: Wiley.

Hewison, Robert. 1987. *The heritage industry: Britain in a climate of decline*. London: Methuen.

Hobsbawm, Eric J. 1992. *Nations and nationalism since 1780: Programme, myth, reality*. Cambridge: Cambridge University Press.

Hobsbawm, Eric J., and Terence Ranger. 1983. *The invention of tradition*. Cambridge: Cambridge University Press.

John, Angela V. 1991. *Our mother's land: Chapters in Welsh women's history, 1830–1939*. Cardiff: University of Wales Press.

Jones, Dot. 2000. The coming of the railways and language change in North Wales 1850–1900. In *The Welsh language and its social domains 1801–1911*. ed. Geraint H. Jenkins, 131–150. Cardiff: University of Wales Press.

Kapferer, Judith. 1998. Heritage tourism and identity instruction: Whose heritage? Whose benefit? *Discourse: Studies in the Cultural Politics of Education* 19 (2): 219–232.

Kelly-Holmes, Helen. 2000. Bier, parfum, kaas: Language fetish in European advertising. *European Journal of Cultural Studies* 3 (1): 67–82.

Kelly-Holmes, Helen. 2005. *Advertising as multilingual communication*. Basingstoke: Palgrave Macmillan.

Knox, Dan, and Kevin Hannam. 2007. Embodying everyday masculinities in heritage tourism(s). In *Tourism and gender: embodiment, sensuality and experience*, eds. Annette Pritchard, Nigel J. Morgan, Irtena Ateljevic, and Candice Harris, 263–272. Wallingford: CABI.

Landes, Joan B. 1988. *Women and the public sphere in the age of the French Revolution*. Ithaca, N.Y.: Cornell University Press.

Le Menestrel, Sara. 1999. *La Voie des cadiens: Tourisme et identité en Louisianne*. Paris: Belin.

Lord, Peter. 1993. *Aesthetics of relevance*. Llandysul: Gomer.

Malaborza, Sonia, and Mireille McLaughlin. 2006. Spectacles à grand déploiement et représentation du passé et de l'avenir: L'Exemple de quatre productions canadiennes-françaises en Ontario et au Nouveau-Brunswick. *Cahiers franco-canadiens de l'Ouest* 18 (2): 191–204.

Nagel, Joane. 2001. Masculinity and nationalism: Gender and sexuality in the making of nations. *Ethnic and Racial Studies* 21 (2): 242–269.

National Statistics Office. 2004. *Census 2001: Report on the Welsh language: Laid before parliament pursuant to section 4 (1) Census Act 1920*. London: TSO.

Outram, Dorinda. 1987. Le Langage mâle de la vertu: Women and the discourse of the French Revolution. In *The social history of language*, eds. Peter Burke and Roy Porter, 120–135. Cambridge: Cambridge University Press.

Phillips, Dylan. 2000. We'll keep a welcome? The effects of tourism in the Welsh language. In *The Welsh language in the twentieth century*, 527–550. Cardiff: University of Wales Press.

Picard, Michel, and Robert Wood. 1997. *Tourism, ethnicity, and the state in Asian and Pacific societies*. Honolulu: University of Hawaii Press.

Pietikäinen, Sari, and Helen Kelly-Holmes. 2011. The local political economy of languages in a Sámi tourism destination: Authenticity and mobility in the labelling of souvenirs. *Journal of Sociolinguistics* 15 (3): 323–346.

Piller, Ingrid. 2001. Identity constructions in multilingual advertising. *Language in society* 30 (2): 153–186.

Pitchford, Susan. 2008. *Identity tourism: Imaging and imagining the nation*. Bingley, U.K.: Emerald Group Publishing Ltd.

Pratt, Mary Louise. 2002. Modernity and periphery: Toward a global and relational analysis. In *Beyond dichotomies: Histories, identities, cultures, and the challenge of globalization*, ed. M. Elisabeth Mudimbe-boyı, 21–48. Albany: State University of New York Press.

Pritchard, Annette, and Nigel J. Morgan. 2001. Culture, identity and tourism representation: Marketing Cymru or Wales? *Tourism Management* 22 (2): 167–179.

Pujolar, Joan. 2006. *Llengua, cultura i turisme: Perspectives a Barcelona i a Catalunya*. Barcelona: Turisme de Barcelona.

Pujolar, Joan, and Kathryn Jones. 2011. Literary tourism: New appropriations of landscape and territory in Catalonia. In *Language in late capitalism: Pride and profit*, ed. Alexandre Duchêne and Monica Heller. Oxford: Routledge.

Purcell, Kate. 1997. Women's employment in UK tourism: Gender roles and labour markets. In *Gender, work and tourism*, ed. M. Thea Sinclair, 35–59. London/New York: Routledge.

Puri, Jyoti. 2004. *Encountering nationalism*. New York: Wiley-Blackwell.

Sinclair, M. Thea, ed. 1997. *Gender, work and tourism*. London, New York: Routledge.

Takashi Wilkerson, Kyoto, and Douglas Wilkerson. 2004. Tourism and Japanese national identity: 'J' and the exotic. In *La Communication touristique: Approches discursives de l'identité et de l'altérité*, ed. Fabienne Baider, 103–116. Paris: L'Harmattan.

Urry, John. 1995. *Consuming places*. London, New York: Routledge.

Vilalta, Arnau Gonzàlez i. 2006. *La irrupció de la dona en el catalanisme (1931–1936)*. Barcelona: L'Abadia de Montserrat.

Walby, Sylvia. 1997. *Gender transformations*. London: Routledge.

Williams, Colin H. 1994. *Called unto liberty! On language and nationalism*. Clevedon: Multilingual Matters.

Williams, Raymond. 1975. *The country and the city*. Oxford: Oxford University Press.

Yuval-Davis, Nira. 1997. *Gender & nation*. London: SAGE.

Yuval-Davis, Nira, Floya Anthias, and Jo Campling. 1989. *Woman-Nation-State*. London: Macmillan.

CHAPTER 5
Heteroglossic Authenticity in Sámi Heritage Tourism

SARI PIETIKÄINEN

This chapter focuses on the multilingual indigenous Sámi village of Inari in Finnish Lapland as a peripheral site of multilingual complexities. Lapland, also known as Sápmi, Sámiland, Lapponia, and North Calotte, has long been considered as a periphery on the edge of the world in the imaginations of the nation-state—system, tourism, and literature. However, seen from the perspective of centre–periphery dynamics, this seemingly stable position transforms. While Sámiland may seem peripheral when looked at from the heartlands of the nation-state, it is central to indigenous Sámi. Further, the current conditions of globalization in Sámiland, with a novel type of mobility, relocalization, and circulation, open up new opportunities for commerce, identity, and multilingual language practices while at the same time stirring up the previous relations and categories in terms of what is considered central and what is considered marginal multilingualism (cf. Coupland 2010; Pietikäinen 2010).

Looking at Inari village through a lens of evolving centre–periphery relations provides a revealing nexus (Scollon and Scollon 2004) to examine tensions and innovations emerging in the multilingual interaction of practices and discourses. A powerful principle organizing relations, resources, and practices in Inari is the transforming, contested, and guarded boundary between what is perceived as indigenous Sámi culture and language practices and what is taken as local and national Finnish culture and language practices. Today, the village is a multilingual, polycentric place with different sets of norms, opportunities, and resources, some open to all, some only to a few (Pietikäinen 2010). For Inari, this creates its own peripheral local political economy of resources (Pietikäinen and Kelly-Holmes 2011).

Within this economy, authenticity has become a necessary capital for both political mobilization and economic development (see e.g. Coupland 2003; Heller 2003, 2011; McLaughlin, this volume). It has become an invested and ideologized resource circulating across the political spaces of Sámi identity politics and indigenous rights into the economic spaces of heritage tourism and popular culture. It is also appropriated in the domains of Lapland tourism and in local arts and handicrafts. In this circulation, various understandings, representations, and practices of authenticity are constructed and consumed, and it is these dynamics that I wish to focus on in this chapter. Further, these dynamics can be fruitfully seen, I believe, as a simultaneous play of centripetal and centrifugal forces (Bakhtin 1982), standardizing and creating language and discourse practices related to what is taken as authentic in the Sámi tourism context. The centripetal authenticities are perceived as unified, unquestionably 'real', and typically indexed by a Sámi family connection, tradition, and personal history. In contrast, the centrifugal authenticity, emerging at the crossroads of tradition and innovation, is more ambiguous, carnivalesque, and fluid, mixing local and indigenous traditions and practices with novel, often global formats, resources, and practices.

To examine the dynamics between centrifugal and centripetal authenticities, I will draw on my longitudinal discursive and ethnographic research[1] on multilingualism in Sámiland (Pietikäinen and Dufva 2006; Pietikäinen 2008, 2010, forthcoming; Pietikäinen et al. 2008). In particular, I explore what gets constructed as authentic in one particular Sámi tourism site, marketed as an authentic reindeer farm,[2] and what kind of tensions and creativity the touristic capitalization of authenticity generates. The data drawn on in this article relating to the reindeer farm include several on-site observations of tourism interaction between 2008 and 2011; interviews with the hosts; informal discussions with hosts, tourists, and guides; and multimodal and discursive data (linguistic landscape, printed materials, etc.). Here, I will focus in particular on the use of Sámi resources in authentication practices at the farm visit. I will next give a brief description of the village of Inari before moving on to discuss authenticity as discursively constructed. Then I will present an analysis of authentication practices at the reindeer farm and conclude with a discussion of authentication in heritage tourism.

POLYCENTRIC PERIPHERY: THE CASE OF THE INDIGENOUS SÁMI VILLAGE OF INARI

In common with many of the sites of interest in this volume, Inari village displays many of the characteristics of centre–periphery dynamics. It is distant and peripheral in terms of its relationship to larger urban centres, but it is a locally central and active space. While it is over 350 kilometres to the nearest hospital or McDonalds, Inari is a locally important centre for trade, tourism, and administration, especially for the indigenous Sámi community. The Sámi people (approx. 60,000–80,000 people) are a recognized indigenous people living in Scandinavia and North-West Russia, and their culture and the indigenous Sámi languages are protected by various legal instruments and to a varying degree, depending on the nation-state concerned (for more details, see Pietikäinen et al. 2010). Today, nine different Sámi languages are still spoken, but they are all endangered, with estimated numbers of speakers varying from just a few people up to approximately 30,000 speakers of Northern Sámi, the biggest Sámi language (Kulonen, Seurujärvi-Kari, and Pulkkinen 2005). There are no monolingual Sámi speakers left, but rather Sámi languages have different positions in people's linguistic repertoires, varying from mother tongue to knowledge of a few words. Inari village is one of the symbolic and institutional focal points for the Sámi languages, and the major site of Sámi language practices on the Finnish side of the Sámiland. Many of the central Sámi institutions are in Inari, including, for example, Sámi medium education, the Sámi Parliament, Sámi media, and the Sámi museum Siida, making Inari a centre for Sámi language speakers and practices.

Inari village is thus a site of multilingual dynamics, where the hierarchies, categories, and boundaries between indigenous and other languages and their speakers are under construction and often also contested. This relates, on the one hand, to the shifting position of Sámi languages in people's language practices linked to language endangerment and revitalization. On the other hand, the ongoing transformation from the traditional livelihoods (fishing, reindeer herding, forestry) to the service sector (especially tourism), has brought new languages and novel linguistic needs into the area (for other minority language contexts, see e.g. contributions by Jaffe, this volume; Kelly-Holmes, this volume; and Pujolar, this volume). Nowadays tourism, with indigenous Sámi culture as its major selling point, is a rapidly growing industry. Besides its economic impact, tourism also has an influence on what kind of multilingualism is needed, valued, and expected in the area.

Within this dynamic multilingual environment, two important and interrelated processes, relevant for the argument I wish to develop in this chapter, occur: First, some new ways of using Sámi resources are now changing their traditional values and functions. Secondly, authenticity, in its various forms and meanings, has become a new commodity, used and invested in multiple ways. This transition brings about tensions and creativity related to what is perceived to be authentic in the context of Inari, and how this is discursively constructed. Inari can thus be seen as a polycentric space of peripheral multilingualism, where various logics and norms of different 'centres'—(the nation-state, Sámi indigenous politics, market forces) intersect and interact, centralizing certain identities, languages, and practices while peripheralizing some others. In this sense, Inari is a nexus (Scollon and Scollon 2004) of centre–periphery dynamics. The shifting ideas of desired or 'unwanted multilingualism' or valued and 'tacky' authenticity point to the relativity of centres and peripheries, their spatial and temporal variation and their codependence. Next, I will discuss in more detail how these dynamics are played out in relation to the question of authenticity.

AUTHENTICITY IN MULTILINGUAL SÁMILAND

Authenticity is no doubt a complex and conflicted concept used not only in various academic disciplines, language, and tourism studies (see e.g. Bruner 2001; Eckert

2003; Coupland 2010; McLaughlin, this volume; Pujolar, this volume) but also employed in a wide range of sites, practices, and events in peripheral multilingual sites. Despite its ambiguity, authenticity remains, as Coupland (2003: 417) argues, 'a quality of experience that we actively seek out', an aspect often commodified in tourism. In a shifting multilingual peripheral site such as Inari, authenticity is also in high demand in the categorization of people, practices, and products as more or less 'authentic' or 'inauthentic'. The concept also figures prominently in the conflicted concept of 'native speaker', especially in various indigenous politics, language revitalization, documentation, and maintenance discourses (cf. Moore, Pietikäinen, and Blommaert 2010).

In an attempt to build on an approach that helps to examine the various and shifting meanings and usages of authenticity in heritage Sámi tourism in Inari, I draw on some of the previous sociolinguistic and discourse analytical work on language and authenticity (see e.g. Coupland 2003; Bucholtz 2003; Johnstone and Kiesling 2008; King and Wicks 2009; Pietikäinen and Kelly-Holmes 2011) in seeing authenticity as a discursively constructed resource put to work in the service of various interests.

The discursive conceptualization of authenticity foregrounds three important aspects of authenticity, relevant for this chapter. First, it emphasizes the relativeness of authenticity (cf. e.g. Bruner 2001; Coupland 2001, 2003; Eckert 2003). It comes in different shades and modes, linked to the variation depending on context and participants, as well as on the particular time and space. Thus, there is no one single, monolithic authenticity, but it is subject to change. The relativeness and situatedness of authenticity stresses that we can only examine discourses, representations, and practices of authenticity. To underline this, Bucholtz (2003) suggests that rather than studying 'authenticity' we need to focus on the processes of authentication: the various ways in which certain languages, bodies, practices, places, and objects become authenticated in a particular time and space. These are important sociolinguistic and language ideological processes (cf. Coupland 2010; Pietikäinen, forthcoming). Authenticity is thus seen as emergent from encounters, interactions, socio-cultural situations, and the personal life history of the participants (cf. Scollon and Scollon 2004; Otsuji and Pennycook 2010; Pietikäinen, forthcoming).

Secondly, and importantly for the argument I wish to develop in this chapter, the understanding of authenticity as a discursively constructed resource and as emergent in interaction, foregrounds the importance of language and other semiotic resources as a means for authentication (Coupland 2003; Pietikäinen and Kelly-Holmes 2011). Multilingualism in Sámi communities usually receives a conflicted perception. This is complicated by the disjunction between what is perceived as beneficial for endangered Sámi languages and the recent economic development in the particular area, drawing heavily on tourism, requiring multilingual, incomplete, and changing language repertoires.

Also, the utilization of multimodal Sámi resources, such as Sámi colours, flag, dress, and ornaments, in authentication of products and places has caused frictions, particularly related to what is considered as a 'proper' or 'respectful' way to use them. Another cause for debate is the question of who has valid access to these resources. This discussion is especially tense in tourism, where there is a long history of debating how Sámi heritage culture can be used and by whom (cf. Länsman 2004).

Finally, authenticity implies, as powerfully argued by Coupland (2003, 2010), a value system. The value system connected to authenticity can be seen to be constantly on the move, continuously evolving, albeit not unconstrained and certainly not without consequences. The circulation of Sámi resources stirs up existing language relations, categories, and hierarchies and, at the same time, creates new multimodal and linguistic environments, practices, and users (cf. Pietikäinen 2010). In the context of Sámi authentication, different spaces may share or vary in what kinds of orientations, norms, and practices in relation to Sámi authenticity are valued and validated. This relates to the understanding of space as a complex and dynamic social construction (cf. Lefebvre 1991; Pennycook 2010; Jaworski and Thurlow 2010; Busch, this volume) produced and experienced in human interaction. This dynamic view of authenticity sees it in relation to time and place. The temporal aspect emphasizes the historicity and change, while the spatial aspect underlines the variation and multiplicity. Together they create the dynamics of authentication. We can see temporary affordances and subscriptions of/into a certain type of Sámi authenticity, as well as different ideas of Sámi authenticity operating at the same time in the same place, sometimes in harmony, sometimes in conflict.

These dynamics of Sámi authenticity in a complex multilingual and shifting situation can, I would like to suggest, be fruitfully examined with the help of concepts of heteroglossia and the closely related concepts of centripetal and centrifugal forces (see e.g. Bakhtin 1981: 294). Although *heteroglossia* is nowadays often used as an overall expression for linguistic diversity, I would like to emphasize heteroglossia as a fundamental characteristic of language, underlying its relational nature (as opposed to seeing it as a closed system) and seeing it as a spatio-temporal whole—a kind of chronotope to borrow the concept by Bakhtin (see Bakhtin 1981; also cf. Dufva and Pietikäinen, forthcoming). The point here is that heteroglossia refers not only to the coexistence of 'languages' within a language, but their coexistence and temporal and spatial characteristics in a juncture of centralizing and decentralizing forces. These competitive forces, borrowing from physics, are referred to as *'centripetal' and 'centrifugal' forces*. They serve to promote the continual evolution of language and language practices. The centripetal and centrifugal forces within heteroglossia are what change the 'official', centralized and standardized language of a culture over time, usually by infusing diverse, unofficial forms of language into official forms via the speech of various literary characters (Bakhtin 1981). These forces offer a way, taken up in this chapter, to examine centre–periphery dynamics in relation to authenticity in a peripheral multilingual site of Sámi heritage tourism.

When applied to Sámi tourism contexts, centripetal forces can be seen to be working to render authenticity as monoglossic and unifying, linked to hierarchies and normativity, while centrifugal forces bring in situationally changing and creative meanings of authenticity. The 'central' authenticity is typically perceived as 'real' and 'genuine', indexed, for example, by a Sámi family connection, Sámi language skills, and personal history. The 'peripheral' authenticity is more ambiguous and carnivalesque (Bakhtin 1981), mixing local and indigenous traditions and practices with global formats, genres, and practices. The former can be seen as an 'authoritative' authenticity, while the latter is perceived more as an 'emerging' authenticity.

Both centripetal and centrifugal authenticities invest and feed into the reinventing of the bodies, practices, and resources that may index such authenticity. This calls into question the understandings and perceptions of the role and value of Sámi languages in the practices and experiences of creating and marking authenticity. Especially the emerging markets for Sámi cultural and language resources, particularly in popular music, art, and tourism, bring forth new versions and usages of Sámi authenticity (cf. Pietikäinen 2008; Pietikäinen and Kelly-Holmes 2011). At the moment of the simultaneous existence of centripetal and centrifugal authentication forces, there are situations where the historically standardized markers of Sámi authenticity—the family connection, the dress, the flag, the reindeer, and the language—encounter emerging markers of Sáminess: multilingual, transnational family ties, a Sámi dress with a twist, a multilingual repertoire without any Sámi in it.

A DISCOURSE APPROACH TO AUTHENTICATION: PRACTICES IN SÁMI TOURISM

In attempting to understand this centripetal–centrifugal tension, I adopt a discourse analytical approach to examine shifting authenticities under centre–periphery dynamics in transforming, peripheral multilingual Sámiland. In particular, I apply some of the ideas of transdisciplinary discourse analysis, called Nexus Analysis, introduced by Scollon and Scollon (2001, 2004). Nexus Analysis is a form of multidimensional discourse analysis aimed at analysing the complexity and multiplicity of situated events and actions by examining the simultaneous coming together of participants, discourses, and interactional normativities in any moment of language use. To capture this idea Scollon and Scollon use the term 'nexus', by which they mean 'a point at which historical trajectories of people, places, discourses, ideas, practices, experiences and objects come together to enable some action which in itself alters those historical trajectories in some way as those trajectories emanate from this moment of social action' (Scollon and Scollon 2004: 159; for applications see e.g. Hult 2009; Lane 2010; Pietikäinen 2010; Pietikäinen et al. 2011).

The Sámi village of Inari can be seen as a nexus of many current and overlapping authentication practices related to, for example, the new economy, globalization, mobility, and indigenous language rights and revitalization, each impacting on how authenticity is constructed. This results in emerging ways of organizing and exploiting Sámi resources for authentication in a specific, situated interaction and with particular participants. These simultaneous processes have an impact on what kind of authenticity is perceived as centripetal (i.e. 'central' and 'normative') and what is considered as centrifugal or 'peripheral' (i.e. creative, unexpected, and carnivalesque). However, as the concepts are under ongoing construction, there are usually overlapping, conflicting, and even paradoxical understandings and criteria as regards perceptions of authenticity. To me this suggests looking at authentication through discursive practices, not only limited to the use of Sámi languages but including representations, discourses, particular spaces, and particular participants related to Sámi authentication. Thus, my focus is on what authenticity comes to mean: what is constructed and taken as authentic in a given situation.

To examine how some of the dynamics of Sámi authentication play out in the tourism context, I will focus here on one particular site, namely a Sámi reindeer farm, which is a popular tourist attraction in the area. The farm is in the business of circulating Sámi resources and in making claims about and representations of Sámi authenticity. The Sámi reindeer farm is the home of a multilingual Sámi family, who turned it into a successful Sámi heritage tourism business decades ago. Now they are making their living out of the business which is organized around claims, performances, and experiences of Sámi authenticity. This Sámi tourism business is at the core of the dilemmas related to creating and consuming Sámi authenticity. Living at the heartlands of the Sámi culture and being a recognized Sámi family, they are engaged in a permanent balancing act to make an economically viable tourism product for volatile markets but in a way that taps into local norms regarding the commodification of Sámi culture, and hence becomes locally validated. Working with both requirements means a continuous and delicate balancing act between centripetal and centrifugal authenticity: blending the authoritative, standard(ized) Sámi authenticity and recognized heritage tourism practices with creative and unique local resources to create a recognizable yet distinctive and locally accepted heritage tourism attraction.

Their main tourism product is a pre-booked, guided tour with various activities in the surroundings of their home. The visit to the reindeer farm is typically part of a holiday programme for a larger tourist group, who often travel with their fellow-nationals and arrive in large groups by bus. Depending on the day and the tourist season, the tourists may come from France, the Netherlands, Germany, Hungary, and so on. Language practices are decided depending on the tourist group: in most cases the host will use mainly English as a lingua franca for tourists of various nationalities. However, at times the tourists will have their own guide with them, who translates the host's English into the language of the tourists.

The ethnographic and discursive data used here are based on my long-standing ethnographic and discourse analytic research with this particular tourism attraction and with the family running it. The data comprise ethnographic observations, photographs, and video- and audio-recordings of several on-site visits, interviews,[3] and informal discussions with the family members, tourist operators, and tourists. I have also made use of various tourism and media texts featuring this touristic attraction. The ethnographic nature of this research means that it is done in cooperation with the family and other participants, and they have been important and valuable resources in planning, carrying out, and reflecting on this particular research. The individuals running this tourism business have given their permission to be recognized (e.g. via connection to place, product, language practices, etc.), and to use their names, telling me that the publicity for their tourism business as well as the unique characteristics of their product mean that publicity and recognizability are part of their business and daily life regardless of this particular research. However, to put emphasis on the authentication practices in this context, rather than on individual decisions and experiences, I have anonymized the visit and participants to some extent: I will not use names and I have left out some immediately identifying details.

To examine authenticity as emerging in the interaction, I am not building on any assumed connections between language, culture, authenticity, or geography (cf. Otsuji and Pennycook 2010). Rather, my aim is to explore how such relations are discursively produced, resisted, defied, or rearranged. I will next focus on two interrelated discursive authentication practices simultaneously at play in the visit, namely (1) visual consumption of Sámi resources and (2) discourses and language practices related to Sámi languages.

AUTHENTICATION PRACTICES IN A SÁMI TOURISM PERFORMANCE

The Stage

The Sámi tourism product, the visit to the reindeer farm, can be seen as being created and consumed as a co-performance between the hosts and tourists (cf. Bruner 2001; Sheller and Urry 2004; Salizar 2010). This scripted and repeated co-performance requires awareness of the rules of touristic performances and willingness from all participants to submit themselves to this play of authenticity. In the play the tourists are cast as reindeer caretakers, lasso throwers, reindeer drivers, language learners, singers, and consumers while the hosts are hailed as teachers, singers, sellers—and above all, authenticated, embodied Sámi. To meet the varying criteria of a worthwhile tourism experience, a profitable tourist product and local legitimacy in heritage tourism business, the performance needs to be skilfully performed and carefully managed and yet be open to some variation.

This means that the visit is performed in a juncture of centripetal and centrifugal authentication practices. On the one hand, the performance needs to be standardized and unified to some extent for it to be repeatable and manageable. On the other hand, the performance also needs to vary and adapt, for example, according to the tourist group (e.g. shared language resources, number of tourists, their preferences) and to weather conditions (if there is snow, how cold it is, etc.), as well as to the resources of the particular host for a particular visit. As a result, the visit is both repetitious and unique. Figure 5.1 illustrates the repeated key activities in the visit and their temporal order and location at the space of this tourism performance.

In the following, my aim is to briefly describe the key activities, and their standardized (i.e. centripetal) and varying (i.e. centrifugal) characteristics.

Figure 5.1:
Key activities in the reindeer farm visit and their temporal order

(1) **Welcoming:** The tourists arrive by their buses and are greeted by the host, typically one of the family members or hired helpers called 'a friend of the family'. Without exception, the host is wearing the Sámi dress.

(2) **Feeding the reindeer:** After welcoming, the host offers the tourists lichen from a bag for feeding the reindeers on a leash nearby. Typically, the tourists enthusiastically feed the reindeers and equally enthusiastically take pictures of this activity.

(3) **Teaching/learning about reindeers:** After a while the host routinely gathers the tourists in a semi-circle around reindeers and gives a relatively standardized lesson on reindeers; on their nutrition, survival in the arctic nature, ear marking system, etc. The tourists are invited to ask questions and quite often few are put forward, often regarding the biology of the reindeer. In the background, some of the tourists ignore this activity and continue feeding the reindeers and taking pictures.

(4) **Teaching/learning lassoing:** Next, the tourists are invited to learn lassoing, a skill needed in reindeer herding. The training is done with a help of a mock reindeer and a lassoing teacher. There is variation around who does the teaching: sometimes it is the host, sometime an older man, dressed invariably in a Sámi dress and talking only in Sámi (for details, see below). This subversion of the participatory roles in lassoing is often a moment of laughter and clowning. After some hesitation, most of the tourists participate in this activity quite eagerly, but some withdraw to the background and observe the event. Another activity going on all the time is extensive photographing and videotaping.

(5) **Driving a reindeer sledge:** During the winter the tourists have an option (for an extra fee) to have a reindeer sledge drive in the snowy forest right next to the house. The hosts prepare the reindeers for the drive and guide the tourists in the sledges and give directions on how to drive. The reindeers are tamed and trained as sledge reindeers and they dutifully walk or slowly run the approximately 500 meter long circle-shaped track. The tourists seem to enjoy the excitement, take lots of pictures during the drive and give encouraging shouts to each other and to the reindeer. Later, they will be given a humorous 'Reindeer driving licence', a small card with a picture of the Sámi host and a reindeer against a wintery scene. The 'licence' states that the holder has passed the examination and is entitled to drive in the wilds of Lapland. The license is 'authorized' by a date and the signature of the host. The tourists typically greet the cards with amusement.

(6) **Visiting the *kota*:** After the outside activities, the tourists are guided inside a *kota*, which resembles the traditional Sámi 'tepee', but this modern version is much larger and made of wood. Inside the *kota* the standard refreshments include coffee, tea, and a biscuit traditional to the region. While enjoying the coffee, the host tells stories about the Sámi culture, with an emphasis

on handicrafts and languages. The latter part of the visit centres around singing: first, a member of the family performs a few Northern Sámi joiks, a traditional form of Sámi throat singing. After this, the tourists are taught 'easy' joiks and all sing together. The closing sequence of singing varies depending on the particular group of tourists. The tourists are asked to sing a song from their native country in their native language. This request gets mixed responses from the tourists: the big groups of tourists with the same nationality usually pick up the song relatively quickly and end up singing a well-known song to everyone. The situation varies even more when the tourist group is multilingual and multinational or a very small group of people are put on the spot. At times, there might not be that much singing, at other times the solution is to sing a song that everyone knows (like Brother John), and everybody sings in their own language.

(7) **Souvenir shopping**: Next, the tourists are guided to a small souvenir shop next to the *kota*. In the shop, all kinds of Sámi and Northern souvenirs are sold (e.g. knives, items made of reindeer antlers or skin, wooden items, stones, postcards, etc.). Many of the sold items are made by the family members.

(8) **Farewell**: The host guides the tourists back to the front of the house where the bus is waiting for them. The tourists climb in and the host waves to everyone.

The visit to the reindeer farm is put into play in relation to other places and previous tourism experiences. In this sense, the visit to the reindeer farm takes place in a trans-local tourism space. It draws on trans-local connectivity by indexing, using, and moulding recognized tourism genres, scripts, and performances, resulting in what Sheller and Urry (2004: 1) describe as 'relational mobilization of memories and images, emotions and expectations'. This is achieved by using strategically selected, central local resources of Sámi culture and Northern nature, and mixing them with globalized tourism resources. As a result, we have a construction of an authenticated performance, produced in the tension between centripetal and centrifugal forces, in a localized space of Sámi tourism. Next, I will focus on two interrelated discursive authentication practices simultaneously at play, namely (1) visual consumption and (2) discourses and language practices related to Sámi languages. Both show the interplay between centripetal and centrifugal tendencies in authentication.

VISUAL CONSUMPTION OF AUTHENTICITY AT SÁMI TOURISM PERFORMANCE

Visual consumption refers to strategic visual communication central to the experience economy, such as tourism, marketing, and media (Schroeder 2002). In tourism, the ability to both strategically produce and make available visual representations, on the one hand, as well as the ability to 'take in' visual signs and circulate them, on the other hand, constitutes a key attribute of the tourism product and experience (cf. Urry 2002). Tourism experience is very much also a visual experience, including visual practices, notably photographing. The reindeer farm visit performance draws on three central visual domains: Northern nature, iconic Sámi culture, and home, illustrated in Figure 5.1. The picture illustrates how the landscape of the Northern periphery functions as a wider framing for the performance. The farm is geographically located outside the village, in the middle of 'nowhere', where an accidental tourist would not 'happen' to end up. It makes use of the wealth of Northern peripheral resources: untouched nature; snow, darkness, and silence during the winter; a running stream and white nights during the summer.

The family house as the background of the many tourist activities (see Figure 5.1) makes the visual and material connection between the touristic visit and the home space: although the tourists do not actually go inside the house, they walk around it while taking part in the various tourism activities. The living home is a very efficient resource for authentication of the visit. Everyday life going on in the house, evident from the accidental toys and bicycles in the yard and occasional glances from the family members, making this tourism product distinctive. In several tourism destinations throughout Lapland it is possible to 'visit' a Sámi or Lappish (usually) man, who comes, dressed up in a Sámi dress or a modification of it (Lappish costume), and with a reindeer or two to a tourist resort for tourists to see and take pictures. To be able to come and visit the real, living home of a Sámi family contributes to the feeling of being a guest and having a unique opportunity to see something 'authentic'.

The visual consumption of Sámi culture includes the Sámi flag, the Sámi tepee *kota*, the sauntering reindeers, reindeer antlers, and reindeer skins. However, the most obvious—and authenticating—visual consumption is the Sámi dress. With its different colours and ornaments, the Sámi dress speaks of locality for the local people and authenticity for the tourists. For those familiar with the language of Sámi dress, the visual elements in the dress index the particular region in Sámiland from which the person comes and consequently which Sámi language (potentially) s/he speaks. Traditionally, the Sámi people wore these dresses every day, but more recently the dresses are typically used only for various festivities (Lehtola 1997) with the exception of tourism work. Moreover, only members of the Sámi community are entitled to wear the dress, even though, again, there are exceptions at times in tourism. At the reindeer farm, the hosts are marked as Sámi by the stylized Sámi dresses they are wearing, which simultaneously differentiate them from the tourists. Their bodies become authenticated as genuine Sámi: the dress lends centripetal, authoritative authenticity to the hosts, and the tourists have, perhaps for the first time, a chance see the Sámi dress—and Sámi people, certified by the dress—with their own eyes.

The visual consumption of the dress as a part of the performance is no accident, but a very conscious and strategic decision made earlier when establishing the reindeer farm tourism business decades ago. In the interview extract[4] below, the host, one member of the family explains how the idea of the Sámi reindeer farm started:

Isäntä: Sittenhän mulla oikeastaan alkoi himottamaanki tämä homma. kun olin täällä [yrityksen nimi] töissä niin jatkuvasti tuli ihmisiä kysymään että missä näkis poron. [sanoin] jotta tienvarressa niitä sattuu näkymään ni siinä on ainut mahollisuus. sitten ne kysy missä näkis saamelaisia minä että tässä on ensimmäinen. ne katto pitkään mutta sitte ne muutti se [kysymyksen] että missä näkis lapinpukusen ihmisen. [minä] että kyllä täällä saamelaisia on mutta ku ei niillä ole lapinpukua päällä ni että jos joku vanhempi ihminen tullee. siihen aihaan ruukas vanhemmat ihmiset tuli aina kylälle ni heillä oli lapinpuvut päällä. minä että jos joku vanhempi ihminen sattuu kylälle tulemahan se on ainut mahollisuus mutta muuten en tiiä sitä sanoa. sitten mulla tosin koko ajan mielessä kytiki siinä että minä tehen sellasen yrityksen että aina saa sanoa että siellä on lapinpukune ihminen siell on poro (nauraa).

Host: Well then, this whole business started to interest me when I was working here in [name of a company]. All the time people came and asked me where they could see a reindeer. I said that you might happen to see them on the roadside. That is really the only chance. Then they asked where they could see Sámi and I answered that here is the first one. They looked at me for a long time and then they changed their question and asked where they could see a person wearing a Sámi dress. I said that there are Sámi people around here but they do not wear Sámi dress. Only if an older person comes—at that time the older people always used to wear some dress when they came to the village. So I said that if an older person happens to come to the village, that is the only chance, at least as far as I know. But all the time, I was playing with an idea in my mind that I would establish that kind of business, so that one can always say that there is a person wearing Sámi dress there, and that there is a reindeer there (laughing).

The host's account illustrates two interrelated points that are relevant for authentication practices at the farm. First, as a Sámi family, this particular tourism enterprise has local legitimacy as regards Sámi culture and access to Sámi resources and their commodification—an issue that is problematic for many in Lapland's tourism business. The use of Sámi resources is a hot topic in Lapland tourism and many tourism products have been criticized for misuse of Sámi culture (see e.g. Saarinen 1999; Länsman 2004), and some products make use of Northern or Lappish resources instead to avoid trying to claim access to or ownership of Sámi resources (cf. Pietikäinen and Kelly-Holmes 2011). Secondly, the extract illustrates the recognition and reflection of the fact that tourists collect signs (Urry 2002): compulsory and compulsive photographing is an important element in tourism, and providing a scene for this activity opens up a business opportunity. Locally legitimate access to the commodification of Sámi resources for the tourist gaze (Urry 2002) means organizing the tourist practices for the consumption of what is taken to be authentic by tourists, regardless of what the performances may mean or how they may be treated by locals or the family members themselves.

Another resource used for authentication of the reindeer farm visit is the discourse of Sámi languages and language practices in/around Sámi. While the most used language resources for interaction during the visit are English and Finnish, and at times other languages with the help of the interpreting guide of the tourist group, Sámi languages and discourses about them are also used in two key activities: the lassoing (activity 4) and the *kota* visit (activity 6). Next I will focus on the former case.

The lassoing activity centres on the idea of the tourists learning the 'key skills of a reindeer herder', used to catch a single reindeer from a running herd. In the tourist version, the 'reindeer' is a wooden, immobile model and the tourists try to 'catch' it by throwing the lasso from a distance of approximately 20 meters. Typically in this interaction, the key participants are the host, the lasso teacher (an older male member of the family), and the tourists. The activity starts with the host explaining what is going to happen. What is interesting in terms of authentication practices is the use of Sámi language in this interaction. Dressed up in a Sámi dress and as a skilful lasso thrower, the teacher is an embodied authentic older Sámi man. This image is further reinforced by the teacher's language choice in this activity. Regardless of his multilingual repertoire, here he chooses to use only Sámi, a language totally incomprehensible to most of the visitors. The teacher talks only Sámi, for example, when inviting tourists to take part, when explaining the various throwing techniques, and asking about their previous experiences in lassoing. After some hesitation, most of the tourists appear to take part in the activity rather enthusiastically, even if with some self-consciousness, indicated by facial expressions and laughter. The tourists respond to the teacher's talk in Sámi typically with a mixture of laughter, cheering, and replying to him either non-verbally (nodding, gestures) or in their own language. This is a carnivalesque moment of subversion and laughter (Bakhtin 1981; see also Blackledge and Creese 2009; Pietikäinen, forthcoming). Learning a Sámi activity (lassoing) and being taught in an endangered, indigenous language by a Sámi man wearing a Sámi dress is a rich point of authentication in the visit. It also serves as a high visual point for many tourists, who take lots of pictures and videotape the activity.

In his interview with the researcher, the teacher himself reflects upon the requirement of authenticity as regards Sámi language practices. He starts to explain his language choice by telling a story he has heard of a Finnish man, hired in one of Lapland's tourist resorts to perform a joik (traditional Sámi singing). The man had sung a 'fake joik', using Finnish lyrics 'Hallikoira haukkuu hau hau hau (a dog barks woof woof woof)'. These words did not have any obviously relevant meaning in the context or any link to joiking, but rather the choice of these particular words and syllables presumably drew on their phonetic similarity to an aural stereotype of joiking. According to the story, the tourists were very excited and clapped enthusiastically, oblivious to the fact that the performance was not joik at all, nor an 'authentic' Sámi performance. The lasso teacher says in the interview that some people have also said to him that his job is easy as he, too, can say whatever he wants or just nonsense in Sámi when teaching lassoing. However, he does not approve of the suggestion of using Sámi only emblematically, but wants to keep the informational function at the centre of his performance:

> Opettaja: Siihen ei koskaan voi luottaa [ettei kukaan ymmärtäisi] että siellä on seassa aina semmosia jotka ymmärtääkin että se pittää olla hyvin tarkka että siinä ei kannattais tyhjiä puhua (nauraa). joo moniki on sanonu mulle että johan sulla on helppo ku sie saat höpiskellä mitä haluavat (epäselvää) mie että kyllä kai se nii että siinä on (epäselvää) (nauraen-) vapaa että siinä voi kyllä kokkeilla että jos sillä kovin kauan ei pärjää ni sillon on tyhjää höpissy sitte (-nauraen).

Teacher: One can never trust that (nobody understands). Among the tourists there might be people who understand. One must be very careful not to talk nonsense (laughing). Well, many have said to me, you have it easy as you can say whatever you want (unclear). I (reply) that I guess one is (unclear, laughing) free, that one can surely try but if one does not make it (in the tourism business) for long, then one must have talked nonsense (laughing).

The teacher's story and opinion about the 'false' authentication show his awareness of and reflection about the authentication practices under local conditions. Even though it may well be that, for the vast majority of the tourists, his language is emblematic, functioning like a well-chosen sound track (cf. Kelly-Holmes 2005) and from that perspective he could say anything. However, to him and potentially for a few guests, the Sámi language is a communicative resource and hence the content of his talk needs to make sense. This multifunctionality of Sámi resources in the lassoing context makes it ambivalent and multi-voiced (Bakhtin 1981), authenticating the performance for the tourists and connecting locally with the value of the Sámi language as a living language.

DISCUSSION: REPETITION, REFLEXIVITY, AND PERIPHERAL MULTILINGUALISM

Multilingualism under the centre–periphery dynamics in a peripheral site of Sámi tourism links to the centripetal and centrifugal authentication practices. Centripetal authentication practices pull Sámi, local, and tourism practices and resources together tightly into a repeatable, standardized performance, while centrifugal forces propel them into unexpected and creative combinations and order. Together, these forces create an ambivalent and heteroglossic authenticity performance, a nexus of historical and new meaning, value and function of Sámi resources.

This multilingual performance also highlights the dynamics and potential of repetition and creativity in heritage tourism. For example, Pennycook (2010: 36), when talking about cultural production and relocalization in relation to time and place, argues that repetition and creativity are not opposite to each other, but rather repetition can be seen 'as an act of difference, relocalization, renewal.' Copying a style, activity, or genre, for example, and repeating the same performance over and over can be seen as a creative relocation practice (Pennycook 2010: 42), amplified by the flow of time and the uniqueness of individual experience. In the context of Sámi tourism, we can see repetition as complementary to creative innovation in authentication practices, making the same reindeer farm performance different every time.

The experiences of the hosts in the Sámi reindeer farm visit bring out the importance of reflexivity in tourism. The capacity to reflect on their own actions and choices seems to allow the tourist service providers to make a link between the particular local conditions of producing a tourism product and the needs of the tourism markets. This seems to be particularly relevant as regards access and ownership of Sámi resources and their commodification. In addition, reflexivity can be used as a resource in the actual performance: the use of humour, irony, and laughter can help in creating a space in which the playfulness and the performative characteristics of the product are recognized and put in relation to other spaces and performances. Also, the interaction between the tourists and the hosts can facilitate a joint moment of experiencing the play but in a way that allows various distances and distinctions.

The multilingual complexities in indigenous Sámi communities oblige speakers, locals, and visitors alike, to adapt, develop, and strategize with their linguistic and discursive resources and lead to both language-ideological tensions and creativity. Seeing multilingualism through a periphery-centre lens highlights the dynamics of language change. As geographical, economic, political, and cultural centres and peripheries are constantly renegotiated, language categories and practices also become dynamic and are in a constant dialogue with the previous and current transitions. In the Sámi reindeer visit, all these trajectories, norms, practices, and bodies come together, resulting in a heteroglossic tourism performance, simultaneously repeated and unique.

NOTES

1. This article is based on two research projects, Northern Multilingualism (http://www.northernmultilingualism.fi) and Peripheral Multilingualism (http://www.peripheralmultilingualism.fi), both funded by the Academy of Finland.
2. I wish to warmly thank the individuals who have allowed me to do ethnographic research related to their multilingual everyday life in Inari.
3. Research assistant Hanni Salo collected some of these interviews.
4. The extracts from the interviews have been edited for readability. The transcription of the interview interaction represents all the words spoken that

could be identified. Unidentifiable words are in empty single parentheses and audible paralinguistic communication like laughter is represented in double parentheses. In the English translation, idiomaticity is a higher priority than literal translation.

REFERENCES

Bakhtin, Mikhail. 1981. *The dialogic imagination: Four essays by M. M. Bakhtin.* Trans. C. Emerson and M. Holquist. Austin: University of Texas Press.

Blackledge Adrian, and Angela Creese. 2009. Meaning-making as dialogic process: Official and carnival lives in the language classroom. *Journal of Language, Identity, and Education* 8 (4): 236–253.

Bruner, Edward. 2001. The Maasai and the Lion King: Authenticity, nationalism, and globalization in African tourism. *American Ethnologist* 28 (4): 881–908.

Bucholtz, Mary. 2003. Sociolinguistic nostalgia and the authentication of identity. *Journal of Sociolinguistics* 7 (4): 398–416.

Coupland, Nikolas. 2003. Sociolinguistic authenticities. *Journal of Sociolinguistics* 7 (4): 417–431.

Coupland, Nikolas, ed. 2010. *Handbook of language and globalization.* Cambridge, Mass.: Blackwell Publishers.

Eckert, Penelope. 2003. Dialogue, sociolinguistics and authenticity: An elephant in the room. *Journal of Sociolinguistics* 7 (4): 392–431.

Heller, Monica. 2003. Globalization, the new economy, and the commodification of language and identity. *Journal of Sociolinguistics* 7 (4): 473–492.

Heller, Monica. 2011. *Paths to post-nationalism: A critical ethnography of language and identity.* New York: Oxford University Press.

Hult, Francis M. 2009. Language ecology and linguistic landscape analysis. In *Linguistic landscape: Expanding the scenery,* ed. Elana Shohamy and Durk Gorter, 88–104. London: Routledge.

Jaworski, Adam, and Crispin Thurlow, eds. 2010. *Semiotic landscapes: Language, image, space.* London: Continuum.

Johnstone, Barbara, and Scott Fabius Kiesling. 2008. Indexicality and experience: Exploring the meanings of /aw/-monophthongization in Pittsburgh. *Journal of Sociolinguistics* 12 (1): 5–33.

Kelly-Holmes, Helen. 2005. *Advertising as multilingual communication.* Basingstoke and New York: Palgrave Macmillan.

King, Ruth, and Jennifer Wicks. 2009. 'Aren't we proud of our language?' Authenticity, commodification, and the Nissan Bonavista television commercial. *Journal of English Linguistics* 37 (3): 262–283.

Kulonen, Ulla-Maija, Irja Seurujärvi-Kari, and Risto Pulkkinen, eds. 2005. *The Sámi: A cultural encyclopaedia.* Helsinki: Suomalaisen Kirjallisuuden Seura.

Lane, Pia. 2010. 'We did what we thought was best for our children': A nexus analysis of language shift in a Kven community. *International Journal of the Sociology of Language* 202: 63–78.

Länsman, Anni-Siiri. 2004. *Väärtisuhteet Lapin matkailussa: Kulttuurianalyysi suomalaisten ja saamelaisten kohtaamisesta.* [Host-guest relations in tourism in Sápmi (Finland). A cultural analysis of the encounter between Finns and Sámi]. Inari: Kustannus Puntsi.

Lefebvre, Henri. 1991. *The production of space.* Oxford: Blackwell.

Lehtola, Veli-Pekka. 1997. *Saamelaiset: Historia, yhteiskunta, taide.* Jyväskylä, Finland: Gummerus.

Moore, Robert E., Sari Pietikäinen, and Jan Blommaert. 2010. Counting the losses: Numbers as the language of language endangerment. *Sociolinguistic Studies* 4 (1): 1–26.

Otsuji, Emi, and Alastair Pennycook. 2010. Metrolingualism: Fixity, fluidity and language in flux. *International Journal of Multilingualism* 7 (3): 240–254.

Pennycook, Alastair. 2010. *Language as a local practice.* London: Routledge.

Pietikäinen, Sari. 2008. Sami in media: Questions of language vitality and cultural hybridisation. *Journal of multicultural discourses* 3 (1): 22–35.

Pietikäinen, Sari. 2010. Sámi language mobility: Scales and discourses of multilingualism in polycentric environment. *International Journal of Sociology of Language* 202: 79–101.

Pietikäinen, Sari. forthcoming. Multilingual dynamics in Sámiland: A system of discourses about language change. *International Journal of Bilingualism.*

Pietikäinen, Sari, and Hannele Dufva. 2006. Voices in discourses: Dialogism, Critical Discourse Analysis, and ethnic identity. *Journal of Sociolinguistics* 10 (2): 205–224.

Pietikäinen, Sari, and Helen Kelly-Holmes. 2011. The local political economy of languages in a Sámi tourism destination: Authenticity and mobility in the labelling of souvenirs. *Journal of Sociolinguistics* 15 (3): 323–349.

Pietikäinen, Sari, Riikka Alanen, Hannele Dufva, Paula Kalaja, Sirpa Leppänen, and Anne Pitkänen-Huhta. 2008. Languaging in Ultima Thule: Multilingualism in the life of a Sami boy. *International Journal of Multilingualism* 5: 77–89.

Pietikäinen, Sari, Leena Huss, Sirkka Laihiala-Kankainen, Ulla Aikio-Puoskari, and Pia Lane. 2010. Regulating multilingualism in the North Calotte: The case of Kven, Meänkieli and Sámi languages *Acta Borealia* 27 (1): 1–23.

Pietikäinen, Sari, Pia Lane, Hanni Salo, and Sirkka Laihiala-Kankainen. 2011. Frozen actions in the Arctic linguistic landscape: A nexus analysis of language processes in visual space. *International Journal of Multilingualism* 2011, iFirst Article: 1–22.

Saarinen, Jarkko. 1999. Representations of indigeneity: Sami culture in the discourses of tourism. In *Indigeneity: Constructions and re/presentations*, ed. James N. Brown and Patricia M. Sant, 231–249. New York: Nova Science Publishers.

Salizar, Noel B. 2010. *Envisioning Eden: Mobilizing imaginaries in tourism and beyond.* New York. Berghahn Books.

Schroeder, Jonathan E. 2002. *Visual consumption.* London: Routledge.

Scollon, Ron. 2001. *Mediated discourse: The nexus of practice.* London: Routledge.

Scollon, Ron, and Suzie Wong Scollon. 2004. *Nexus analysis: Discourse and the emerging Internet.* London and New York: Routledge.

Sheller, Mimi, and John Urry. 2004. Places to play, places in play. In *Tourism mobilities: Places to play, places in play*, ed. Mimi Sheller and John Urry, 1–10. London: Routledge.

Thurlow, Crispin, and Adam Jaworski. 2010. *Tourism discourse: Language and global mobility.* Basingstoke and New York: Palgrave-MacMillan.

Urry, John. 2002. *The tourist gaze.* 2nd edn. London: Sage Publications.

CHAPTER 6
Linguistic Creativity in Corsican Tourist Context

ALEXANDRA JAFFE AND CEDRIC OLIVA

INTRODUCTION

In Corsica, as in other peripheral multilingual contexts, changing economic practices and circulating discourses about plurilingual, European and global markets, and forms of citizenship are creating new frameworks within which people understand and enact their linguistic and cultural identities (Heller 2003, 2010; Boudreau and White 2004; Da Silva, McLaughlin, and Richards 2007; Blommaert 2009; Duchêne 2009; Heller and Pujolar 2009; McLaughlin and LeBlanc 2009). This chapter takes up the complex interrelationship between language practices, the construction of place/space, and processes of minority language identification. The specific focus is on how linguistic boundaries and statuses are negotiated through Corsican along with other languages in the commercial and tourist spheres.

The focus on boundary work includes the historically salient boundary between the minority language, Corsican, and the dominant language, French. But it also encompasses Corsican's relationship with its closest neighbouring language, Italian. This represents a shift away from viewing Corsican only within the frontiers of the French nation: as a 'periphery' that contrasts with a Parisian or continental French 'centre'. Rather, this analysis addresses the varied historical and new meanings that accrue to the multilingual resources in Corsican speakers' repertoires. The analysis focuses on the way that Corsican, a minority language, is positioned within public and tourist texts and interactions. In these texts, social actors produce, reproduce and potentially challenge notions of both centre and periphery by attending to or backgrounding processes of differentiation through language, and by construing various kinds of speakers, writers, and audiences. This dynamic process through which minority languages are positioned and imagined is productively explored through the lens of multilingualism, because a multilingual framework disrupts dominant, historical conceptions of monolingual centres and (trivially) bilingual peripheries. The multilingual speaker or community, on the other hand, has a potential relationship to multiple linguistic and cultural centres and peripheries. The 'minority' language can thus be 'reimagined' through its relationship(s) with a variety of languages and speakers.

Data collected on the uses and representations of Corsican in commercial and tourist spheres show evidence of ideological continuity with dominant, monolingual ideologies of language and identity and are articulated within a historical, Corsican-French oppositional relationship. At the same time, texts in this domain show evidence of linguistic creativity in which language (and identity) boundaries are expressed and experienced as a relatively fluid continuum. The findings also suggest the ways in which Corsican may be repositioned, in contemporary discourses and practices, as a form of 'added cultural value' in a tourist market, and the possibilities and tensions of identity that this new market framework present for speakers of the minority language. Finally, from a theoretical perspective, the analytical approach taken in this chapter problematizes the notions of 'centre' and 'periphery', showing them not so much as places, but as stance objects evoked in discourses and practices.

LANGUAGE SHIFT AND REVITALIZATION: DOMINANT AND ALTERNATIVE IDEOLOGIES OF LANGUAGE

Over the last century, Corsican, like many minority languages in Europe, has gone from being an unmarked code of everyday communication, to a stigmatized 'dialect' subordinated to French, to a highly charged symbol of cultural belonging and authenticity. French language ideologies, transmitted through the school system, played a large part in the cultural devaluation of Corsican. At the same time, the economic value of French was an integral part of the picture for Corsicans who aimed for economic and social horizons beyond the limits of sheepherding and small-scale agriculture. French was indeed a tool of social and economic advancement for Corsicans who left the island in increasing numbers to work in France or its colonies, as well as in an island economy that shifted definitively after the Second World War to the tertiary sector. In these conditions, language shift towards French accelerated.

The Corsican language revitalization movement, which began in the early 1970s, was profoundly influenced by the French political and institutional context, as well as by the dominant nation-state language-ideological framework. In this framework, languages are conceptualized primarily as bounded, autonomous formal linguistic codes with an 'essential' or natural relationship with collective identities and territories (Blommaert and Verscheuren 1998; Wright 2004; Gal 2006; Heller 2006). This influenced Corsican language activists' understandings of what a legitimate language and speaker are: that is, they measured the authority and authenticity of their language with respect to an ideal of an 'autonomous' code, free from influence from other languages, characterized by a single authoritative written and oral standard. In this framework, a legitimate speaker is someone who speaks the minority language without 'interference' from other languages, and only legitimate speakers can lay claim to a full minority cultural identity. Struggles for language rights within the French State also imposed these ideologies of language, since Corsicans were compelled to demonstrate that Corsican was a language on French terms: showing that it had internal linguistic unity and was clearly differentiated from both French and Italian.

In previous work on Corsica, Jaffe has traced the influence of this dominant ideological formation in a variety of discourses and practices that emphasize the fixity of language (and identity) boundaries and articulate Corsican language rights on the basis of an essential link between Corsican and a bounded Corsican ethnic community (Jaffe 1999). This dominant ideological framework surfaces in policies and practices that endorse or enact parallel, authoritative monolingualisms (Corsican and French), promote language purism, a single written and oral standard in both languages, and sanction code-switching and language mixing (Jaffe 2007a). Corsican bilingual education is structured in part around this ideological formation in its effort to create parallel, equally authoritative curricula and practices in Corsican and French.

At the same time, research on Corsican has also documented an alternative ideological formation—a discourse of plurilingual identities and competencies, of 'polycentric' and 'polynomic' languages in which the emphasis is on language practice (and its expressive and communicative functions) as opposed to linguistic form and on fluidity rather than fixity of language boundaries (Jaffe 2007a). The notion of 'polynomy' has been most fully articulated as an alternative ideology by Corsican sociolinguists (Comiti 1992; Marcellesi 2003; Thiers 2008; see also Pietikäinen 2010 and Swigart 2001; Jacquemet 2005; Benor 2010 for 'fluidity' as a principle of sociolinguistic practice). Marcellesi's definition of a 'polynomic' language describes its unity as 'abstract': located in the recognition by its speakers of the equal legitimacy and status of different dialectal varieties (Marcellesi 1989: 170). In addition to not requiring a single dialectal norm, the notion of polynomy has also been interpreted by Thiers as allowing for the potential recognition and legitimation of mixed linguistic codes that arise from language contact between dominant and minority language (Thiers 2003).[1] Along with other scholars, Jaffe's work has documented reflections of this ideology in Corsican popular culture (including broadcast media), as well as in highly reflexive educational practices (Cortier and Di Meglio 2004; Jaffe 2007b, 2008).

While the dominant language ideological formation, above, comes out of a long history of minority language speakers' experiences in schools and in the political sphere, the alternative and plural ideological orientation is also grounded in those speakers' experiences, and their inherently multiple and mixed linguistic and cultural character. It also grows out of material and ideational shifts associated with processes of globalization: these include new forms of circulation of people, goods, ideas, and communicative flows, as well as shifts in the language ideological discourses articulated in centres of European language planning and policy-making (see Coupland 2010).

In particular, contemporary Corsican language planning and educational discourse has been influenced by the Council of Europe's promotion of the notion of the 'plurilingual citizen', where 'plurilingualism' is defined as a 'complex or even composite' communicative competence based on 'varying degrees of proficiency in several languages and experiences of several cultures' (Council of Europe 2001: 4, 168). Plurilingualism is thus the ability to make flexible use of a linguistic repertoire in intercultural communication. Here, citizenship is predicated on *participation* through multiple languages, at various levels of competency: both language boundaries and monolingual norms are deemphasized. The focus, in the following analysis, is thus on the ideological work that takes place around constructing and deconstructing language boundaries (see Makoni and Pennycook 2007; also Busch, this volume): on both continuity and change with respect to dominant language ideologies.

LANGUAGE-IDEOLOGICAL CONTINUITY AND CHANGE IN TOURIST SPACES

Corsican language revitalization in the educational sphere is framed almost exclusively with respect to institutionalized French language policy and language ideologies and, in more recent years, supranational models of plurilingual citizenship (Jaffe 2010). In contrast, in the domain of tourism, the market is the frame for both linguistic practices and the values attributed to different languages. Language is thus both a tool for market-based practices (a means to an economic end) and a potential commodity itself. The commodification of language itself is particularly clear in sites of heritage tourism (see e.g. Boudreau and White 2004; Heller 2003; Coupland, Garret, and Bishop 2005; also Pietikäinen, this volume), but language is also susceptible to commodification in destinations where cultural difference has been made salient outside a self-conscious 'heritage' framework (Pietikäinen and Kelly-Holmes 2011). In Corsica, there is little heritage tourism, but Corsican cultural and linguistic difference from mainland France has long figured as a central element of the island's identity in the public and tourist imaginary both in and outside of France (Antonmarchi et al. 2010).

An emerging line of research (Coupland, Bishop, and Garret 2003; Heller 2003; Boudreau and White 2004; Boudreau 2005; Jaworski and Pritchard 2005; Moïse and Roy 2006; Pujolar 2006, this volume; Duchêne 2009; Heller and Pujolar 2009; McLaughlin and LeBlanc 2009; Pietikäinen and Kelly-Holmes 2011; as well as contributions by Coupland; Kelly-Holmes; Pietikäinen; and Pujolar to this volume) focuses on tourism as a nexus for the study of how processes of globalization reconfigure the economic and symbolic/identity values of minority languages and varieties. As Heller points out, in globalized economies, the state is no longer alone in setting language hierarchies: language as a commodity 'redefine(s) the relationship between language and identity and produce(s) new forms of competition and social selection' (2003: 473). One of the characteristics of tourist encounters that makes them ripe for a sociolinguistics of globalization is that they make visible both the circulation of people and the circulation of language(s) in the tertiary sector, and draw attention to multilingualism and other forms of linguistic variation. This critical sociolinguistics of tourism is concerned both with the role of language in the constitution of identity, power, and social difference in the context of tourism and mobility (Jaworski and Thurlow 2010) and with the way that tourist encounters and displays are implicated in 'the production, distribution and attribution of value to symbolic resources' (Heller and Pujolar 2009: 178) that include language and culture. As a consequence, the sociolinguistics of minority language tourism looks at how minority language communities are discursively produced in sites of contact between 'outsiders' and 'insiders'.

In the Corsican tourist context, there are conditions that favour both language ideological continuity and change. On the one hand, conventional models of linguistic and cultural authenticity can be brought into play by tourists or be anticipated by Corsican tourist providers as product expectations and then reproduced in tourist interactions (see also Pietikäinen, this volume). This favours the commodification of Corsican as a bounded, exotic, possibly archaic code or valorizes the use of Corsican as a marker of authenticity or identity by tourist providers. Secondly, the practical obligation of the tourist provider to accommodate to the tourist client can result in normative language choices. Those norms may be anchored in global frameworks in which English is predominant and in which Corsican is unimaginable as a language of tourist exchange. This has the potential to suppress the use of Corsican in favour of English as a lingua franca, or lead Corsican-speaking tourist providers to use only their knowledge of major Romance tourist languages to communicate—that is, not to involve the tourist in the effort of 'intercomprehension' between Corsican and related languages. Finally, there is continuity with diglossic ideologies that not only rank but compartmentalize minority vs. dominant language practice. Corsican has historically been absent from the commercial sphere as a language of tourist exchange, even though it has been nominally present as a language of identity in a symbolic or 'emblematic' way, predominantly in business names displayed on signs. The default language of interaction with outsiders has long been French, with English making some modest inroads during the last decade. In general, there is also a striking absence of marketing of Corsican language and culture for tourist consumption. Corsican has thus more or less remained an 'insider' code, detached from the tourist enterprise.

At the same time, there are several elements of the tourist context that have the potential to encourage change, including the use of Corsican, as well as creative, hybrid language practices. First of all, most tourist interactions on Corsica take place outside of formal structures of linguistic control, evaluation, and surveillance. This is important in a context where the use of the minority language has become part of the academic institutions at all levels and has thus disseminated notions of Corsican language 'purity' and 'authenticity' and 'correctness' that typically stigmatize mixed codes. The tourist domain thus has the potential to be a space for the use of the Corsican language for Corsicans who are reticent about using Corsican with other (more proficient) Corsican speakers who might negatively evaluate the quality of their language. In a related vein, the fact that tourist interactions take place outside Corsican identity politics creates conditions in which Corsicans may use the language without any of the secondary entailments (including political affiliation) that its use might have in other intra-Corsican contexts. Even though there is relatively little cultural tourism on Corsica, there are some signs (see data below) of increased awareness of Corsican linguistic and cultural distinctiveness as a possible tourist product. While this has the potential to reproduce stereotypes, it also has the potential to valorize the knowledge and use of Corsican (see Boudreau and White 2004). Finally, many tourist interactions have a primarily practical/communicative rather than an ideological focus, and tourists and tourist professionals have relative goal congruence: achieving understanding simultaneously meets tourists' needs and facilitates the sale of tourist products. This shared pragmatic focus authorizes and validates 'imperfect' and hybrid language practices.

PRELIMINARY OBSERVATIONS: CONTINUITY AND CHANGE IN TOURIST SPACES

The following findings are the result of preliminary observations and recordings of tourist interactions and signage in tourist shops, tourist information centres, airports, boats/ports, hotels and cafes conducted in the summer of 2009 and 2010 by the authors. Commercial sites were located in one interior mid-sized town, a coastal town, and one of the two major cities on the island. One fairly striking form of ideological continuity is when Corsican tourist providers fail to consider Corsican a possible language of exchange with Italian tourists, even when English is not working well as a lingua franca. This is something that we have observed and have also had reported to us. Another is a purely emblematic use of Corsican on signs, mostly business names. On the side of change and creativity, we have documented other forms of public signage where Corsican is positioned as a language of communication and identity, or is the subject of metalinguistic play linked to the tourist framework. Finally, we have also found evidence of the use of Corsican and mixed forms of Corsican and Italian being used between Corsican tourist providers and Italian tourists. In the following sections, we look at progressively more creative forms of language use in these domains.

Contemporary linguistic landscape research, launched by Landry and Bourhis (1997), has focused on the way that signage—both 'public' and 'private'—reflects local economies of language including political and ideological processes and negotiations surrounding the relative status of different languages present in a particular context (see, among others, Backhaus 2007; Ben-Rafael et al. 2006: 8; Shohamy and Gorter 2009; Stroud and Mpendukana 2009). For minority languages, public signage is a site for the affirmation of language status and rights (see e.g. Cenoz and Gorter 2006; Huss 2008; Coupland 2010; Pietikäinen et al. 2011; Busch, this volume). Signs can counteract the historical exclusion of minority languages from public space by making them visible. Once visible, a variety of forms of semiotic positioning (using resources of colour, size, placement, etc.) with respect to other languages (particularly, dominant ones) also reflects and confers (relative) status and contributes to the discursive construction of public space (Hult 2009). Minority languages are also positioned in public signage by the genres in which they are used (Pietikäinen et al. 2011) and the functions those signs fill. The approach to Corsican signage developed in this section follows these lines of analysis to address issues of the status of Corsican relative to French and other foreign languages as reflected in commercial and public signage. The analysis also incorporates a model of signage as a space of *virtual or imagined interaction*. In this framework, the choice of languages and their functions *presupposes* and/or *stages* imagined linguistic communities, audiences, and linguistic interactions. In particular, I focus on the distinction between signs that project Corsican as a language of communication (among Corsicans or between Corsicans and speakers of other languages) and signs that display Corsican in a primarily 'emblematic' way, as an identity marker. As Jaworski and Piller's work on the representation of languages in travelogues shows, tourists and travel writers associated 'lived', rather than 'displayed' minority language use as authentic (2008: 310): the mere 'display' of the language fails to exemplify the sociolinguistic authenticity of being 'fully owned and unmediated' (Coupland 2003). The emphasis in the discussion below is on the visual representations of Corsican that are accessible to tourists on high-use transportation routes and in businesses where they are likely to shop.

LANGUAGE IDEOLOGICAL CONTINUITY: EMBLEMATIC SIGNAGE

One of the most common emblematic uses of Corsican in signage that tourists encounter is in business names. In Figure 6.1, Corsican is used in the main business sign, which reads 'Produtti di Corsica' (Corsican Products), followed by 'Artisgianatu' (Crafts). Corsican, however, is not used to communicate specific consumer information: the list of products available is written in French, German, and English on the sign to the right of the door to the shop (e.g. 'Chacuterie, Wurstwaren,

Figure 6.1:
Emblematic signage

Salumi'). This limited use of Corsican for business names is extremely widespread and cannot escape the notice of the tourist consumer. It is thus both conventional, and recognizable as a use of the language to mark local identity. At the same time, it does not present Corsican to tourists as a language of communication.

The distinction between the symbolic and communicative functions is also found and displayed to tourists in two other pieces of language addressed to tourists. The first example is illustrated in the contrast between official and more 'vernacular' signs on the Italian-run Moby Lines ferry linking Corsica and Italy. On these boats, permanent/official signs in the ladies' toilets (cautioning against throwing objects in the WCs) and in the hallways (identifying different lounges and services on the boat) address passengers in French, German, English, Italian, and Corsican.[2] However, despite the official decision of the Moby Lines company to use Corsican as a language of informational content, an employee-made sign on the same boat (Figure 6.2) belies this symbolic message by communicating essential information in French, Italian, and English only, sidelining both the Corsican and German that appear in the official company signs.

Corsica Airlines has also adopted a policy of bilingual announcements in French and Corsican. The departure text given to flight attendants to read goes as follows:

Salute à tutti, ghjunghjeremu in _____ trà un ore è mezzu, fate un bon' viaghju.

Welcome everyone, we will arrive in _____ in an hour and a half. Have a nice trip.

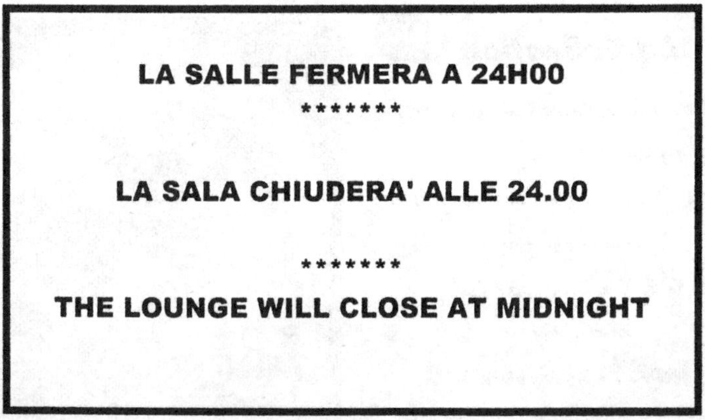

```
LA SALLE FERMERA A 24H00

*******

LA SALA CHIUDERA' ALLE 24.00

*******

THE LOUNGE WILL CLOSE AT MIDNIGHT
```

Figure 6.2:
Trilingual employee-made sign on Mobylines Ferry

However, once these announcements have been made, safety instructions and any other important informational content are broadcast in French and English only. All other routine oral interactions between flight attendants and passengers take place in French or occasionally English. In summary, the airline announcements and the kinds of official signage found on the Moby Lines boat mentioned above are conventional in two senses. First, they are normative and widespread. Secondly, they are ideologically conventional in their function of using Corsican to symbolize Corsican identity. They differ from the long-standing practice of naming businesses in Corsican in the degree to which they foreground the symbolic and political aspect of displaying linguistic heritage.

LANGUAGE IDEOLOGICAL CHANGE

Evidence of more consequential language ideological change can be found in signage that positions Corsican (to varying degrees) as a language of communication.

This can be seen in the large format electronic signboards erected on main highways and road junctions by the Regional Collectivity. They feature generic public service messages, alternating the French and Corsican versions of the message every 30 seconds or so. In the summer of 2011, one of these messages was 'Let's not burn Corsica; let's protect it'—in French, 'Ne brulons pas la Corse, protégeons-la' and in Corsican, 'Un brusgemu a Corsica; paremula di u focu.' In the same year, bilingual parking meters were installed in the city of Bastia. The electronic message on the meter's screen read: 'Tempu passatu: Amenda 1 €; Passata 1 H, 35 €' (Time expired: Fine, 11€, 1 hour past expiry 35 €).

While motorists can access all of these messages in French, these signs symbolically position Corsican as a language of salient everyday public communication equal to French.[3] The functions of these signs (issuing warnings/advice, notifying

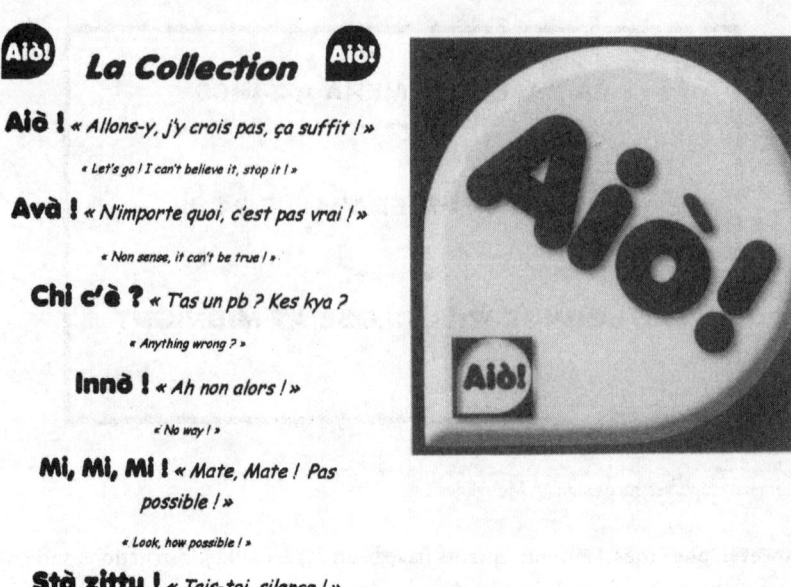

La Collection

Aiò ! « Allons-y, j'y crois pas, ça suffit ! »

« Let's go ! I can't believe it, stop it ! »

Avà ! « N'importe quoi, c'est pas vrai ! »

« Non sense, it can't be true ! »

Chi c'è ? « T'as un pb ? Kes kya ?

« Anything wrong ? »

Innò ! « Ah non alors ! »

« No way ! »

Mi, Mi, Mi ! « Mate, Mate ! Pas
possible ! »

« Look, how possible ! »

Stà zittu ! « Tais-toi, silence ! »

« Be quiet ! »

Figure 6.3:
Corsican language sticker and packaging

about fines, etc.) also position Corsican along with French as a language of social control (see Dann 2003).

LANGUAGE PLAY, FLUID BOUNDARIES, AND A PLURILINGUAL FRAMEWORK

In this section, we explore some examples of language use in the tourist contact zone that engage tourists as plurilingual consumers and position Corsican as one of the languages in play in plurilingual repertoires and interactions.

In the first example (Figure 6.3), the Corsican language is the product being marketed in a series of stickers featuring brief Corsican expressions. The full list (printed on the back of each individual package) includes the Corsican term printed on the sticker along with French and English translation (Table 6.1).

The fact that the expressions are all interjections evokes Corsican as a language of local exchange—in fact, as a language that carries a significant affective load and is used for high social-interactional purposes. In fact, 'ordinary' (that is, non high-affect) translations are left out in the case of '*Innò*', which can be translated simply 'No', and '*Chi c'è?*' The latter expression is translated relatively neutrally in English, but the French version has an accusatory tone, reading 'What's your problem? What's the matter?'

Table 6.1 CORSICAN LANGUAGE STICKERS

Corsican	French	English
Aiò!	Allons-y; j'y crois pas; ça suffit!	Let's go; I can't believe it; stop it!
Innò!	Ah non alors!	No way!
Mi Mi Mi Mi!	Mate, mate! Pas possible!	Look, how possible!
Avà!	N'importe quoi, c'est pas vrai!	Nonsense, it can't be true!
Chi c'è?	T'as un pb? Kes kya?	Anything wrong?
Stà zittu!	Tais-toi! Silence!	Be quiet!

It is also worth noting that the French translations are also colloquial. For example, the translation of 'Aiò' includes 'j'y crois pas', and the translation of 'Avà' includes 'c'est pas possible'. In both these cases the 'ne' of the standard form of the negative ('je n'y crois pas;' 'ce n'est pas possible') is left out in a reflection of everyday oral usage and conventional 'vernacular' writing. The French translation of 'Chi c'è?' also includes French text-messaging abbreviations ('pb' for 'problem' and a phonetic, abbreviated spelling—'kes kya' in place of the standard 'qu'est ce qu'il y a?'). These translations also function to position Corsican as a colloquial language used for every day, even high-tech functions.

This is the explicit message sent by a large poster situated in the departures area of one of the two main airports of the island in the summer of 2011. It featured a list of about twenty Corsican versions of common text messages, translated variously into English, French, German, Italian, Spanish, and Breton. This material was also printed as a glossy flyer that was distributed in many tourist offices across the island, as well as in some highly frequented businesses in the summer of 2011 and was made available on line at http://www.afcumani.org. The banner text on the front page of the flier and poster was written in five languages in block letters and read:

(Corsican) *I MIO TESTO I SCRIVU IN CORSU*
(German) *MEINE SMS SCHREIBE ICH AUF KORSISCH*
(English) *I WRITE MY SMS IN CORSICAN*
(Spanish) *ESCRIBO MIS SMS IN CORSO*
(French) *J'ECRIS MES SMS EN LANGUE CORSE*

Below this banner, the text listed ten text messages, each written in Corsican plus one other language, each preceded by a humorous text message category expressed in Corsican. The first one, for example, was an '*SMS Farniente*', where 'farniente' refers to lazing around (evoking both summer leisure and stereotypes of Corsican 'laziness'). This text was in Corsican and French, with the message (translated here but not on the flier) 'Arrived safely. Kisses from Corsica'.

(Corsican) *Ghjunti bè. Basgi da Corsica*
(French) *Bien arrivés. Bisous de Corsica*

Another text was labelled 'SMS Paghjella', referring to a traditional, and sometimes melancholy, Corsican song form. This one was in Corsican and English:

(Corsican) *N'ùn ti scurdà di mè ben ch'è luntanu.*
(English) *Don't forget me far away.*

An 'SMS Facebook' paired Corsican and German for the message 'How are you? Greetings from Corsica':

(Corsican) *Cumu stai amicu(a)? Ti salutu da Corsica.*
(German) *Wie geht's? Grüsse aus Korsika.*

The intent of the billboard is explained in Corsican and French in two text boxes on the bottom of the panel (the same message appeared on the back page of the flier). The following is my own English translation:

> The Corsican language is like a magnificent, forgotten garden signposted 'Forbidden to the public'... such a beautiful, lush, and useful garden, full of secrets and forgotten herbs that can nourish and heal us. Let's create that desire to pull down the sign 'No Access'; let's rejoice in the pleasure of opening up the garden. Let's conjure up the strength to cultivate it with know-how, love, and experience. Language is the 'house of being': it belongs to everyone. Let's have the courage to make it flourish, to offer and share it.

This discourse identifies Corsican simultaneously as a privileged, essential element of Corsican identity and heritage and as a token of exchange and interaction with speakers of other languages, including another minority one (Basque). These tourist visitors are invited 'into the garden' with text messages that locate the sender on Corsica (which is the 'deictic centre' of messages) and the messages as going to friends and family elsewhere. Thus Corsican is positioned as the language that both welcomes the visitors and anchors their experience to a tourist place, and as the language that does the work of connection and affective communication 'back home' and thereby authenticates the tourist trajectory and experience. The message of the essential unity of language and identity is ideologically conventional, but the imagined role of the language in the tourist experience represents ideological change in the representation of the plurilingual tourist adopting a minority language that is not his/her own for purposes of communication both inside and outside the tourist host society.

In the stickers mentioned earlier and in the text messages, Corsican is also positioned as a language of light-hearted, playful communication and as a specific focus of metalinguistic play (see Kelly-Holmes and Atkinson 2007; Jaffe 2000; Atkinson and Kelly-Holmes 2011). The very implausibility of a Basque speaker texting 'home' in Corsican underscores this ludic quality and establishes another potential point of convergence between host (author) and tourist (audience): the elite reflexivity needed to create and understand metalinguistic humour.

What is striking is that this play is packaged—at least potentially or partially—for an outside audience, indexed by the translations and by where the texts are located (tourist shops; airport). The target outside market is also reflected in the commentary of the owner of a tourist shop where the stickers were sold. When asked how they were selling, she said that they were not selling too well, and that in her view they needed to put a visual symbol of the island on each sticker so that tourists who bought them could display their Corsican origin outside the island. In essence, she voices the principle that Pietikäinen and Kelly-Holmes articulate for the labelling of souvenirs in Sámiland: that the 'ideal' tourist product should both cue the authenticity of place and assure its mobility (2011: 325). So, for the potential French- or English-speaking buyer, the Corsican language on the stickers authenticates the localness and the exoticness of place. This is a form of ideological continuity, both in terms of the use of the language and the positioning of Corsican as a culturally specific tourist destination.

At the same time, these particular stickers also index something else: a potential kind of intimacy of the buyer and the linguistic context without which it would be hard to imagine the consumer value or appeal of the product. In one scenario, the buyer can be imagined as having heard or heard of one or more of the terms evoked on the stickers, and made a purchase to validate that brush with insider knowledge. Alternatively, the tourist could buy the sticker with no prior knowledge of the terms and use the purchase as a springboard for future acts of listening. Both of these scenarios at least imagine non-Corsicans in interaction with the Corsican language. This is a new form of sociolinguistic imagination that extracts Corsican from its historical status as a uniquely insider code.

These products are also inherently multivalent, because they have other potential sources of consumer value for more than one category of consumer. With respect to the stickers, there is an obvious emblematic dimension to these stickers: they are linguistic tokens of Corsicanness, and Corsicanness is already heavily typified in the French national imagination. Thus, it is possible that both the producers and consumers view the expressions on the stickers not so much as fragments of a Corsican-speaking world, but rather as humorous elements of a regional variety of French. This view is not unfounded, since these expressions are used by speakers with a wide range of competencies in Corsican, and are used in both Corsican, French, and mixed utterances. In this respect, the stickers can be consumed as confirmations of fundamentally negative stereotypes. Secondly, the stickers are not uniquely targeted at or bought by tourists, so they also have to be interpreted as 'insider' consumables purchased by Corsicans living on the island permanently, as well as those who live on the French continent and visit in the summer.

Finally, the purchase of these stickers, like the consumption of the text message poster and pamphlet may also serve to authenticate the 'elite' tourist through the appropriation of 'local language' in ways that position those tourists as 'cosmopolitan internationals' who engage with local cultures and languages in superficial ways (Jaworski and Piller 2008: 304).

The final example of linguistic creativity in the commercial domain is an advertisement for a Corsican wine, documented on a large poster in one of the island's main airports. The poster had a dark background, with three wine glasses 'hanging' upside down from its top right corner and a silhouette of the shape of the island against a small pink text box with the word 'Corse' (Corsica) on the bottom right. The central part of the poster is filled with three words in very large, pink typeface (Calibri), followed by three bits of text in smaller typeface. They read, and are placed as follows:

Nielluciu*
Niélouchou
Nilouxou
c'est l'intention qui compte
*cépage Corse
FORCEMENT INATTENDUS

As in the stickers, we have another relatively rare instance of the presence of Corsican being explicitly signalled as the object of creative play that engages an outside audience. The first line is the name of the grape: 'Nielluciu', written in Corsican. The asterisk following the word identifies it as a genuine Corsican varietal. The second two lines are faux-phonetic transcriptions, followed by 'c'est l'intention qui compte' (it's the thought that counts) in French. One presupposition embedded in this humour is the unpronouncability of Corsican (see also Kelly-Holmes and Atkinson 2007). This is, of course, a form of authentication—linguistic exoticism signals an authentically other place, and authentically other, native speakers who can say it correctly. This in turn authenticates and adds value to the wine itself as an authentic, local product (Kelly-Holmes 2005; Pujolar 2006). The advertisement also makes a tongue-in-cheek intertextual reference to tourist guide books and lexicons and the language-of-purchase-specific pronunciation guides. These guides presume fleeting interlinguistic encounters and a tourist who will likely never advance beyond an approximation of native pronunciations. All of this can be considered ideological continuity relative to language in tourist spaces.

At the same time, the advertisement defines and positions several potential audiences/consumers. The matrix language of the advertisement is French, which is the language of all of its text apart from the two faux transliterations. French-speaking audiences are thus positioned as its primary audience. This audience is differentiated, however, by the first transliteration of the pronunciation of the word as 'Niélouchou' which follows French spelling conventions. This positions continental (non-Corsican) French speakers simultaneously as consumers (of the ad and the wine) and as the targets of a joke to be consumed by Corsicans who, while French speakers, do not need the transliteration to recognize and pronounce the name of the wine variety. The spelling 'Nilouxou' indexes non-French tourists from a variety of possible (but unspecified) places with languages in which the 'x' is pronounced [tʃ]. These tourists are less plausibly consumers of the ad; rather they are positioned as underspecified exotic visitors. They authenticate the island as a tourist destination and are symbolically aligned with continental French tourists as targets of the humour and as 'outsiders', thus highlighting the 'insiderness' and 'not-Frenchness' of Corsica and Corsicans.

With respect to the themes of ideological continuity and change, there are two simultaneous, and conflicting, frames introduced by this ad. On the one hand, 'It's the thought that counts' frames any pronunciations produced via other-language faux-phonetic transcription as imperfect, and thus emphasizes linguistic and cultural boundaries. Outsiders cannot penetrate Corsican as a code. At the same time, the ad evokes a frame in which there are potential tourists in Corsica who are interested in pronouncing a Corsican word and who might use the transliterations to do so, as well as Corsican hosts who are willing to accept imperfect pronunciations as good-faith efforts to accommodate to the presence of Corsican. In other words, the advertisement invokes a space of linguistic exchange that allows boundary transgressions and is not premised on perfect competencies.

This is particularly interesting because it contrasts with the history of representations of non-native pronunciations in Corsica. The speaking of Corsican with foreign accents has been the subject of radio and stand-up comedy sketches by 'other' foreigners for a Corsican audience (see Jaffe 1999). Non-native pronunciations of Corsican have also been the focus of Corsican opposition to the use of Corsican spellings and proper names on maps and road signs (now de facto norm). Objectors claimed either that tourists 'couldn't understand' Corsican place names and would get lost, or objected to the potential for tourists, especially French ones, to mangle Corsican pronunciations. In both of these discourses, linguistic boundaries are represented as impermeable by nature or by preference.

FLUID LANGUAGE USE IN TOURIST INTERACTION

The last piece of data we wish to examine is a partial transcript of a tourist interaction between tourists who were accompanied by Cedric Oliva (identified as 'F' in the transcript) during a visit to a Corsican shepherd who sells cheese on a heavily travelled tourist route up a mountain (Transcript 6.1). Oliva habitually uses Italian or English with these acquaintances, who do not speak French. In addition to French, Corsican, English, Italian, and Spanish, the coding on the transcript indicates two other categories: 'bivalent' utterances that are pronounced exactly the same in Italian and Corsican and 'mixed' utterances in which a word or phrase has elements of more than one language.

The transcript shows that for the shepherd, the default language of tourist interactions is French, which the tourists don't understand. Hearing Oliva's English explanation on line 9, the shepherd asks, 'English'? They counter with 'or Italian', to which he responds (line 11) in Corsican that he will speak Corsican to them and they will 'understand each other better': better, presumably, than if he tried to speak English. So we can see that the shepherd assumes mutual intelligibility of Corsican and Italian. He does indeed use Corsican with them, and it seems to work. He also produces several mixed utterances, listed in Table 6.2. In all cases, these mixed utterances involve phonological accommodation to Italian, thus an effort to make his Corsican more understandable to his clients. So in lines 19 and 22, he pronounces 'ricotta/ricorta' (fresh cheese) with an intervocalic [k] and [t], whereas in Corsican, a phonological process of vowel lenition produces the sounds [g] and [d] in the same contexts. The expression is 'mixed' because he uses the Corsican article

Transcript 6.1 TOURIST TRANSCRIPT

1	S	*Messieurs, entrez*	*Gentlemen, come in.*
2		*Messieurs, dames.*	*Ladies and gentlemen.*
3		*Mettez votre main comme ça,*	*Put your hand out like this, ladies*
4		*messieurs-dames, je vous fais*	*and gentlemen. I will give you a*
5		*gouter le brocciu.*	*taste of brocciu (cheese)*
6	F	He says to put out your whole	He says to put out your whole
7		hand.	hand.
8	T1	Ok. (she puts out hand) Así?	Ok. (she puts out hand) Like this?
9	S	Ok, English?	Ok, English?
10	T2	O italiano?	Or Italian?
11	S	Taliano? Allora vi parlu u	Italian? Then I'll speak
12		corsu, s'emu da capisce megliu.	Corsican to you, we'll
13			understand one another better.
14	T1	Si.	Yes.
15	T2	Si, corso va bene.	Yes, Corsican will work.
16	T1	Che buono !	This is so good!
17	T2	Si.	Yes.
18	F	*Merci.*	*Thank you.*
19	S	a ricotta, italiano,	the ricotta, in Italian,
20		*c'est ça* ?	*right*?
21		- (No response) -	- (No response) -
22	T1/2	Ricorta, in taliano ?	Ricorta, in Italian?
23	S	Ricorta, si. (tasting)	Ricorta, right. (tasting)
24	T1	Che buon-! (last vowel indistinct)	This is so good!
25	S	H/è bonu, deliciosu.	It's good, it's delicious.
26	T1	Delicioso/u, è incredibile! Che	Delicious – it's incredible. What
27		cosa possiamo fare?	can we do with it?
28	F	Possiamo mangiarla con acqua di	We can eat it with liqueur and
29		vita e zucchero	sugar
30		- (Several seconds of no talk,	- (Several seconds of no talk,
31		tasting) -	tasting) -
32	S	Fromagiu di pecura (/pɛkura/),	Sheep's cheese,
33		dui mesi (/dz/).	two months (old).
34	T	Dui mesi (/z/).	Two months.
35	S	Di u ghjornu stessu, d'oghie	(this one is) freshly made today

S=Shepherd; T1=Female tourist; T2=Male Tourist; F= Researcher friend of couple

Italian	**Corsican**	**Bivalent**	
Mixed	*French*	English	Spanish

Table 6.2 MIXED UTTERANCES IN TOURIST EXCHANGE

Line #	MIXED UTTERANCES	Italian	Corsican	French
19	a ricotta /a rikɔta/	la ricotta /la rikɔta/	a ricotta /a rigɔda/	
22	'taliano' pronounced /taliano/	/italiano/	/talianu/	
22	'ricorta' pronounced /rikorta/	/rikɔta/	/rigɔda/ or /rigɔrta/	
24/26	'buon- ?' and 'delicios-?'	-o	-u	
32	'fromagiu' (cheese)	formaggio	furmagliu/casgiu	fromage
32	'pecura' (sheep) pronounced /pɛkura/	/pɛkora/	/bɛgura/	

'a' instead of the Italian 'la'. On line 32 he again avoids Corsican consonant lenition in the word for 'sheep', producing [p] and [k] where in Corsican, the consonants are pronounced [b] and [g]. This word remains 'mixed' because he does not modify the Corsican vowel [u] to the Italian [o]. He does, however, attend to the contrast between [o] and [u] in the word for 'Italian' (line 22), beginning the word with a Corsican pronunciation (an initial 't' instead of an initial 'i') but ending it with the Italian 'o' instead of the Corsican 'u'. Finally, he produces a mixture of French and Corsican for the word for 'cheese' on line 32. This is not as clear a form of accommodation to Italian, since the resonances between Corsican and Italian and French and Italian for this word are very different, but of the same order. However, it is likely that his habitual word for 'cheese' in Corsican is 'casgiu,' since it is the generic word for cheese that he uses on the sign for his business. In this respect, he may be seen as accommodating to his clientele by mixing French with the Corsican vocabulary word that is closer to Italian than the one he features on his sign.

On the part of the tourists, there is a lot of echoing of the words 'good' and 'delicious' in the sequence as they try the cheese. On lines 24 and 26, the pronunciation of the woman tourist was heard by both authors as having a—u, or Corsican ending, although both also found the stimulus ambiguous in multiple listenings. It is thus noted here as a *potential* act of accommodation to the shepherd.

This transcript shows the space of tourist interaction to be a linguistically flexible one, in which both the tourists and the shepherd make mutual accommodations in both the production and reception of language, instantiating a mixed discourse and mixed codes that allow them to reach a variety of shared, or at least congruent social, experiential, and commercial goals. Future data collection will reveal the extent to which this kind of interaction is the norm, and what kinds of configurations of participants (types of tourists and tourist providers) and events/activities facilitate hybrid, creative, and multilingual practice. What we glimpse in the transcript is the realization, in the interactional sphere created by a tourism of 'proximity', of the kind of exchange indexed by the stickers, text message poster and the *Niellucciu* wine ad. In this kind of exchange, tourists and Corsicans engage in communicative exchanges in ways that include Corsican as a language linked to 'authentic' place but also include Corsican as a language used as a bridge to interlinguistic conversations with other romance language speakers. In the same way that the textual materials analysed above presuppose savvy audiences, these kinds of interactions also position their participants as multilingual and reflexive social actors: as sharing metalinguistic awareness and orientations.

CONCLUSIONS AND PERSPECTIVES

Corsican sociolinguistic history has left a dominant language ideological legacy. The drive for linguistic legitimacy that has marked the last several decades of Corsican language activism favours the reproduction of dominant models of language as a bounded code with an essential, iconic relationship with a bounded cultural identity. This model of language is activated and reproduced within the French national context, which serves as an important frame for tourists and tourist professionals alike. In the public, visual domain, we see this in the bilingual signage that is accessible to tourists, which positions Corsican as 'not French'. The activation of this contrastive value reproduces dominant language ideologies because it focuses attention on language boundaries. In tourist spaces, the display and commodification of the Corsican language as a marker of authentic heritage and place also tends to reproduce 'essentialist' models of the relationship between language and identity. This can be seen in all the emblematic uses of written Corsican in the commercial domain, as well as in much public domain signage that is not exclusively targeted at tourists but is nevertheless part of the linguistic landscape that they consume. Tourist spaces also reproduce language hierarchies and differentiation of function that are also linked to dominant language ideologies associated with minority languages. That is, the commodification of 'heritage' as a possible product tends to confine Corsican—and other minority languages—to emblematic functions and does not disrupt the default assumptions and conventional expectations that tourist encounters take place in 'major' languages or lingua francas (a point made by Kelly-Holmes 2005, with respect to minority languages in advertising). The still limited interactional data collected suggest that many Corsicans still need to be prompted to view Corsican as a language of tourist offer: one that can be displayed more extensively in the public sphere, one that can be used among Corsicans in front of tourists, and used with those tourists who speak other romance languages. The potential for Corsican to be used as a bridge to communication with Italians is present in the collective experience (see Oliva 2011) but is often articulated as 'being able to speak Italian', rather than being able to use Corsican. All these features have the effect of reinforcing 'peripherality' as an element of Corsica and Corsican's positioning in the international context. We have seen the reflection of this perspective in the relative and historical exclusion of Corsican as a language of international, commercial transactions in the public sphere: in signage that restricts the use of Corsican to emblematic/symbolic functions and uses French or other major languages as vehicles for communicative content. While evidence is still very preliminary, it is also attested in tourist providers' habitual recourse to French or English as the default, matrix languages of interactions with tourists.

At the same time, tourist contexts are also sites in which ideological change is possible. The data that we have collected include texts and interactions that at least implicitly validate a communicatively oriented, 'repertoires'-based notion of the multilingual person and presume or anticipate plurilingual zones of contact where speakers with multiple language competencies of various kinds and levels engage in fluid, creative language practices. This is an interesting extension of the 'polynomic' approach to intra-Corsican sociolinguistic variation. We have seen traces of this kind of linguistic engagement and sociolinguistic imaginary in the advertisements that involve metalinguistic play and evoke and position multiple audiences, as well as in the fragment of interaction between the shepherd and his clients presented in the last section. Within the actual and perceived constraints and regimentation imposed by the economic market, tourist spaces thus offer some opportunities for both language play and unregimented, convivial social interactions in which fluid and varied uses of Corsican, Italian (and potentially other languages) can emerge.

The comparison and contrast of tourist data with previous research conducted by Jaffe in Corsican bilingual schools (Jaffe 2008, 2009) suggests that it may be useful to distinguish between different kinds of linguistic regimentation: that associated with commercial markets (the commodification of heritage, the homogenization of products and services and the ranking and valuation of languages and language skills) vs. the regimentation associated with public institutions. Market-driven language ideologies may reproduce some, but not all institutional ones, since the ultimate objective is not symbolic or political but commercial. The commercial imperative, in particular contexts, may thus 'free' social actors to engage in mixed language practices that may be sanctioned or undervalued in some official minority language contexts and practices; further data collection is needed to assess the extent to which this happens on Corsica. The commercial (stickers and wine ad) and semi-commercial (text message billboards and pamphlets) texts discussed above also show the ludic potential of communication put on display in the linguistic landscape accessed by tourists. These creative and playful texts create virtual linguistic ecologies, imagined interactions, and participation structures in which Corsican plays a central role as a language of exchange. These creative stagings of Corsican represent it as a language that does not just symbolize a static Corsican identity, but is a tool in the active expression of that identity in interaction with outsiders. These uses of Corsican exhibit features of *sociolinguistic authenticities*, positioning Corsican as 'fully owned, unmediated language' and as language that 'indexes authentic cultural membership' (Coupland 2003). They also index a key feature of *sociolinguistic authorities*: metalinguistic control (Jaffe 2011).

These forms of representational legitimacy are, however, complicated by the dynamics of reception and evaluation in tourist spaces, where their meanings are subject to being reentextualized in ways that escape the control of their authors. While this is true of many forms of expression, the fact that tourist audiences are also *consumers* implicitly gives them an edge, since they ultimately control the act of buying (whether a product or an experience) that underpins all tourist relationships. Similarly, the circulation of Corsican in a global market of words and images has the potential to both attenuate and emphasize its peripherality. An island and language that is 'peripheral' to the French hexagon is not necessarily so when positioned as a bridge to nearby languages (like Italian) or as a different kind of representational tool with more distant speakers and languages (indexed by the text messaging poster). However, the positioning of the language as a transnational index of cultural authenticity can both confer and undermine its status and legitimacy. This is because the tourist consumers of Corsican circulate in contexts whose legitimacy is external to the island, contexts in which local, exotic, and 'small' languages are powerful tools in the creation of elite, cosmopolitan identities. These identities are potentially also available to Corsicans involved in producing tourist texts of various kinds. These kinds of complexities, we argue, are emblematic of emerging uses of minority languages in tourist contexts. In the end, it is a question of the particular balance achieved and experienced in specific moments of use, exchange, and evaluation: this chapter sketches the parameters needed for a full ethnographic account of those moments of action.

NOTES

1. Although he seems to have pulled back from this position in more recent statements (Thiers 2010).
2. This message of symbolic parity through identical positioning in multilingual signage is practiced routinely in numerous instances of public and private (including commercial) signage on the island that, due to space limitations, cannot be described in detail here.
3. With respect to the billboards, however, an analysis of them over several months (that is, beyond the limited time of the typical tourist visit) revealed that whenever there is time-sensitive, specific information to report (e.g. a road closure) the information is presented in French only.

REFERENCES

Antonmarchi, Florence, Toni Casalonga, Charlie Galiber, Franck Michel, and Jean-Didier Urbain. 2010. Imaginaire, île, tourisme, Corse: Voyage à plusieurs voix. *Autres Voies* 6. Online journal: http://www.deroutes.com/AV6/num6.htm. Accessed 10 December 2011.

Atkinson, David, and Helen Kelly-Holmes. 2011. Codeswitching, identity and ownership in Irish radio comedy. *Journal of Pragmatics* 43 (1): 251–260.

Backhaus, Peter. 2007. *Linguistic landscapes: A comparative study of urban multilingualism in Tokyo.* Clevedon: Multilingual Matters.

Benor, Sara. 2010. Ethnolinguistic repertoire: Shifting the analytic focus in language and ethnicity. *Journal of Sociolinguistics* 14: 159–183.

Ben-Rafael, Eliezer, Elana Shohamy, Muhammad Hasan Amara, and Nira Trumper-Hecht. 2006. Linguistic landscape as symbolic construction of the public space: The case of Israel. *International Journal of Multilingualism* 3 (1): 7–30.

Blommaert, Jan. 2009. *A sociolinguistics of globalization.* Cambridge: Cambridge University Press.

Blommaert, Jan, and Jef Verschueren. 1998. *Debating diversity: Analysing the discourse of tolerance.* London: Routledge.

Boudreau, Annette. 2005. Le Français en Acadie: Maintien et revitalisation du français dans les provinces Maritimes. In *Le Français en Amérique du Nord: état présent,* ed. Albert Valdman, Julie Augerand, and Deborah Piston-Hatlen, 439–354. Québec: Les Presses de l'Université Laval.

Boudreau, Annette, and Chantal White. 2004. Turning the tide in Acadian Nova Scotia: How heritage tourism is changing language practices and representations of language. *The Canadian Journal of Linguistics / La Revue canadienne de linguistique* 49 (3/4): 327–351.

Cenoz, Jasone, and Durk Gorter. 2006. Linguistic landscape and minority languages. *International Journal of Multilingualism* 3 (1): 67–80.

Comiti, Jean-Marie. 1992. *Les Corses face à leur langue: De la naissance de l'idiome à la reconnaissance de la langue.* Aiacciu: Squadra di u Finusellu.

Cortier, Claude, and Alain Di Meglio. 2004. Le Dépassement du conflit diglossique en Corse: Implications pédagogiques et didactiques chez les maîtres bilingues de l'école primaire. *Repères* 29: 185–206.

Council of Europe. 2001. *Common European Framework of Reference for Languages.* Online. Available HTTP: http://www.coe.int/t/dg4/linguistic/Source/Framework_EN.pdf. Accessed 9 August 2009.

Coupland, Nikolas. 2003. Sociolinguistic authenticities. *Journal of Sociolinguistics* 7 (3): 417–431.

Coupland, Nikolas. 2010. Introduction: Sociolinguistics in the Global Era. In *Handbook of language and globalization,* ed. Nikolas Coupland, 1-28. Malden: Wiley-Blackwell.

Coupland, Nikolas, Hywel Bishop, and Peter Garret. 2003. Home truths: Globalization and the iconizing of Welsh in a Welsh-American newspaper. *Journal of Multilingual and Multicultural Development* 24 (3): 153–177.

Coupland, Nikolas, Peter Garret, and Hywel Bishop. 2005. Wales underground: Discursive frames and authenticities in Welsh mining heritage tourism events. In *Discourse, communication and tourism,* ed. Adam Jaworski and Annette Pritchard, 199–222. Clevedon: Multilingual Matters.

Dann, Graham. 2003. Noticing notices: Tourism to order. *Annals of Tourism Research* 20 (2): 465–484.

Da Silva, Emanuel, Mireille McLaughlin, and Mary Richards. 2007. Bilingualism and the globalized new economy: The commodification of language and identity. In *Bilingualism: A social approach,* ed. Monica. Heller, 183–206. New York: Palgrave.

Duchêne, Alexandre. 2009. Marketing, management and performance: Multilingualism as commodity in a tourism call centre. *Language Policy* 8 (1): 27–50.

Gal, Susan. 2006. Contradictions of standard language in Europe: Implications for the study of publics and practices. *Social Anthropology* 14 (2): 153–181.

Heller, Monica. 2003. Globalization, the new economy, and the commodification of language and identity. *Journal of Sociolinguistics* 7: 473–492.

Heller, Monica. 2006. *Linguistic minorities and modernity: A sociolinguistic ethnography.* New York: Continuum Press.

Heller, Monica. 2010. Language as a resource in the globalized new economy. In *The handbook of language and globalization*, ed. Nikolas Coupland, 349–365. Malden: Wiley-Blackwell.

Heller, Monica, and Joan Pujolar. 2009. The political economy of texts: A case study in the structuration of tourism. *Sociolinguistic Studies* 3 (2): 177–201.

Hult, Francis. 2009. Language ecology and linguistic landscape analysis. In *Linguistic landscape: Expanding the scenery*, ed. Elana Shohamy and Durk Gorter, 88–104. London: Routledge.

Huss, Leena. 2008. Scandinavian minority language policies in transition: The impact of the European charter for regional or minority languages in Norway and Sweden. In *Sustaining linguistic diversity: Endangered and minority languages and language varieties*, ed. K. King, N. Schilling-Estes, L. Fogle, J.J. Lou, and B. Soukup, 129–144. Washington, D.C.: Georgetown University Press.

Jacquemet, Marco. 2005. Transidiomatic practices: Language and power in the age of globalization. *Language and Communication* 25: 257–277.

Jaffe, Alexandra. 1999. *Ideologies in action: Language politics on Corsica*. Berlin: Mouton de Gruyter.

Jaffe, Alexandra. 2000. Comic performance and the articulation of hybrid identity. *Pragmatics* 10 (1): 39–60.

Jaffe, Alexandra. 2007a. Minority language movements. In *Bilingualism: A social approach*, ed. Monica Heller, 50–70. Basingstoke: Palgrave Press.

Jaffe, Alexandra. 2007b. Corsican on the airwaves: Media discourse, practice and audience in a context of minority language shift and revitalization. In *Language in the Media*, ed. Sally Johnson and Astrid Ensslin, 149–172. London: Continuum Press.

Jaffe, Alexandra. 2008. Language ecologies and the meaning of diversity: Corsican bilingual education and the concept of 'polynomie.' In *The encyclopedia of language and education*, ed. Angela Creese, Peter Martin, and Nancy Hornberger, vol. 9: 225–237. Frankfurt: Springer.

Jaffe, Alexandra. 2009. Stance in a Corsican school: Institutional and ideological orders. In *Stance: Sociolinguistic Perspectives*, ed. Alexandra Jaffe, 119-145. New York: Oxford University Press.

Jaffe, Alexandra. 2010. Critical perspectives on language-in-education policy: The Corsican example. In *Ethnography and language policy*, ed. Teresa McCarty, 205–231. New York: Routledge.

Jaffe, Alexandra. 2011. Sociolinguistic diversity in mainstream media: Authenticity, authority and processes of mediation and mediatization. *Journal of Language and Politics* 10 (4): 562–586.

Jaworski, Adam, and Ingrid Piller. 2008. Linguascaping Switzerland: Language ideologies in tourism. In *Standards and norms in the English language*, ed. Miriam A. Locher and Jürg Strässler, 301–321. Berlin: Mouton de Gruyter.

Jaworski, Adam, and Annette Pritchard, eds. 2005. *Discourse, communication and tourism*. Clevedon: Multilingual Matters.

Jaworski, Adam, and Crispin Thurlow, eds. 2010. *Semiotic landscapes: Language, image, space*. London: Continuum.

Kelly-Holmes, Helen. 2005. *Advertising as multilingual communication*. London: Palgrave.

Kelly-Holmes, Helen, and David Atkinson. 2007. When Hector met Tom Cruise: Attitudes to Irish in radio satire. In *Language in the media*, ed. Sally Johnson and Astrid Ensslin, 173–187. London: Continuum.

Landry, Rodrigue, and Richard Bourhis. 1997. Linguistic landscape and ethnolinguistic vitality. *Journal of Language and Social Psychology* 16 (1): 23–49.

Makoni, Sinfree, and Alastair Pennycook. 2007. *Disinventing and reconstituting languages.* Clevedon: Multilingual Matters.

Marcellesi, Jean-Baptiste. 1989. Corse et théorie sociolinguistique: Reflets croisés. In *L'île miroir,* ed. Georges Ravis-Giordani, 165–174. Ajaccio: La Marge.

Marcellesi, Jean-Baptiste. 2003. *Sociolinguistique: Epistémologie, langues régionales, polynomie. With Thierry Bulot and Philippe Blanchet.* Paris: L'Harmattan.

McLaughlin, Mireille, and Melanie LeBlanc. 2009. Identité et marché dans la balance: Le Tourisme mondial et les enjeux de l'acadianité. *Francophonies d'Amerique* 27: 21–51.

Moïse, Claudine, and Sylvie Roy. 2009. Valeurs identitaires et linguistiques dans l'industrie touristique patrimoniale (Ontario et Alberta). *Francophonies d'Amerique* 27: 53–75.

Oliva, Cedric. 2011. 'Minority languages and their evolutions with and within people: The case of the Corsican language in the Romance-speaking world'. Doctoral dissertation, University of Corsica.

Pietikäinen, Sari. 2010. Sámi language mobility: Scales and discourses of multilingualism in polycentric environment. *International Journal of Sociology of Language* 202: 79–101.

Pietikäinen, Sari, and Helen Kelly-Holmes. 2011. The local political economy of languages in a Sámi tourism destination: Authenticity and mobility in the labelling of souvenirs. *Journal of Sociolinguistics* 15 (3): 323–346.

Pietikäinen, Sari, Pia Lane, Hanni Salo, and Sirkka Laihiala-Kankainen. 2011. Frozen actions in the Arctic linguistic landscape: A nexus analysis of language processes in visual space. *International Journal of Multilingualism* 8 (4): 277–298.

Pujolar, Joan. 2006. *Language, culture and tourism: Perspectives in Barcelona and Catalonia.* Barcelona: Turisme de Barcelona.

Shohamy, Elana, and Durk Gorter, eds. 2009. *Linguistic landscape: Expanding the scenery.* New York: Routledge.

Stroud, Christoper, and Sibonile Mpendukana. 2009. Towards a material ethnography of linguistic landscape: Multilingualism, mobility and space in a South African township. *Journal of Sociolinguistics* 13 (3): 363–386.

Swigart, Leigh. 2001. The limits of legitimacy: Language ideology and shift in contemporary Senegal. *Journal of Linguistic Anthropology* 10 (1): 90–130.

Thiers, Jacques. 2003. Language contact and Corsican polynomia. In *Trends in Romance linguistics and philology, vol. 5: Bilingualism and linguistic conflict in Romance,* ed. Rebecca Posner and John Green, 253–270. Berlin: Mouton de Gruyter.

Thiers, Jacques. 2008. *Papiers d'identité.* Aiacciu: Albiana.

Thiers, Jacques. 2010. Interview with Albiana Publishers. http://www.albiana.fr/Jacques-Thie rs-a-propos-de-Papiers-d-identite-s_a409.html. Accessed 5 October 2011.

Wright, Sue. 2004. *Language policy and language planning: From nationalism to globalisation.* Basingstoke: Palgrave Macmillan.

CHAPTER 7

'Translation in Progress'

Centralizing and Peripheralizing Tensions in the Practices of Commercial Actors in Minority Language Sites

HELEN KELLY-HOLMES

INTRODUCTION

This chapter is concerned with examining how the tensions between centralizing and peripheralizing ideologies are reflected in the practices of individual commercial actors in sites of peripheral multilingualism. My starting point is the following: given the importance of tourism and craft industries in sites of peripheral multilingualism, as outlined in the introduction to this volume, the role of individual commercial actors in these sectors can be a significant one in these sites, and their language practices may have an important impact. The linguistic decisions and practices of individual commercial actors can be seen as involving guesswork in terms of credibility and acceptability (Bourdieu 1991) within the boundaries of prevailing language ideologies. Their practices may thus constitute a challenge to or a reaffirmation of these ideologies (cf. Kelly-Holmes 2010 for a discussion of this). Of course, commercial actors are also members of speech communities and share language ideologies of those speech communities. Thus, they may not always act in strictly rational ways—in economic terms—with respect to the language choices they make in their marketing, advertising, and so on (Atkinson and Kelly-Holmes 2006). Consequently, the role of the individual commercial actor in creating, following, maintaining, or challenging language trends and language regimes is all part of the political economy of language in sites of peripheral multilingualism (Kelly-Holmes 2010; Pietikäinen and Kelly-Holmes 2011).

The focus here is on two particular interrelated questions: First, do individual actors in sites of peripheral multilingualism attempt to centralize or peripheralize Irish (e.g. do they attempt to draw it into the centre of their everyday business and commerce as a type of normalization, or do they peripheralize it by confining it to particular functions and domains)? I understand centralizing here as the opposite of peripheralization and thus as a form of linguistic normalization (cf. Bastardas and Soler 1988), whereby the use of Irish in a commercial domain is driven by the desire to have it used as a normal and unremarkable language of daily life and commerce. Centralizing, then, involves taking on the trappings of modernity: for example, corpus planning, using, disseminating and adhering to standards, 'correction' of linguistic landscapes in minority language contexts, and use of the language in commercial or other high prestige domains (cf. Strubell 1998; Atkinson and Kelly-Holmes 2006). Peripheralizing, then, is the other side of the coin: using Irish in a marked, exceptional, and non-essential way, which may add symbolic value, but which reinforces its status as something that is peripheral and not part of the 'real', 'modern' world.

Secondly, do individual commercial actors in sites of peripheral multilingualism adopt centre/centrist practices and ideologies (understood here as norm-driven policies and practices based on parallel monolingualism and modernist concepts) or peripheral practices (understood here as hybrid processes, based on individual practices). As outlined in the introduction to the volume, peripheral multilingualism is driven by the concept of linguistic repertoire (e.g. Makoni and Pennycook 2007; Blommaert 2010; Pennycook 2010). In contrast to the centre, which is seen as the source of norm creation and norm (re)enforcement, the periphery involves multiple sites of normativity (cf. Blommaert et al. 2005). Centre multilingualism is concerned with geographically or socially demarcated speech communities, whereas peripheral multilingualism involves communities of practice (cf. Rampton 2006, 2009). The concept of 'bilingualism as deficit' is fundamental to centre multilingualism, whereas peripheral multilingualism assumes a 'bilingualism as added value' (Jaffe 2006) approach. Significantly, in terms of the focus here on individual commercial actors, we can understand centre multilingualism as making use of 'available forms' and 'available classifications', whereas peripheral multilingualism involves 'individual acts of sign-making' (Kress and van Leeuwen 2006: 12), and, in common with many contributors to the current volume, it is to those 'individual acts of sign-making' that we turn our attention in this chapter.

The particular site is the website for a pottery workshop in the *Corca Dhuibhne Gaeltacht*/Dingle Peninsula, a designated Irish-speaking area, in the South-West of Ireland. I begin by discussing Irish in relation to the concept of peripheral multilingualism before going on to describe the sociolinguistic context of the peripheral multilingual site of interest, in particular in relation to centralizing and peripheralizing tensions. The chapter then focuses on the case of one particular commercial actor, Louis Mulcahy Pottery, and examines the practices on the website for that company.

The first thing to say about Irish in relation to the concept of peripheral multilingualism is that we are not dealing with a 'straightforward' case of a peripheralized language community in a peripheral location. Irish is both central and peripheral at one and the same time in contemporary Ireland. The respective centralization or peripheralization can vary depending on the actors, location, context, and so on. This complexity, however, exemplifies the tensions that characterize centre–periphery relations in the contemporary era, and how these impact on multilingualism. In a context such as that of Irish, the periphery–centre dynamic involves constant change and renegotiation: it cannot really be understood in terms of a system that is unchanging or subject only to very slow change, in the way in which, for example, Wallerstein (2004) has conceived centre–periphery economic and geographic relations, or, de Swaan (2001) has metaphorized centre–periphery relations between languages (as discussed in the introduction to the volume). In fact, it is almost impossible to classify a language such as Irish in terms of de Swaan's 'World Language System', since 'peripheral languages', according to de Swaan, are generally oral and without status in education, government, and so on, something which is clearly not the case for Irish, while 'central' languages are national languages with all the associated functions, again something which Irish falls short of for a variety of reasons (cf. e.g. Mac Giolla Chríost 2005; Ó Laoire 2008; Walsh 2011).

The concept of a 'privileged minoritized language' (Kelly-Holmes 2006a) sums up this ever-changing, constantly renegotiated status between centre and periphery. As a 'privileged minoritized' language, Irish is both central and peripheral to everyday life in Ireland. It is clearly central in some domains, being the first official language of the country, and given a privileged status in the education system and other official domains of life. However, it is certainly peripheral in other areas (e.g. in mainstream entertainment, mainstream media, commerce, and advertising). Most significantly, it is not the everyday language of communication for the majority of people in Ireland, although many people do use Irish on a daily basis (cf. e.g. Mac Giolla Chríost 2005; Ó Laoire 2008 for an overview of the situation). For Irish, as for many languages in a similar sociolinguistic situation, periphery–centre relations are determined on the basis of context (who, what, where, how, why) and are fluid rather than fixed.

Education is a good example of the centralizing–peripheralizing tensions. While Irish can be seen to be at the core of the national curriculum, particularly for primary schools—it is a compulsory subject throughout schooling and is usually required for matriculation purposes—its status in education is the subject of constant debate. Its forced centrality almost makes it a target for those who argue that its peripheral status in everyday life and in the 'real world' should be reflected in its status in educational and official domains. As Gal and Woolard (2001) point out, normalization is a marked way of using a language in order to make use of the language less marked. Irish in its many contradictions and complexities also shows how the drive to normalize and centralize a language by reversing an existing language hierarchy can often in fact highlight and reinforce its peripherality (cf. Gal and Woolard 2001).

In addition, norm-setting for Irish is not a straightforward case of rules being set by the centre and followed by the periphery. In matters of spoken language, the native speaker from the geographically peripheral *Gaeltacht* was traditionally seen as the expert and so those geographically remote areas (like the Dingle Peninsula) were in fact seen as central for that process. However, much of the emphasis in status planning for Irish has been on written language, and the norms for this have tended in recent years to be derived by elites living outside the periphery. In debates on terminology, the speakers from the *Gaeltacht* may either be absent or may adopt a more laissez-faire attitude to mixing between the languages—an example of 'peripheral multilingualism' in terms of this volume—whereas 'language ideological brokers' (Blommaert 1999) are more concerned with boundary work between the two languages (cf. e.g. Lenihan's (2011) study of the Irish language Facebook site). Unsurprisingly, there is resistance to adopting new terminology, designed in and disseminated from the centre, among *Gaeltacht* speakers (cf. Ní Ghearáin 2011).

Finally, while Irish has long been stigmatized and peripheralized in the modern era and not associated with economic advancement (cf. Walsh 2011 for extensive and comprehensive overview of these issues), there has, since the founding of the state, been an advantage to Irish-English bilingualism for those in the centre, although not always for those in the periphery (who were expected to remain monolingual in the *Gaeltacht* to provide linguistic resources for the centre, particularly to support and aid the objectives of acquisition planning). So, discourses of 'bilingualism as deficit' and 'bilingualism as added value' (Jaffe 2006) have managed to co-exist in Ireland.

THE CONTEXT: THE DINGLE PENINSULA AS
PERIPHERAL AND CENTRAL

Like the Irish language, the Dingle Peninsula, where the Louis Mulcahy workshop is located, is also both peripheral and central. Significantly for Dingle, its peripherality and its centrality are interrelated and interdependent. Dingle is central as a key tourist destination (listed frequently in the top 10 European tourist destinations); many larger centres (e.g. Limerick) are bypassed by tourists and holidaymakers (domestic and international) on their way to Dingle; and Dingle is also a centre for the Irish language as part of the *Gaeltacht* area, which is made up of designated Irish-speaking or bilingual Irish-English areas. For its locality, Dingle town is also a centre of trade, particularly fishing, and provides shops and other facilities for the hinterland. Crucially, it is also central to the Irish nation's imagining of itself as bilingual and to the marketing of Ireland abroad; the image of the Dingle peninsula is an iconic one both in the Irish imagination and in the marketing discourse about

Ireland as a tourist destination. However, Dingle is also peripheral, in its geographical isolation, distance from larger urban centres and from the capital, and limited access to health, infrastructure, and so on.

Dingle like other minority language spaces has been the subject of language policy and language planning initiatives—most explicitly in the establishment of the *Gaeltacht* areas, which can be seen as an attempt to create boundaries around the communities and the language practices of these peripheries in an attempt to keep them monolingually Irish or at least predominantly Irish-speaking, regardless of the sociolinguistic realities within the area.

The case of the *An Daingean*/Dingle renaming controversy highlights the tension that arises from the need for the area to be imagined as a monolingual periphery by the centre and the imposition of centralizing (monolingual) norms in order to achieve this. As part of the Official Languages Act (2003), a major piece of status planning for Irish, there was a move to change the change the name of Dingle town on signage and to impose a monolingual Irish name—*An Daingean*—with English only or bilingual signage to be removed. The move was resisted by a large number of local people, one of the main objections being that the erasure of the English name (Dingle) would adversely affect tourism, given the value of the brand internationally (cf. Moriarty 2011 for a discussion). The renaming controversy can be seen as an attempt to impose centrist norms—norms of parallel monolingualism—onto chaotic and fragmented language practices, and to impose boundaries between the Irish and the English languages. As discussed in the introduction to the volume, Wallerstein (2004) sees peripheries as being created and maintained by centres as a source of primary resources (cf. Heller, this volume). Dingle and the other *Gaeltacht* areas in Ireland have to be maintained as monolingual peripheries not only to act as a linguistic resource for the rest of the nation (e.g. for language tourism and the language industry) but also to provide a resource to legitimize Irish claims to be different from the rest of the Anglophone world and to be 'genuinely' bilingual. Another recent example of an attempt, driven by centre ideologies, to impose monolingual norms on language practices in peripheral sites, was the 'C' status afforded to Dingle in Ó Giollagáin et al.'s (2007) survey of Irish language usage in *Gaeltacht* areas. The town of Dingle was classified as a 'C' location, meaning the lowest level of Irish language usage on a day-to-day basis. However, the survey can, like the renaming attempt described above, be seen to represent an attempt to impose centrist norms on multilingual realities, since it is conceptualized on the basis of bounded languages and 'clean' (i.e. one language or the other) language practices.

In common with many of the peripheral sites under examination in this volume (e.g. Inari, Acadie), the tourism and crafts industry in Dingle grew out of a need for an alternative economic development strategy for the area, which was adversely affected by structural changes in the national and global economy. Peripherality underpins Dingle's popularity and appeal as a tourist destination for both domestic and international tourists, again, in common with many of the sites examined in this volume.

PERIPHERAL MULTILINGUALISM AND POTTERY

Louis Mulcahy is described as 'one of Ireland's most eminent potters' and 'the best-known Irish potter' (http://www.louismulcahy.com). His creations are not just for tourists: as one Dublin customer comments on the company's website, he offers 'inspirational pieces to lighten up our homes' (http://www.louismulcahy. com). Significantly, he moved his business from Dublin, the capital, to the Dingle peninsula in the 1970s. This could be understood as a type of opting out and moving from the centre to the periphery. However, if we do not accept a fixed notion of centre–periphery, we can see the move actually as an attempt to centre the business even more, by locating it in an area which, while being geographically peripheral, is also central in terms of the tourist trail and the craft route. The area is also of iconic centrality, as outlined above, in the imagining and marketing of Ireland for Irish people and for tourists, and so the locating of his pottery workshop on this site can be seen in fact as a definite centring move as well as one that at the time challenged the established norms of the centre–periphery relationship.

The business is, we are told, a key economic actor in the area, employing forty people, and the impact of the businesses relocation to the Dingle Peninsula 'on the morale and economy of the local *Gaeltacht* community has been enormous'. The continued location at a time when many of the better-known Irish craft industries are contracting out work to cheaper labour markets overseas gives his work an added authenticity: 'Despite the high Irish labour costs, Louis continues to make all his pots at his workshop in Dingle.' He is described as 'the last of the big potteries making all their pottery exclusively in Ireland'. Amid pictures of iconic scenery and pottery—with the potter emerging from the sea with one of his creations in one image—visitors to the website are given the message on the homepage that Louis Mulcahy is 'one of the last workshops making every piece by hand at their base in Dingle' (http://www.louismulcahy.com).

The discourse of the website involves a strong marketing of place (Urry 2005), and peripherality is a key resource in the marketing discourse and clearly adds value to the brand. The pottery is 'a great keepsake from Dingle' and 'his work is distinctively Irish and reflects the magnificent scale and wonderful colours of the landscape of his chosen home' (http://www.louismulcahy.com). Thus, if he were to leave this geographically peripheral site and move back to the centre of Ireland, Dublin, or a larger urban area, he would in fact be peripheralizing his work. This example shows the danger of falling into a fixed notion of central–peripheral relations: as stated previously, centre–periphery dynamics are being constantly negotiated and renegotiated and are entirely context-dependent.

The marketing discourse not only highlights the peripherality that is at the heart of the brand's distinctiveness, it also traces the causes, and references the fragility and vulnerability of peripheral economies. For example, the closure of any factory in the West of Ireland is often followed, almost instantaneously, by emigration of those workers to other countries for work, and to a lesser extent to larger urban centres in other parts of Ireland. The closure of a factory in a larger centre is unlikely to lead to such a massive change—especially not in the short term—as people have more opportunities to find alternative employment in their location. While Appadurai's (1996) ethnoscapes may bring to mind large cosmopolitan and industrial centres, because of the conditions of peripheralities, there has always been movement into and out of these areas. Previously, the movement was predominantly outward in the form of labour emigration, with some inward movement in terms of lifestyle migration or the return of emigrants. Nowadays, tourists make up the biggest inward flow, as well as those with their own property in the area as part-time residents.

The marketing discourse is also a discourse of peripherality in the sense that it can be seen to borrow from and rely on endangerment discourses (Duchêne and Heller 2007) about the Irish language. This key business located in this peripheral site, which is also a minority language site, and so a site where endangerment discourses are played out, is also presented in heroic terms: the economy is being saved and the language is being saved also:

> [I]n 2004 he became the first Irish craftsman ever to receive an honorary degree from the National University of Ireland in recognition of his artistry and the prosperity it has brought to his community, together with his support of the local culture including the endangered Irish language. (http://www.louismulcahy.com)

It is interesting that Irish is described on the website as endangered, as in the extract above, even in what is considered and proclaimed to be its centre and heartland (i.e. the *Corca Dhuibhne Gaeltacht*). The pottery's efforts to save the language, to revitalize it, and to centralize it are told within a peripherality discourse:

> The fact that, despite the long hours spent in building their internationally known business, the family took the time and effort to learn the local language and speak it in their home and business lives showed a dedication to the well-being of their community.

The language was learned, not as a necessary means of doing business, employing local people, and so on—it was in fact learned despite this. Learning it was an additional burden and distraction from building up the business and enjoying family life—both of which are presented as vital, normal activities that do not need Irish. Learning Irish is presented as an act of solidarity with the local community. The 'international' world of business is juxtaposed with the 'local' language. Thus, even though the act of putting Irish on the global website and also making metalinguistic discussion about Irish part of the content of the website and part of the marketing of the pottery can be seen as a centralizing, modernizing move, the net effect is that the language gets re-peripheralized through the endangerment-type discourse on the website.

The default homepage is in English, but some Irish is used throughout this default version (versions in Irish and Danish are available and these will be discussed below). Irish is used in the slogan of the company, the sparrow pottery: *potadói-reacht na caolóige*. Here the slogan is written in the old Gaelic alphabet, which was in use up to the middle of the twentieth century, but is now used only in symbolic and marked contexts. The slogan also alludes to nature (the sparrow pottery), again strongly indexing place, although no translation is given and the meaning, even for speakers of school Irish, might not be obvious to most visitors to the site. The choice of an Irish slogan for the marketing of the company can be seen as a type of centralizing or normalizing. Marketing on the web involves a global audience, and consequently many companies opt for English as their default language, even when the product or company does not originate in an English-speaking company (Kelly-Holmes 2006b). Thus, the decision to use an Irish slogan, without an English translation, in this global, high status domain could be seen as a normalizing move which presents Irish as being as fit for this purpose as any other language, particularly its rival English. However, the position of the slogan and the use of old Gaelic script mark the usage as graphic rather than textual (for a wider discussion of this, cf. Kelly-Holmes 2005). It is irrelevant whether the Irish version is understood. It still enhances the product because it looks authentic and different—this, it could be argued, continues to peripheralize Irish.

As well as the slogan for the pottery workshop itself, Irish is used in a number of product names, for example, the *Smoilín* range; and it is also used in product names which are also descriptions (e.g. *Dearg* for red). Again, we can see this use, on the one hand, as centralizing. It involves a high status domain (i.e. branding), which is a central part of the business and its identity, and it is on this basis that tourists and customers are attracted to the workshop and enticed to buy the products. In addition, the Irish names are not marked by italics, thus in paralinguistic terms, they are normalized, and the use of Irish for technical details such as colour (which can be seen as part of the 'housekeeping' and serious business of a sales website) and its use on the front page can all be seen as centralizing. However, we can also see this usage as peripheralizing. The usage is generally fetishized (Kelly-Holmes 2005), or functions as a type of linguascaping (Jaworski et al. 2003), since the use of Irish on the front page is limited to a number of tokens, with the main or serious business taking place in English, thus reinforcing the linguistic status quo: it makes sense in relation to the norm, which is English, from which it departs (cf. Bourdieu 1991).

One of the questions to be addressed in this chapter is the extent to which this particular commercial actor adopts centralizing or peripheralizing practices in commercial linguistic choices and language practices. As mentioned earlier, the Louis Mulcahy site is provided in an Irish and also a Danish version. The choice of the former version can be seen to be a rational choice in terms of the discourse of the site—its strong indexing of place and neo-Whorfian discourse (Jaffe 2006) about the relationship between product, place, and language. Not to have an Irish language version, in the context of having linked the business so strongly to its locality, would be a marketing blunder. The provision of a Danish site would appear to be motivated by Lisbeth Mulcahy, who is herself Danish. Danish does not frequently appear as an option in tourist language selections and can be considered in world-systems terms as relatively small and even peripheralized in certain contexts (e.g. international tourist domains). The provision of two 'small' languages (one very small and one 'central' in de Swaan's (2001) terms) alongside English sends an interesting, destabilizing message in terms of the received norms of commercial multilingualism—the normal expectation being that languages such as French, German, and Spanish, for example, would be provided (cf. Kelly-Holmes 2006b).

The provision of Irish and Danish versions can be seen as an attempt to centralize them, and, not surprisingly, this centralizing move relies on a parallel monolingual ideology. For example, in the section where the language choice is made, the user is presented with a symbolic line separating all the languages:

English | Gaeilge | Dansk

The strict separation between *Gaeilge* and English in this particular location does not in fact reflect everyday life and local practice in this site of peripheral multilingualism, as outlined above, or in fact the everyday existence of both languages in Ireland.

The visitor, having chosen Irish, is then presented with the following statement in all three languages:

Translation in Progress

Much of this website is available in Irish now, and most of it will be. However, there will be occasional words or phrases in English, which is unavoidable.

Here we can see that a centrist ideology is being adopted in relation to the translation of the site. The provider states the need for separate, parallel versions; the Irish site needs 'purity' and should be used with caution until the site is complete. Being 'complete' means a site that is only in Irish and from which all English words have been eradicated. This reflects an ideology of 'functional completeness' (Moring 2007), which is seen as necessary in order for minority languages to be taken seriously. The respective language must be able to fulfil all functions in all domains and only then will it be normalized. However, the reality of everyday life in sites of peripheral multilingualism such as Dingle, is, in common with many of the sites discussed in this volume, very much one of mixed up, bilingual and hybrid language practices, which are very hard to separate and demarcate. However, on this commercial site, we can still see the ideal, which is that of parallel monolingualism (Heller 1999), and which reflects a centrist concept of multilingualism, involving bounded languages (as discussed in the introduction to the volume). The user must choose his/her language preference; a bilingual option (i.e. a mixed Irish and English version) is not possible. The centrist ideology of parallel monolingualism is reinforced by the search engine, Google, which saves the language preference of individual users and automatically enforces it on the user on their next visit, strengthening the message that people speak one language, people prefer to speak one language (and only one at a time), and people only speak one language for one particular domain. In addition, if the user selects the Irish version of the site, the Google Translation toolbar automatically pops up with a warning that the site is in Irish and asks if the user wants to use the application to translate it back into the 'normal' language of that user (i.e. English).

The Irish version of the site is an identical, parallel version of the default English site with all the same features. As the user hovers over the list of links on the right hand side, synopses in English appear. In addition, Irish and English co-exist on this site, which is in fact a bilingual or mixed one, rather than a strictly monolingual one. For example, the link to join the mailing list includes instructions partly in English and in Irish, within a frame that is partly in English (including ads for the products and marketing discourse about the pottery) and partly in Irish (headings for tabs and links). English product names are used in descriptions that are written in Irish, and vice versa. The heading for the mailing list form is in English: 'Join our mailing list/newsletter sign up', while particulars such as email, name and country as well as instructions for completing the form are given in Irish only.

A customer comment in English is posted above an Irish text encouraging customers to click on the hyperlink to read more testimonials and customer comments:

Excellent Service—loved the pottery making.

Féach ar a thuilleadh rudaí a dúirt custaiméirí eile (My translation: Have a look at what other customers say)

Only one of the many customer posts featured is in Irish:

Tá ceann de na mugs a cheannaigh me i 1980 agam fós Sean O Broin (My translation: I still have one of the mugs I bought in 1980)

Interestingly, this particular poster uses 'mugs' rather than an Irish equivalent in his otherwise Irish language sentence, again highlighting the mixed language practices that are a feature of everyday life.

Peripheral practices are then in evidence throughout the designated *Gaeilge/* Irish language website, which is more mixed than the English version. In the English default site, Irish is used mainly for graphic/symbolic purposes, whereas in the designated *Gaeilge*/Irish language site, it fulfils unremarkable functions, as well as these symbolic functions. This takes place in a mixed, hybrid context where the frame is sometimes Irish, sometimes English, and sometimes both. However, as the 'Translation in Progress' warning indicates, this hybridity is seen as transitional phase, on the way to complete and separate versions; it is something that needs to be excused by the commercial actor, even though it actually works.

DISCUSSION

As well as borrowing from globalized trends in terms of language practices on commercial websites, the louismulcahy.com site can also be seen to make its own norms: Danish is a chosen language for the site, not because of demands from foreign tourists, size of the language or number of speakers, but because it is an available resource and an individual initiative. The Irish-English practices on the website reflect a bottom-up initiative by an individual actor who will get the job finished (i.e. complete the translation) eventually, when there is time; but there is also an implicit acknowledgement that from a pragmatic point of view an unfinished, partially Irish site can work and be acceptable (Bourdieu 1991) and can add value to the brand. Peripheral multilingual practices can be a reflection of a way of life that is removed from centres of norms and centres of power; they may also be a reflection that is at odds with the image that the centre has of this place as monolingual, peripheral, uncomplicated, and homogeneous (see the discussion in the introduction to the volume). In the current context of a language ideological shift from 'bilingualism as deficit' to 'bilingualism as added value' (Jaffe 2006: 51), and even more than this, a 'valorization of multilingualism' at the global level, and the development of global markets for 'the expression of "authentic" minority language identities' (p. 51), 'transidiomatic practices' (Jacquemet 2005) and having a little bit of the language can be enough to add difference and authenticity, no matter how fleeting.

Peripheral multilingualism thus offers the possibility to valorize the chaotic coexistence of languages and heteroglossic practices (cf. Pietikäinen, this volume). However, as we can see in the case of the Dingle/*An Daingean* renaming controversy, central authorities seek to impose order on such chaotic practices and carry out the necessary restorative boundary work (Bauman and Briggs 2003). Even for individual commercial actors and community members, while practices may be multilingual and mixed, ideologies and metalinguistic comment, as evidenced by the endangerment discourse and the invoking of a parallel monolingual discourse by www.louismulcahy.com, can reinforce and maintain centrist ideologies. Furthermore, while new technologies and means of production allow linguistic and other resources to circulate in more unregulated and fragmented ways (cf. Pietikäinen 2010), new modes and new technologies do not mean that centre ideologies automatically give way to more fluid ones.

The pottery website also shows how the 'neo-Whorfian discourse' (Jaffe 2006), the same one used in endangerment discourses (Duchêne and Heller 2007) and by minority language movements, can be utilized to appeal to tourists, consumers of crafts and cultural products. In this way businesses can create a 'unique selling proposition' in marketing discourse based on a 'primordial language-culture connection in bounded communities' (Jaffe 2006: 59). And thus, 'minority and indigenous communities can reposition their identity as a commodifiable resource in the interconnected fields of tourism and cultural production' (da Silva, McLaughlin, and Richards 2006: 186).

Relations between centre and periphery, between the majority and minority language, are, according to Aracil (1983), governed by a type of 'linguistic interposition', which means that relations are always determined from the perspective of the dominant language; in our terms from a centrist rather than a peripheral perspective. More than this, however, Pujolar (2006: 79) argues that linguistic interposition

> generates a categorical division between the dominated and dominating languages that ends up influencing any situation perceived in any way to be 'foreign'....And beyond this, any forum for interaction between that which is one's own and that which is foreign is to be treated as a vacuum, an impossibility or as simply not existing.

In some ways, we can see the tokenistic use of Irish on the website and the 'incomplete' translation of the Irish version as evidence to support the persistence of 'linguistic interposition' and the continuing 'impossibility' of addressing a global audience directly through the minority language, thus leading to further peripheralization of Irish. However, if we look at this from an alternative point of view, the website represents the reality of the global-local connection, which, in this case at least, negates the peripherality of the physical site and bypasses the national level. For example, this is the first site to appear in the Google search engine if the term 'Irish pottery' is entered. The 'traversals' (Lemke 2002) that are enabled in cyberspace thus present a considerable challenge to established notions of peripherality and centrality. Furthermore if we abandon a centrist/monolingual ideology in measuring this interposition and imagine instead that it can happen through mixed language practices, then we can see new possibilities opening up in current practices.

As argued in the introduction to the volume, peripheral multilingual sites are also spaces for reinventing and reconfiguring borders and values of languages and their speakers, linked to the economy of local resources. As da Silva, McLaughlin, and Richards (2006) point out, 'the very act of commodification can be seen as destabilizing' and can have unexpected consequences not just for the relevant minority language. For example, even where the dominant (national/majority) language in a relationship of peripheral multilingualism is English, as in the case of Irish, its role as a tourist lingua franca gives it new meaning in its use and selection by www.louismulcahy.com and other commercial actors. Its selection can take on the meaning of speaking to a global rather than/in addition to a national audience, thus possibly justifying its use as a positive rather than as a negative (i.e. not as an imposition by a dominant language in the national context or because of an individual's lack of competence in the relevant minority language).

Finally, let us return to our concern with the individual commercial actor and his or her role in peripheral multilingualism. The current case reminds us that the individual commercial actor is not always straightforward, predictable, and rational when making decisions about language in relation to his/her products, marketing, and so on. As Kress and van Leeuwen (2006: 12) point out:

> We have available the culturally produced semiotic resources of our societies, and are aware of the conventions and constraints which are socially imposed on our making of signs. However {we} are guided by interest, by the complex condensation of cultural and social histories and of awareness of present contingencies.

The linguistic decisions of individual actors such as www.louismulcahy.com can be seen in terms of 'the complex condensation of cultural and social histories and of awareness of present contingencies'. Kress and van Leeuwen (2006) capture wonderfully the complexity of decision-making in a commercial environment, particularly involving individual actors in small communities, where ideological, social, cultural historical and other factors all play a part, but so too does pragmatism. Out of this messy and imperfect combination, creativity and individual acts of sign-making can be born, and this creativity seems key to understanding peripheral multilingualism.

REFERENCES

Appadurai, Arjun. 1996. *Modernity at large: Cultural dimensions of globalization*. Minneapolis: University of Minnesota Press.

Aracil, Lluís V. 1983. *Dir la realitat*. Barcelona: Edicions dels Països Catalans.

Atkinson, David, and Helen Kelly-Holmes. 2006. Linguistic normalisation and the market: Advertising and linguistic choice in El Periódico de Catalunya. *Language Problems and Language Planning* 30 (3): 239–260.

Bastardas, Albert, and Josep Soler, eds. 1988. *Sociolingüística i Llengua Catalana*. Barcelona: Editorial Empúries.

Bauman, Richard, and Charles L. Briggs. 2003. *Voices of modernity: Language ideologies and the politics of inequality*. Cambridge: Cambridge University Press.

Blommaert, Jan, ed. 1999. *Language ideological debates*. Berlin: Mouton de Gruyter.

Blommaert, Jan. 2010. *The sociolinguistics of globalization*. Cambridge: Cambridge University press.

Blommaert, Jan, Nathalie Muyllaert, Marieke Huysmans, and Charlyn Dyers. 2005. Peripheral normativity: Literacy and the production of locality in a South African township school. *Linguistics and Education* 16 (4): 378–403.

Bourdieu, Pierre. 1991. *Language and symbolic power*. Oxford: Polity Press.

Da Silva, Emmanuel, Mireille McLaughlin, and Mary Richards. 2006. Bilingualism and the globalized new economy: The commodification of language and identity. In *Bilingualism: A social approach*, ed. Monica Heller, 183–206. Basingstoke and New York: Palgrave Macmillan.

De Swaan, Abram. 2001. *Words of the world: The global language system*. Cambridge: Polity Press.

Duchêne, Alexandre, and Monica Heller, eds. 2007. *Discourses of endangerment: Ideology and interest in the defence of languages*. London: Continuum.

Gal, Susan, and Kathryn A. Woolard. 2001. Constructing languages and publics: Authority and representation. In *Languages and publics: The making of authority*, ed. Susan Gal and Kathryn A. Woolard, 1–12. Manchester: St. Jerome's Press.

Heller, Monica. 1999. *Linguistic minorities and modernity: A sociolinguistic ethnography.* London: Longman.

Jacquemet, Marco. 2005. Transidiomatic practices: Language and power in the age of globalisation. *Language and Communication* 25: 257–277.

Jaffe, Alexandra. 2006. Minority language movements. In *Bilingualism: A social approach,* ed. Monica Heller, 50–70. Houndsmills: Palgrave Macmillan.

Jaworski, Adam, Crispin Thurlow, Sarah Lawson, and Virpi Ylänne-McEwen. 2003. The uses and representations of local languages in tourist destinations: A view from British TV holiday programmes. *Language Awareness* 12: 5–28.

Kelly-Holmes, Helen. 2005. *Advertising as multilingual communication.* Basingstoke and New York: Palgrave Macmillan.

Kelly-Holmes, Helen. 2006a. Irish on the World Wide Web: Searches and sites. *Journal of Language and Politics* 5 (2): 217–238.

Kelly-Holmes, Helen. 2006b. Multilingualism and commercial language practices on the Internet. *Journal of Sociolinguistics* 10 (5): 507–519.

Kelly-Holmes, Helen. 2010. Language trends: Reflexivity in commercial language policies and practices. In *Applied Linguistics Review* 1 (1), ed. Li Wei, 67–84. Berlin and New York: Mouton de Gruyter.

Kress, Gunther, and Theo Van Leeuwen. 2006. *Reading images: The grammar of visual design.* London and New York: Routledge.

Lemke, Jay. 2002. Travels in Hypermodality. *Visual Communication* 1 (3): 299–325.

Lenihan, Aoife. 2011. 'Join our community of translators': Language ideologies & Facebook. In *Digital discourse: Language in the new media,* ed. Crispin Crispin Thurlow and Kristine Mroczek, 48–64. Oxford: Oxford University Press.

Mac Giolla Chríost, Diarmait. 2005. *The Irish language in Ireland: From Goídel to globalisation.* London: Routledge.

Makoni, Sinfree, and Alastair Pennycook. 2007. Disinventing and reconstituting languages. In *Disinventing and reconstituting languages,* ed. Sinfree Makoni and Alastair Pennycook, 1–41. Clevedon: Multilingual Matters.

Moriarty, Máiréad. 2011. Language ideological debates in the linguistic landscape of an Irish tourist town. In *Minority languages in the linguistic landscape,* ed. Durk Gorter, Heiko Marten, and Luk Van Mensel, 74–88. Basingstoke and New York: Palgrave MacMillan.

Moring, Tom. 2007. Functional completeness in minority language media. In *Minority language media: Concepts, critiques and case studies,* ed. Mike Cormack and Niamh Hourigan, 17–34. Clevedon: Multilingual Matters.

Ní Ghearáin, Helena. 2011. The problematic relationship between institutionalised Irish terminology development and the Gaeltacht speech community: Dynamics of acceptance and estrangement. *Language Policy* 10 (4): 305–324.

Ó Giollagáin, Conchúr, Seosamh Mac Donnacha, Fiona Ní Chualáin, Aoife Ní Shéaghdha, and Mary O'Brien. 2007. *A comprehensive linguistic study of the use of Irish in the Gaeltacht: Principle findings and recommendations.* Dublin: Department of Community, Rural and Gaeltacht Affairs.

Ó Laoire, Muiris. 2008. The language situation in Ireland: An update. In *Language planning and policy in Europe 3: The Baltic States, Ireland and Italy,* ed. Robert Kaplan and Richard Baldauf, 193–261. Clevedon: Multilingual Matters.

Official Languages Act. 2003. *Irish Statute Book.* Dublin: Office of the Attorney General.

Pennycook, Alastair. 2010. *Language as a local practice.* London: Routledge.

Pietikäinen, Sari. 2010. Sámi language mobility: Scales and discourses of multilingualism in polycentric environment. *International Journal of Sociology of Language* 202: 79–101.

Pietikäinen, Sari, and Helen Kelly-Holmes. 2011. The local political economy of languages in a Sámi tourism destination: Authenticity and mobility in the labelling of souvenirs. *Journal of Sociolinguistics* 15 (3): 323–349.

Pujolar, Joan. 2006. *Language, culture and tourism: Perspectives in Barcelona and Catalonia*. Barcelona: Turisme de Barcelona.

Rampton, Ben. 2006. *Language in late modernity: Interaction in an urban school*. Cambridge: Cambridge University Press.

Rampton, Ben. 2009. Speech community and beyond. In *The new sociolinguistics reader*, ed. Nikolas Coupland and Adam Jaworski, 694–713. Basingstoke: Palgrave Macmillan.

Strubell, Miquel. 1998. Language, Democracy and Devolution in Catalonia. *Current Issues in Language and Society* 5 (3): 146–180.

Urry, John. 2005. The 'consuming' of place. In *Discourse, Communication and Tourism*, ed. Adam Jaworski and Annette Prichard, 19–27. Clevedon UK: Multilingual Matters.

Wallerstein, Immanuel. 2004. *World-systems analysis: An introduction*. Durham, N.C.: Duke University Press.

Walsh, John. 2011. *Contests and contexts: The Irish language and Ireland's socio-economic development*. Bern: Peter Lang.

CHAPTER 8

Welsh Tea

The Centring and Decentring of Wales
and the Welsh Language

NIKOLAS COUPLAND

INTRODUCTION

Wales has sometimes seemed to be a peripheral kind of place.[1] Wales is joined in the 'Celtic fringe' of North-West European nations and regions by Scotland, the Isle of Man, Ireland, Cornwall, and Brittany, all with complex but interlinked histories of linguistic and cultural distinctiveness, but with this distinctiveness also having been radically challenged by cultural incursions—in the British instances from England. Raymond Williams (2003) euphemistically summarizes the history of cultural relations between England and Wales as Wales having been regularly 'penetrated' by England since the 1536 Act of Union that incorporated Wales into the English state and removed the public legitimacy of the Welsh language (see Colin Williams 1990, for a historical review of the Anglicization of Wales). Wales's peripherality might therefore be understood in terms of cultural and linguistic subordination, as well as geographical marginality, not to mention its 'smallness'—a population of about three million contrasting with the 52 or so million inhabitants of England, 'the old enemy'. If the Welsh language is perceived to be peripheral, again in the sense of being a 'marginal' (= 'small' or 'non-mainstream') British language, this might lie in the fact that virtually the whole population of Wales is fluent in English while only around half a million people report themselves (at the decennial census) to be competent users of Welsh in Wales.

This reading of peripheral Wales and Welsh, however, needs to be challenged on many grounds. Relativities of 'small' versus 'big' languages are, of course, framed in ideological terms from particular perspectives and in the service of particular points of view. Raymond Williams (2003) invited us to consider *how* 'big' a nation might need to be to be thought culturally viable or worthy of critical consideration, and he considered Wales to be more than holding its own through its literary heritage and its history of vibrant cultural self-interrogation. Williams in fact saw a legacy of Welsh cultural resilience emerging from centuries of minoritization. Colin Williams (2000, 2008; see also Coupland and Aldridge 2009) documents the revitalization of the Welsh language in recent decades, with census data (for all their limitations) suggesting that the historic decline of Welsh-speaking in Wales has been reversed. Linguistic and cultural revitalization has been bolstered by political devolution (since 1998) from the Westminster/London government to an ambitiously minded National Assembly for Wales (*Cynulliad Cenedlaethol Cymru*). In any event, Wales has its own historic centring narratives—what Raymond Williams (1985) referred to as its two competing 'truths'. The first truth is based in the continuity of language and literature from the sixth century, where Welsh stands as the ultimate icon of cultural and territorial distinctiveness and successful, heroic resistance to oppression. The second truth is based in quite different metacultural assertions—in (South) Wales's world-leading role as a creative force in the Industrial Revolution and in the labour exploitation and resistance of its coal-mining workforce, amply documented by socialist historians (Morgan 1981; G. A. Williams 1985; Smith 1999).

These 'truths' are the focus of continuous internal debates about where we might establish a 'real Wales'—authenticity contests of the sort that characterize mature cultures as they move through different historical constraints and opportunities. New 'truths' are certainly emerging. They include the emergence of a new and relatively autonomous Welsh polity shaped by the Welsh Assembly Government, and (despite acute local and global economic challenges) the potential for Wales to develop its own voice in European and wider circles. But the 'two truths' debate and those early alternative conceptions of Welshness under the constraint of English hegemonic influence provide the backdrop to the present study, and to the particular topic of 'Welsh tea' that I deal with here.

As a starting point, it is necessary to challenge static and univocal conceptions of centre and periphery, as the complex history of Welsh experiences of 'penetration' and resistance, continuity and fracture, centring and decentring already suggests. While Wales is often described as 'England's first colony', correctly implying recurrent waves of cultural influence and control flowing from the larger to the smaller entity, Wales has not simply been a passive recipient of colonial exploitation. Wales has entertained its own transnational colonial exploits, either linked to English expansionist moves in times of empire, or as a globally mobile culture, and even as a colonizing force in its own name. Below, I discuss two of the most salient of these Welsh moments and contexts of mobility, to show how shifting historical and geographical circumstances have variously positioned Wales and the Welsh language as more and less autonomous, more and less peripheral, within particular cultural economies. The chapter's theoretical significance may therefore lie in helping to demonstrate how core/periphery relations are always relative and subject to radical transformation from one national or international configuration to another, as outlined in the introduction to the volume. I also hope to show how language and languages are woven into relativities of core and periphery, in that Welsh has functioned in ways that belie its status as a 'peripheral minority language'. Welsh came to have quite different symbolic values and social functions under the different conditions we will consider.

I organize the chapter in relation to the (intuitively unconvincing) notion of 'Welsh tea'. It proves to be the case that this curious notion leads us into a nexus of historical, global, and linguistic processes that have centre/periphery relations at their foundation. Tea is, of course, not at all Welsh by provenance; tea is not Welsh, that is, in the sense that lava bread (*bara lawr*, in Welsh, an edible seaweed), cockles, spring water, and even wine can more or less legitimately be said to be Welsh. My schoolmaster grandfather used to assert that 'Tea comes from India, China, Ceylon, and Carolina', and however accurate or inaccurate this teacherly mnemonic was, the list of origins certainly excluded Wales. But the aphorism hints at something British, if not specifically Welsh, in the history of tea—tea as a commodity constructed and exploited under the British Empire. Before I come to the two main scenarios in which 'Welsh tea' does have some documented particular significance, I overview British (and mainly English) colonial involvement in Eastern British India in the late nineteenth century. My general questions in that context are whether and to what extent Welsh colonizers were active in the establishment and management of tea plantations and their spin-off industries back home. Did tea take on any plausible dimension of Welshness in the colonial practices that brought tea to Britain?

The first of the two main scenarios involves the experience of Welsh expatriates in North America, in the nineteenth and twentieth centuries. In this case I am able to point to some direct archival evidence of 'Welsh tea' being at least an available concept. The challenge is to understand how tea, and tea referenced *in* Welsh and now *as* a specifically Welsh commodity, featured in the social lives of Welsh migrants to the New World. What does this contextualization of 'Welsh tea' suggest about centre and periphery in an emerging Welsh diaspora? What part did tea play in the articulation of Welsh and Welsh-American identities? How did tea come to index not only Welshness but a certain valued *sort* of Welshness, relative to cultural norms and expectations about who and what the newly migrant Welsh were?

The second main scenario sees 'Welsh tea' taking on very different symbolic significance in the wake of Welsh people's own 'colony' (*Y Wladfa*)—another Welsh diasporic construction—established in the Chubut Valley in Patagonia, Southern Argentina, from 1865. As we will see, to the present day Patagonian tea houses iconize and celebrate tea-taking as a distinctively Welsh cultural practice, but this time as a feature of the global tourist experience. I want to suggest that each of the two main scenarios leads to a different conception of 'Welsh tea', and that historically shifting practices around tea prove to be a surprisingly rich resource for understanding the ebb and flow of transnational relationships. There is even some trace of a relatively new, 'at home' (within-Wales) understanding of 'Welsh tea' that I briefly consider in a further short section, before concluding.

Tea became a thoroughly colonial and imperial commodity, first in China and later in India, largely through the British East India Company's monopoly of the tea trade from the early eighteenth century (Joliffe 2003). Consolidating British hegemonic rule, Queen Victoria took the title 'Empress of India' in 1876. Pia Chatterjee's (2001) ethnographic, dramatized re-creation of the lived practices of Indian plantation life paints the stark contrast between, on the one hand, tea evolving as a focus for elite and particularly female interest and, on the other hand, tea-picking as an extreme instance of colonial labour exploitation among often female indentured workers.

Chatterjee argues that colonial activity needed to symbolize its own 'success' in a material form and that the cultural meaning of tea should be understood in these terms: 'Cultures of consumption, fed by the very wealth of trade expansion... demanded commodities that signified the success of 'discovery'... Through rituals of consumption, tea signified a new domain of desire in the new global empire' (Chatterjee 2001: 22). Tea became an icon of upper social class and refinement, eventually across Europe and in the colonial parlours of New York and Boston (ibid: 34);[2] Pierre Bourdieu, for example, makes a passing reference to tea-drinking as a mark of upper-class distinction in France (Bourdieu 2010: 13). But first and foremost, tea drinking and tea ceremonialism, as it emerged from the empire, was an English affectation. Tea manufacture in Britain was associated with specific elite companies and the most successful importers were almost all *English*, including Twinings (based in London), Hornimans (also London), Brooke Bond (Manchester), Tetley (Yorkshire, then London; now owned by Tata Tea), Ty-Phoo (branded later than most in the early twentieth century, and named to conjure Chinese associations, based in Birmingham), and Home and Colonial (London), although the Lipton tea empire was based in Scotland (Glasgow). Tea rituals and their associated material culture started to move beyond tearooms into tea museums.[3]

The images of tea advertising placards in Figure 8.1 capture something of the (English, culturally centred) 'home' and the (peripheral) 'colonial' relationships entailed.[4] The Home and Colonial company itself flourished in Britain between 1883 and 1960 and developed into a chain of some 3,000 high street stores, clearly branding itself as a purveyor of the 'fruits of empire'. Note how the placards, taken together, construct India-sourced English tea as an authentic commodity. The Horniman's text visualizes a plantation source for its 'pure tea', and potential users of Hindoola tea, whose name appropriates and orientalizes 'Hindu' culture, are warned to 'Beware of imitations'. Liptons tea is branded as 'By special appointment to His Majesty the King', invoking the force of empire behind the sourcing of tea, which is then thoroughly domesticated in the homely image used in the Ty-Phoo advertisement.

In the contemporary world tea-taking continues to have a predominantly English resonance (in phrases such as 'English tea', 'English breakfast tea', and so

(a)

(b)

(c)

(d)

(e)

Figure 8.1:
Some nineteenth- and twentieth-century tea advertising placards

on). Tea rituals came to include mythologized expertise in the blending of tea, also in tea-tasting and tea-serving, with their associated qualities of connoisseurship and good taste. The story of English/British tea is a paradigmatic instance of colonial exploitation, from the power base at its cultural centre, of human and natural resources in a zone defined to be peripheral ('at the margins of the empire'), with those resources then being ideologically transformed and turned to the colonizers' advantage, both commercially and symbolically. Regions such as Eastern Bengal and Assam, referred to by colonizers at the time as 'wastelands', were offered a modicum of English language and of Christianity, at the cost of servicing a vast industrial-scale tea cultivation enterprise.

Aled Jones (2004) traces the history of Welsh involvement in the tea plantations of these regions, and particularly the role of Welsh Presbyterian missionaries there from 1850 onwards. He comments on the pernicious irony that the plantations were referred to as 'tea gardens', while the Indian plantation project was precisely to develop tea production on industrial principles, the first of them in Malnicherra in the Surma Valley. By 1901 nearly one and a half million acres were under tea cultivation in the districts of Sylhet (now in Bangladesh) and Cachar alone, drawing in migrant workers as so-called 'coolie' workers (Jones 2004: 267). The East Indian tea plantations were a focal point of the British colonial project, carried forward predominantly by English men, but with direct participation by some Welsh and Scottish people. Jones explains that the East India Company's orientation to cultural intervention in India varied over the centuries, but at some periods the Company was strongly committed to promoting the English language (and, of course, not the Welsh language) as part of a wider programme of Europeanization/Anglicization.

Welsh (and Welsh-speaking) missionaries were certainly engaged in evangelical Christianization of local people, and doing this mainly through the English language. Jones concludes that the Welsh missionaries held an 'ambiguous relationship' (2004: 274) with colonial indoctrination, neither fully independent of the colonial mainstream nor standing out consistently against it. There is therefore only very limited reason to believe that there was a distinctively Welsh ideological orientation to colonial practices around tea. (For a wider view, but reaching similar conclusions, see Jones and Jones 2003.) Even though the Welsh language survives fitfully in East India as a relic feature of Welsh missionary involvement there,[5] the Welsh played only a minor part in English-led, British colonial activity, and indeed, British colonial expansion proved to be one of the forces that accelerated the decline of the Welsh language at home through the late nineteenth and early twentieth centuries. We can say, then, that tea *did not* take on a distinctively Welsh quality in tea colonialism, although Welsh people *did* make some contribution to the expansion of the British/English culture centre and the peripheralization of East India that colonial activities engineered. It is against this backdrop that the consolidation of 'Welsh tea' under different conditions is all the more remarkable.

WELSH TEA, SCENARIO 1: THE EXPATRIATE WELSH IN NORTH AMERICA

The idea of tea being meaningfully Welsh seems to have 'brewed' far more convincingly in Welsh-America through the nineteenth and twentieth centuries. 'Welsh tea' (where my quote marks now indicate summary quotation from a source rather than scare-quoting) certainly features regularly in one particularly useful source, the community newspaper *Y Drych* ('The Mirror'), which served the North American Welsh expatriate group and was in continual publication between 1851 and 2001

Figure 8.2:
Advertisement from *Y Drych*, 10 February 1889, page 6

in the United States. From its launch, *Y Drych* carried advertisements designed to appeal to expatriate Welsh people who had settled in the New World.[6] The advertisements in Figures 8.2, 8.3, and 8.4 were typical of those that appeared in the pages of *Y Drych*.[7]

Figure 8.2 gives an indication of the style and placement of *Y Drych* advertisements of the period. It is a bilingual advertisement, at a time when the newspaper's main text genres were predominantly Welsh, with the proprietor's name and address and promotional hook, 'SOLE IMPORTERS' (near the bottom of the advertisement panel), provided in English. Key parts of its Welsh text (below the visual image) translate as follows:

TE Y BRENIN	'The King's tea'
Prawfiad diymwad o ragoroldeb	'Undeniable proof of excellence'
EI WERTHIANT ARUTHROL	'Its prodigious value'
EI BOBLOGRWYDD CYFFREDINOL	'Its accepted popularity'
EI BURDEB DIAMEUOL	'Its indisputable purity'
EI BRYS RHESYMOL	'Its reasonable price'

Figure 8.3 is again bilingual, where *TE'R HEN WLAD* translates as 'The tea of the old country', which is then rendered in an English brand name equivalent in the ad as *Old Country Tea*. The accompanying Welsh text can be translated as follows (keeping the idiosyncratic punctuation of the source text):

You wives and women... do you want cups of tea like the tea you used to drink in Wales, try a pound of Cassidy and Co's 'Tea of the Old Country' just once, then no-one will have to ask you to buy it. You won't be satisfied without it. Ask your shop-keeper for it, Also on sale, a large selection of Congou Breakfast, Assam India, Scented Orange Pekoe and Caper, Formosa Tea, Oolong, Gunpowder, Imperial and Young Hyson, Japan Green Tea and Fired Basket of the best produce and distribution.

The advertisement in Figure 8.4 promotes the same product and distributor as in the Figure 8.2 example. In Figure 8.4 he extols himself, in Welsh, as: 'Distributor of the best products from the South. Amongst them, the world-famous King's Tea.'

Jones and Jones (2001a: 50) note that *Te Y Brenin* and *Te'r Hen Wlad* were supplemented by other brands—*Te Y Ddraig Goch* ('Reg Dragon Tea', so-named because the emblem on the Welsh national flag is a red dragon), *Te Y Werin* (translatable as 'Country People's Tea', although *Y Werin* in Welsh also implies Welsh folk heritage) and *Eryri Tea* ('Snowdonia Tea', in recognition of the North Wales mountain chain that has Mount Snowdon as its highest peak). Millward (2000: 11) also refers to the popularity of *Te Dwyryd* ('Dwyryd [a place in North Wales] Tea'). That source also contains images of print advertisements for *Terwerin Tea* (probably a re-spelling of the Welsh place-name *Trewerin*) and ads constructed by Wales-based importers of *Mazawattee Tea, Dulecmona Tea*, and other brands. However, it was *Te Y Brenin* ('The King's Tea') distributed by G. T. Matthews that dominated the tea ads in *Y Drych* and the Welsh tea market between 1873 and 1932. While the brand-name of *Te Y Brenin* appeals to a royalist Britishness, there is no doubt that *Hen Wlad* ('The Old Country') here refers to Wales not Britain, in that these brands sometimes invoke stereotypically Welsh cultural iconography. For example, the (indistinct) image in Figure 8.2 contains a visual representation of the 'Welsh lady', dressed in what became known as the 'traditional Welsh costume' of a tall black hat, apron and shawl. But the consistent use of Welsh-language brand names explicitly

Figure 8.3:
Advertisement from *Y Drych*, 2 June 1898, page 5

characterizes tea as being Welsh, even though the importers were niche marketers and their businesses were presumably very small relative to the major English colonial brands.

Was the Welshness of tea in this context simply a commercial spin-off from what was more typically an English colonial commodity back in Britain? It is reasonable to see Welsh tea offering a source of British, at the same time as more narrowly Welsh, cultural continuity and reassurance for Welsh people on the move in the New World. But tea took on a much more specifically Welsh metacultural significance too. Jones and Jones (2001b: 66) confirm that tea-drinking was popular and actively promoted among the expatriate Welsh in North America, but specifically as

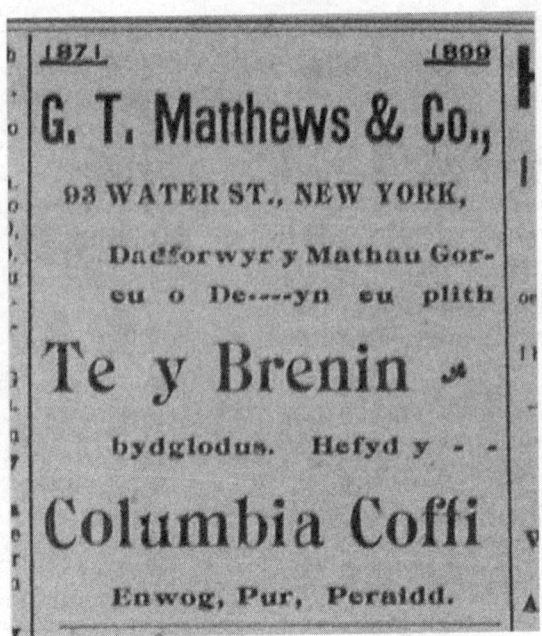

Figure 8.4:
Advertisement from *Y Drych*, 21 December 1899, page 8

an idealization of *Welsh temperance*—a policy of withholding from drinking alcohol and adopting what was called a 'teetotal' lifestyle. The origin of the concept of 'teetotalism' is disputed, although it is generally believed to have no direct connection with the drinking of tea. Nevertheless, tea was able to assume a moral value simply by not being an alcoholic beverage, and this fitted neatly into religious values that were themselves distinctively Welsh. The specific religious tradition in question was Calvinistic Methodism, developed in Welsh-speaking West Wales and promoted through chapel-going as a distinctive branch of Nonconformism (which implied dissention from the Established Anglican Church). For Calvinistic Methodists the drinking of alcohol constituted sinful behaviour and confirmed a fall from grace. *Te'r Hen Wlad* therefore iconized an ideologically 'proper', 'respectable', and *duwiol* (godly) form of Welshness as seen through a dominant and demanding Welsh religious doctrine.

Lambert (1983) gives a detailed history of the temperance movement in Wales through the nineteenth century (see also Kneale 2001), showing that Welsh tea was attracting symbolic value at home too. Lambert explains that, in the early years of the century, drinking water was a dangerous practice, and that 'beer was invariably cheaper than tea' which 'was a rarity in Wales at this time' (1983: 6) and remained so until the 1840s. Notice the foregrounding of tea's affordability in the ad (reproduced in Figure 8.2) for *Te Y Brenin*, but also its purity, probably implying a different agenda of purity from that of the English tea products in Figure 8.1. Welsh tea's purity is very likely to have had both moral and health implications. Welsh tea is mainly promoted in these turn-of-the-century ads as being a good-value, everyday product with the added appeal of moral and cultural asceticism in uncertain times in the New World.

There are further historical reasons for associating tea with Welsh asceticism, and Welsh asceticism with the Welsh language. Lambert analyses the well-known Welsh antagonism between the chapel and the pub (public house), and how the absolutist temperance movement invoked an extreme moralizing discourse, inter-twined with powerful religious but also social class imperatives. To chapel-goers, total abstinence from alcohol was the route to self-improvement on earth, as well as the road to heaven.[8] But the temperance movement also strove to provide social and recreational alternatives to drinking alcohol in pubs, and music and singing (of hymns in Welsh) was a strong theme. From the mid nineteenth century, there were 'temperance *eisteddfodau*' [competitive cultural festivals], held in local chapels (Lambert 1983: 105–6). Lambert says that the temperance movement in Wales was in general 'an intensely religious phenomenon' (1983: 115), strongly commit-ted to resisting the inherent depravity of humankind.

In the last quarter of the nineteenth century Liberals (members of the Liberal [political] Party) were taking a lead in the temperance movement (Morgan 1981: 29; Lambert 1983: 198). William Gladstone himself, four-times Liberal Prime Minister of Britain between 1868 and 1894, endorsed the Welsh Sunday Closing Act of 1881 (making it illegal to open public houses in Wales on Sundays), which Morgan describes as the first distinctively Welsh Act of Parliament. The Act was drafted in response to orchestrated pressure from Welsh (religious) Nonconformists. There was undoubtedly a strong linguistic dimension to all this, not least because Gladstone was an active proponent of the Welsh language and its place in Welsh religious and cultural life, and Welsh was in any case the majority language in Wales at the end of the nineteenth century.

The Welsh language, Welsh Nonconformism, and Welsh tea formed a power-ful ideological triangle, drawing tea away from its English colonial roots and their legacy, and remaking its social value. Welsh tea, together with a distinctively Welsh form of religious worship and Welsh teetotalism, offered a new aspirational vision of Welsh identity, rescuing Wales from its reputation of low sophistication, unruli-ness, and excess as conjured in the Blue Books of 1847 (a damning English report on the state of schooling in Wales): 'Temperance was a theme naturally congenial to the Nonconformist Welsh. The Blue Ribbon movement swept the land in the [eighteen] seventies; 'taking the pledge' [to abstain from alcohol] became for cha-pel boys what the Bar Mitzvah was for Jews' (Morgan 1981: 36).

It is difficult to say whether the New World Welsh were more susceptible to this aspirational vision than their fellow countrymen at home. The 'fresh start' mindset of the expatriate Welsh may well have inclined them that way. Whatever, we see an ideological distinction being forged between (on the one hand) English tea and its exploitative colonial past, and (on the other hand) Welsh tea and a very different aspirational future for the expatriate Welsh. While English tea maintained its colonial cachet of cultural elitism, ceremony, and perhaps femininity, and successfully exported *this* set of associations to America and beyond, Welsh tea came to be associated, at least for a time, with abstinence, cultural asceticism, and a more 'proper' way of being Welsh. The early decades of Welsh-America saw diverse efforts, not least the publication of *Y Drych* as a thriving 'community newspaper', to maintain a Wales-centred and Welsh language-centred experience. This was to hold on into the early twentieth century, particularly in Pennsylvania and in the 'very Welsh' coal-mining town of Scranton in Pennsylvania.[9]

WELSH TEA, SCENARIO 2: TEA TOURISM IN CONTEMPORARY PATAGONIA

Wales's own quasi-colonial experiment in Patagonia, Southern Argentina, ultimately provided another platform for the conceptualization and promotion of Welsh tea, but in a quite different framing of its cultural significance. *Y Wladfa*, the settlement established in the Chubut Valley of Patagonia in 1865, is usually referred to in English as 'The Colony', but it was not an attempt to exploit a remote periphery or to grow a cultural centre at others' expense. It was a self-focused effort to shore up the Welsh language and Welsh cultural traditions that were under threat at home.[10] In that sense it was more of an *anti*-colonial initiative—an effort to resist continuing colonial pressures from England and from the advance of the English language in Wales by establishing a national bridgehead in a far-distant space. For several decades *Y Wladfa* successfully sustained a small ethnolinguistic Welsh group—a supplementary Welsh cultural centre—'in the periphery', in fact in one of the world's 'most remote' locations. Patagonia's remoteness is, of course, an important part of its attractiveness nowadays to tourists, some of whom want to consume aspects of its residual Welsh culture, as well as its expansive natural resources.

The legacy of Welsh language use in Patagonia is generally sparse, although Welsh does have a presence, particularly in ceremonial contexts (such as the annual Welsh cultural festivals or *eisteddfodau*). To some extent Welsh is also visible in the Patagonian semiotic landscape (Jaworski and Thurlow 2010). In an earlier paper Peter Garrett and I have commented on how the bilingual (Spanish-Welsh) landscape in Patagonia, particularly in the more tourism-oriented towns of Gaiman and Trevelin, is organized under different interpretive frames (Coupland and Garrett 2010). Contemporary Patagonian Welshness is a mix of continuing historical indexicalities and new commercial and tourist initiatives. In the earlier study we drew attention to the transformations through which linguistic and cultural Welshness is reworked as a heritage tourism resource (cf. the contributions by Jaffe; Kelly-Holmes; Pietikäinen; and Pujolar to this volume).

Patagonia ceremonializes *casas de té galesas* (Welsh tea houses) (Lublin 2009) as in the four commercial signs and displays in Gaiman that are combined as Figure 8.5.[11]

Welsh tea in Patagonia appeals to tourists, certainly from Wales but probably from different local and global constituencies too, for its heritage value—as one way of remembering the original Welsh settlement of 1865. The images refer back to a non-threatening cultural incursion from Wales that left distinctively 'non-Argentinean' and perhaps 'non-Spanish' cultural forms and practices which have resurfaced in ritualized, touristic, metaculturally Welsh semiotic displays. For Welsh tourists in Patagonia, tea-drinking is not at all an obvious metacultural signifier. But it would have had contrastive cultural significance for earlier, non-Welsh inhabitants of the region who, we can safely assume, were not regular tea drinkers.

There are rather few Welsh linguistic items in the tea house signs. Welsh is mainly restricted to names and titles. *Ty Cymraeg* ('The Welsh House', although in Welsh orthography *Ty* does not normally have circumflex diacritic ^ above <y> as it does in the first image in Figure 8.5) is the name of an establishment run by

Figure 8.5:
Signs and icons displayed outside Welsh tea houses in Patagonia

the Thomas family (and Thomas is a very common family name in Wales), translated into Spanish as *Casa Galesa*. In the second and third images *Caerdydd* is the Welsh name for Cardiff, the capital city of Wales. In the fourth image *Nain* means 'Grandma', and *Ty Nain* ('Grandma's House') is a suitably cosy ethnic and gender stereotype to index the supposedly comfortable familiarity of Welsh tea-taking. Red and green (the dominant colours used in all four images) repeat the colours of the Welsh national flag whose main motif (as we saw earlier) is the red dragon; the dragon is shown in stylized form on the sign in the second image and on the giant teapot pictured in the third image. The language text at the bottom of the second image refers to *Lady Diana Spencer*, and this is another effort to stereotype cultural Welshness, although it is likely to mis-carry for the majority of Welsh people who do not consider the late Princess of Wales to be closely associated with Wales in any significant cultural sense (as opposed to institutionally, through having married into the British Royal Family, becoming the wife of Prince Charles who is designated Prince of Wales).

In other words, several significant semiotic transformations in relation to Wales and Welshness are clearly visible in Patagonian symbolic representations of tea. Tea again takes on some 'old country' values (not unlike those in the *Y Drych* ads), but the old country in question is both Wales itself, the home of the Patagonian settlers, and a Cymrified (Wales-infused) nineteenth-century Patagonia. There is metacultural drift into idealizations of Wales as a culture that reveres its associations with British royalty (when for the most part it does not), and as a culture bathed in warm (*cálido*), grandmotherly (*Nain*), traditional (*tradicional*), and authentic (*auténtico*) sensations. Many national cultures may be prone to imagining themselves in these terms. But we have to remember that these particular representations are creative imaginings by contemporary Patagonians (some of whom may have traceable Welsh ancestry) of a distant and limited Welsh cultural presence that has largely lapsed. These are conditions under which tradition is a matter of selective remembering, if not invention (Hobsbawm and Ranger 1983), and where authenticity needs to be asserted rather than assumed.

The Welsh language here becomes a heritage resource in its own right, indexing an exotic ethnolinguistic difference but needing (in the tea house signs) to be interpreted through Spanish text. In fact there are interesting differences between the textual pragmatics of Welsh and Spanish (in the tea shops data) and Welsh and English (in the *Y Drych* data). For tourist sign readers in Patagonia, Welsh language items are present for the purposes of ethnosymbolic display (Eastman and Stein 1993; Coupland 2012). Tea shop names in Welsh take pride of place as brands in the semiotic structure of the signs' textual construction, whether or not their lexical meanings are intelligible to tourists (and even Welsh tourists may not have the language proficiency to decode them). Spanish elements of these signs, on the other hand, do more interpretive work, either glossing the Welsh formulations, building the cultural values of Welsh tea-taking, or providing more instrumental information such as giving directions (the arrow-text in the first Figure 8.5 image tells readers that *Ty Cymraeg* is 70 metres away). In *Y Drych* ads the branding function is again fulfilled mainly in Welsh, but glossing and interpretive text is also in Welsh, addressing a Welsh expatriate group that is presumed not only to use Welsh as its community language but to sense an intimacy with the product through Welsh being used to promote it. In those ads, English features only in instrumentally referencing suppliers' names and addresses (in the English-dominant context of New York).

In current-day Patagonia, therefore, Welsh tea has some direct and material reference—tourists can drink tea in purportedly Welsh surroundings—but it is also the iconic focus of a metacultural memory or re-enactment. In Patagonia, Welsh tea is heritage-ized. It finds a key place within performative activity that re-creates and stages an aspect of a cultural past, with a complex relationship to what might be considered cultural authenticity (cf. Heller 2010; Pietikäinen and Kelly-Holmes 2011). Heritage reframing is a common characteristic of tourism, although 'heritage tourism', the celebration of 'heritage' meaning a valued past, does not always recognize its own performative dimension. Heritage is also a characteristic of glocalization (Robertson 1995), the globalization of the local and the reconstruction of the local in globalized economies. Patagonian Welsh tea is a ritualized stylization of Welsh cultural practice that reaccentuates aspects of a remembered Wales. This reaccentuation constructs Welsh tea drinking as a homely practice, but spills over into the elite 'colonial English' mode of tea culture too. Fodor's online review of *Casa de Té Caerdydd* ('Cardiff tea house'),[12] for example, is as follows:

> Cypress trees, fountains, and sculpted gardens mark the grounds of Gaiman's largest teahouse, which looks like a mini-palatial estate on the south bank of the Chubut River. It succeeds in impressing, though the dining rooms are larger and less homey than the town's other teahouses.

The *Caerdydd* tea house is grand and said to contrast with more (in American English) 'homey' tea houses. But homey *Ty Nain* is itself celebrated as *'una de las primeras casas de té galés de Trevelin... que mantiene la tradición del té, elaborado con finas hierbas y acompañado con las mas variadas exquiziteces'.*[13] This text recycles elite criteria of not only 'tradition' but 'fineness' in a representation that certainly contrasts vividly with the ascetic associations of 'temperance tea' that we saw earlier.

DISCUSSION

This short historical tour has, I hope, opened up a perspective on how cultural Welshness has shaped and been shaped by different internal and external relationships related to mobility and contact. The Welsh people and the Welsh language (if we feel able to consolidate those categories) are often taken to exemplify a stable, continuous, and indigenous minority experience, but the account of 'Welsh and

Welshness in Wales' is clearly not the whole story. As Welsh people travelled—to India and to North and South America, motivated by very different types of colonial ambitions—what it meant to be Welsh, and what part the Welsh language played in that general process of (re)identification, took on very different qualities. At one level the history of Welsh tea is, of course, highly specific, but in rather unexpected ways it also seems to open a window on much wider social and linguistic realignments. Tea, which emerged as a quintessentially English icon of colonial conquest, also focused cultural meanings for Welshness—the respectable and abstinent Welsh in the New World of the late nineteenth century and the docile, home[l]y colonizers remembered in modern-day Patagonia. What does this history suggest about centre–periphery relations, as they are mediated by language and textual representation? And, first, does the concept of Welsh tea have any continuing resonance in Wales itself?

As I suggested at the outset, the concept of Welsh tea is perplexingly empty without the transnational contextual detail of the above scenarios. One or two commercial efforts to market tea as Welsh do currently exist—the bilingual brand of *Murrough's Welsh Brew/Paned Cymreig* ('The Welsh Cuppa') and the Wales-targeted *Glengettie* tea (whose brand-name indexes Scotland more than Wales). Murrough's brand their packaged tea in Welsh as well as in English, although most of their promotional text (including their web site) is in English only. They use promotional discourse that loosely appeals to 'Welsh tradition':

> There is nothing quite like the welcome afforded by a hot cup of quality tea. Such a welcome has long been the tradition of hospitality in Welsh households. Murroughs Welsh Brew encapsulates the flavour and taste of tea to the traditional standards we recall from years gone by...[14]

The text constructs a veiled national association with Wales, suggesting that Welsh households are welcoming by virtue of offering tea, intertextually referencing the old Welsh song 'We'll keep a welcome in the hillsides... '. Murrough's marketers side-step the ethnic provenance problem by further suggesting (in the same online text, with original spelling) that 'The special blend of quality African and Indian teas, perfectly compliment the waters of Wales'. From their own publicity, Murrough's appears to sell particularly well to the expatriate Welsh and to incoming tourists to Wales, to some extent therefore replaying the marketing strategy of *Te Y Brenin* (in Figures 8.2 and 8.4, above) in the late nineteenth century. So there is some evidence—limited, in that Murrough's is not a particularly prominent brand—that Welsh tea might continue to have some marketability in the interstices of glocalization, reaching outwards from Wales to the Welsh diaspora. Similar marketing strategies support Yorkshire tea and Cornish tea[15], for example, where each of the regional affiliations is similarly tenuous and lacking in metacultural value (notwithstanding that the Tregothnan Estate, the marketing base for Cornish tea, claims that its brand is the only tea *grown* in England).

Overall, the Welshness of tea is neither a matter of cultural inherency nor a matter of opportunistic and simply false cultural attribution; 'Welsh tea' is neither fully authentic nor fully inauthentic in the way it associates a commodity/practice with a national culture. As I noted earlier, my grandfather's aphorism, couched in terms of tea 'coming from' a restricted set of national places, clearly excluded Wales. But when we review the explicit and implicit bases of this sort of association over the different social and historical contexts I have introduced, we see ways in which, under very specific circumstances of time, place, opportunity, and constraint, it has *become* meaningful to claim or disclaim the Welshness of tea.

In all cases, the Welsh language and multilingualism are, in one way or another, corralled into the link between Wales and tea, and each particular association posits a specific relationship between a cultural centre and a periphery—Wales on the fringe of the English colonial core in India, the North American Welsh seeking to perpetuate a sense of home away from home, the contemporary Patagonian Welsh tea house ceremonializing a historic Welsh colony on their own soil and appropriating within-Wales names and images through the mist of tourist priorities. This is why a 'peripheral multilingualism' perspective is helpful in tracking the symbolic complexities of Welsh tea. Like language, tea appears to be a rich but highly malleable metacultural resource, implicated in establishing different versions of Welshness under mobile transnational circumstances.

If we look inside the concept of authenticity, we might gain more critical purchase. In an earlier paper (Coupland 2003) I suggested that a sense of the authentic relies on five interlocking sub-criteria being met: *ontology*, a secure sense of real being; *historicity*, a depth of being that transcends the local and the now; *systemic coherence*, 'making sense' within some specific network of social understandings; *consensus*, the ability to mobilize attention and credibility over a reasonably large field of judgement; and *value*, a shared sense that the object or process 'matters'. In these terms there is, for example, undoubtedly a glibness in Murrough's contemporary appeal to a Welsh tea-drinking 'tradition'. Because historicity is a necessary condition of the authentic, we may feel the need to interrogate the historical depth of this tradition. And, of course, discursive claims to tradition, just like discursive claims to authenticity itself (as in one of the Patagonian tea shop texts) tend to trigger historicity tests rather than being taken at face-value. In any event, historicity is not in itself a sufficient criterion for authentication; history alone, even if it is accurately told, is unable to convincingly warrant the Welshness of tea, any more than the Yorkshireness or the Cornishness of tea. People in all these places have drunk tea, but generally without any meaningful metacultural indexicality.

Tea can only be constructed to be in some sense authentically Welsh if its history incorporates specific values—if there is sufficient consensual appreciation of a historical process that lifts the otherwise mundane product of tea and practice of tea-drinking to a level of metacultural significance. This is precisely what happened when tea acquired salience as a manifestation of discipline and restraint in Welsh contexts where these cultural values had been deemed lacking. Systemic coherence could be appreciated in the contextually significant conflation of the Welsh language, Nonconformist religion, and teetotalism. We might say that the ontological status of tea, as a 'real' and partially defining attribute of Welshness, was scaffolded in the temperance movement. In that context tea could index a certain purity of body and mind, not unlike the singing of Welsh hymns, which was strongly promoted at temperance meetings (which themselves stood in ideological opposition to public houses and disreputable Welshness).

At other moments tea was drawn into long-running cultural antagonisms between Wales and England (which Raymond Williams often characterized in his critical writing), when the vernacular practice of drinking tea in Wales could, this time, stand in opposition to the potentially effete and definitely elite model of the colonial and post-colonial English tea ceremony. England was the motivating centre of the colonial effort in India, and the Welsh, despite their modest colonial involvement in the tea plantations, could to some extent distance themselves from the legacy of English colonial exploitation. Tea could indeed index a distance or peripherality from England that has been appealing to the Welsh, no doubt as a national response to a long history of minoritization.

There is no reason to suppose that the small group of Welsh settlers in South America saw particular cultural value in the tea-drinking practice that they presumably took with them to Patagonia. But centuries after Y Wladfa, mainly Spanish-speaking Patagonians, some of them descendants of Welsh migrants, have been able to construct their own sense of quasi-authentic Welshness, again with tea as its symbolic focus. Historicity was again available—accounts, which are recycled in Patagonian school history lessons, of the Welsh settlers' struggle to survive and to 'stay Welsh' in the arid Chubut Valley—and a cultural coherence could be constructed at the interface between tea, a shakily surviving Welsh language in the Chubut Valley, and other cultural indexicals (e.g. distinctive patterns of house-building, since several of the casas de té galesas do indeed look 'European' more than 'South American').

In different metacultural nexuses, therefore, language, tea, and Welshness have been able to mutually authenticate each other to a reasonable level. The flows of people and symbols that are implied by the term globalization (Coupland 2010) create opportunities and needs for semiotic and metacultural renegotiations of this sort. Globalization often facilitates shifts of scale (Blommaert 2010; Kelly-Holmes and Mautner 2010; Pietikäinen 2010), which I take to mean, at its simplest, that cultural forms and attributes are liable to 'shrink' and to 'grow' in different symbolic economies, from different ideological standpoints. To say that (sometimes bilingual) Welsh people drink tea is an overwhelmingly banal observation. But the fact that tea, and drinking it 'in Welsh' and 'as something meaningfully Welsh', have under some conditions been meaningfully upscaled into national signifiers is suggestive about the flexible semiotics of globalization.

NOTES

1. I am very grateful to the volume editors and to Adam Jaworski for incisive comments on earlier drafts of this text.
2. Celebrating the Britishness of tea in nineteenth-century America would, of course, have carried deep irony for those remembering the Boston Tea Party as a pointed act of resistance against British rule in 1773. The contemporary 'Tea Party Movement' in the United States, a caucus of Republican, conservative, anti-big government politicians, today echoes the politics of the Boston Tea Party.
3. See, for example, the promotional website for Bramah Tea and Coffee Museums at http://www.teaandcoffeemuseum.co.uk/. (All urls cited in the chapter were last accessed in February 2012.) The Bramah Tea Museum valorizes its own tea ceremonials as follows: 'The ceremony of English afternoon tea was popularized throughout the world by the British and is kept alive in our authentic tea room. The five minute wait for the tea to infuse is the heart and soul of English afternoon tea. The ritual had an etiquette which enabled the matriarch of the family to impress and entertain.' There are countless other celebrated English tearooms and tea museums, both in England and globally, including The Twining Teapot Gallery, Norwich Castle Museum, and Babington's English Tea Rooms in Rome. English tea as a concept sells well in the United States today—see http://www.englishteastore.com/ and http://www.veryenglishtea.com/.
4. I am grateful to Alex Renshaw of the Advertising Antiques company for permission to reprint these images, some of which are available at http://www.advertisingantiques.co.uk.
5. See Jenkins (1995) and http://news.bbc.co.uk/1/hi/wales/508582.stm.
6. With colleagues I have written about various aspects of the history of Y Drych, including wider trends in the contents and imagery of its advertisements over time (see Bishop et al. 2005; Coupland et al. 2003; Garrett et al. 2005). My colleagues and I continue to be grateful to successive editors of Y Drych for permission to use the photographic representations of original text that we have archived.
7. I am very grateful to Bill Jones for generously making these advertisement images available from his own collection.
8. Leif Jones, brother of John Viriamu Jones (first principal of the University College of South Wales and Monmouthshire, which became Cardiff University), came to be known as 'Tea Leaf Jones', partly as a pun on his first name but also partly because of his passion for temperance/ teetotalism (Morgan 1981: 107).
9. See the collection of biographies of the Scranton Welsh at http://thomasgenweb.com/scranton_welsh_bios.html.

10. For a historical review of *Y Wladfa* and a semiotic interpretation of the Patagonian-Welsh linguistic landscape, see Coupland and Garrett (2010) and further references in that source.

11. I am grateful to Peter Garrett and Hywel Bishop for making their own photographs of Patagonian semiotic landscapes available to me for this and the earlier study.

12. See http://www.fodors.com/world/south-america/argentina/atlantic-patagonia/review-441199.html.

13. See http://www.patagoniaexpress.com/nainmaggie.html.

14. See http://www.welshbrewtea.com/.

15. See http://www.yorkshiretea.co.uk/ and http://tregothnan.co.uk/.

REFERENCES

Bishop, Hywel, Nikolas Coupland, and Peter Garrett. 2005. Globalisation, advertising and shifting values for Welsh and Welshness: The case of *Y Drych*. *Multilingua* 24 (4): 343–378.

Blommaert, Jan. 2010. *The sociolinguistics of globalization*. Cambridge: Cambridge University Press.

Bourdieu, Pierre. 2010. *Distinction: A social critique of the judgement of taste*. London: Routledge.

Chatterjee, Pia. 2001. *A time for tea: Women, labor and post/colonial politics on an Indian plantation*. Durham, N.C.: Duke University Press.

Coupland, Nikolas. 2003. Sociolinguistic authenticities. *Journal of Sociolinguistics* 7 (3): 417–431.

Coupland, Nikolas, ed. 2010. *The handbook of language and globalization*. Cambridge, Mass.: Blackwell Publishers.

Coupland, Nikolas. 2012. Bilingualism on display: The framing of Welsh and English in Welsh public spaces. *Language in Society* 41: 1–27.

Coupland, Nikolas, and Michelle Aldridge, eds. 2009. Sociolinguistic and subjective aspects of Welsh in Wales and its diaspora. *Thematic issue of International Journal of the Sociology of Language* 195.

Coupland, Nikolas, Hywel Bishop, and Peter Garrett. 2003. Home truths: Globalisation and the iconisation of Welsh in a Welsh-American newspaper. *Journal of Multilingual and Multicultural Development* 24 (3): 153–177.

Coupland, Nikolas, and Peter Garrett. 2010. Linguistic landscapes, discursive frames and metacultural performance: The case of Welsh Patagonia. *International Journal of the Sociology of Language* 205: 7–36.

Eastman, Carol M., and Roberta F. Stein. 1993. Language display: Authenticating claims to social identity. *Journal of Multilingual and Multicultural Development* 14 (3): 187–202.

Garrett, Peter, Nikolas Coupland, and Hywel Bishop. 2005. Globalisation and the visualisation of Wales and Welsh America: *Y Drych*, 1948–2001. *Ethnicities* 5 (4): 530–564.

Heller, Monica. 2010. Language as resource in the globalized new economy. In *The handbook of language and globalization*, ed. Nikolas Coupland, 349-365. Cambridge, Mass.: Blackwell Publishers.

Hobsbawm, Eric, and Terence Ranger, eds. 1983. *The invention of tradition.* Cambridge: Cambridge University Press.

Jaworski, Adam, and Crispin Thurlow, eds. 2010. *Semiotic landscapes: Language, image, space.* London: Continuum.

Jenkins, Nigel. 1995. *Gwalia in Khasia.* Llandysul: Gwasg Gomer.

Joliffe, Lee. 2003. The lure of tea: History, traditions and attractions. In *Food tourism around the world: Development, management and markets,* ed. M. Hall, L. Sharples, R. Mitchell, N. Macionis, and B. Cambourne, 121–136. London: Butterworth-Heinemann.

Jones, Aled. 2004. Gardens of Eden: Welsh missionaries in British India. In *From medieval to modern Wales: Historical essays in honour of Kenneth O. Morgan and Ralph A. Griffiths,* ed. R. R. Davies and Geraint H. Jenkins, 264–282. Cardiff: University of Wales Press.

Jones, Aled, and Bill Jones. 2001a. Y Drych and American Welsh identities, 1851–1951. *North American Journal of Welsh Studies* 1 (1): 42–49.

Jones, Aled, and Bill Jones. 2001b. *Welsh reflections: Y Drych and America, 1851–2001.* Llandysul: Gomer Press.

Jones, Aled, and Bill Jones. 2003. The Welsh world and the British Empire, c. 1851–1939: An exploration. *Journal of Imperial and Commonwealth History* 31 (2): 57–81.

Kelly-Holmes, Helen, and Gerlinde Mautner, eds. 2010. *Language and the market.* Basingstoke: Palgrave Macmillan.

Kneale, James. 2001. The place of drink: Temperance and the public, 1856–1914. *Social and Cultural Geography* 2 (1): 43–59.

Lambert, W. R. 1983. *Drink and sobriety in Victorian Wales.* Cardiff: University of Wales Press.

Lublin, Geraldine. 2009. The war of the tea houses, or how Welsh heritage in Patagonia became a valuable commodity. *E-Keltoi, Journal of Interdisciplinary Celtic Studies* 1: 69–92.

Millward, E. G. 2000. 'Gym'rwch chi baned?' *Traddodiad y te Cymreig.* Llanrwst: Gwasg Carreg Gwalch.

Morgan, Kenneth O. 1981. *Rebirth of a nation: A history of modern Wales.* Oxford: Oxford University Press.

Pietikäinen, Sari. 2010. Sámi language mobility: Scales and discourses of multilingualism in a polycentric environment. *International Journal of the Sociology of Language* 202: 79–102.

Pietikäinen, Sari, and Helen Kelly-Holmes. 2011. The local political economy of languages in a Sámi tourism destination: Authenticity and mobility in the labelling of souvenirs. *Journal of Sociolinguistics* 15 (3): 323–346.

Robertson, Roland. 1995. Glocalization: Time-space homogeneity-heterogeneity. In *Global modernities,* ed. Mike Featherstone, Scott Lash, and Roland Robertson, 27–44. London: Sage.

Smith, Dai. 1999. *Wales: A question for history.* Bridgend: Seren.

Williams, Colin H. 1990. The Anglicisation of Wales. In *English in Wales: Diversity, conflict and change,* ed. Nikolas Coupland, 19–47. Clevedon: Multilingual Matters.

Williams, Colin H. 2000. *Language revitalization: Policy and planning in Wales.* Cardiff: University of Wales Press.

Williams, Colin H. 2008. *Linguistic minorities in democratic context.* Basingstoke: Palgrave Macmillan.

Williams, Gwyn Alf. 1985. *When was Wales?* Harmondsworth: Penguin.

Williams, Raymond. 1985. Community. *The London Review of Books,* January: 14–15.

Williams, Raymond. 2003. *Who speaks for Wales? Nation, culture, identity,* ed. Daniel Williams. Cardiff: University of Wales Press.

CHAPTER 9

The (De-)Centring Spaces of Airports

Framing Mobility and Multilingualism

ADAM JAWORSKI AND CRISPIN THURLOW

Airports are complicated places and demand complicated ways of thinking about not only space and mobility but also about language and languages. Airports also disrupt tidy assumptions about the meanings of core (or centre) and periphery. How does one otherwise account for London's Heathrow airport or Nairobi's Jomo Kenyatta International airport? For all intents and purposes, Heathrow is a powerful core place—the world's busiest international airport serving the political centre of a G8 nation. But what of the trajectories of the 70 million passengers passing through Heathrow each year? The dynamic, human geography of Heathrow is not a homogeneous, uniformly centred one; instead, it is constantly decentred or peripheralized by the flow of people from other global centres or its own post-Imperial peripheries. Speaking of which, with just under 5 million passengers a year, Jomo Kenyatta is Kenya's largest airport and the sixth busiest airport in Africa. As a major hub (i.e. centre) in Africa, it too is not quite so easily located as peripheral, however geographically, financially, and culturally removed from New York, London, or Tokyo it may be (cf. Sassen 1991).

Against this backdrop, we start by grounding our chapter in the following theoretical/critical principles:

(a) space is as much a semiotic and, indeed, linguistic accomplishment as it is a physical or material one (cf. Soja 1989; Lefebvre 1991);

(b) no aspect of contemporary life is ever fully displaced or completely static; our lives are simultaneously sedentary and nomadic (cf. Clifford 1997; Sheller and Urry 2007);

(c) the places of language are no longer neatly contained by the political and cultural geographies of nation states or speech communities (cf. Blommaert 2005; Rampton 2009); and,

(d) binarized approaches to most social phenomena (e.g. identities of race, gender, and sexuality) inevitably give way to more discursive, dialectical, performative understandings (cf. Butler 1990; Hall 1997).

With these principles in mind, and paying particular attention to contemporary multilingualism as 'ideology and practice' (Heller 2007), we present here a visual discourse ethnography of the 'semiotic landscape' of airports (cf. Jaworski and Thurlow 2010; Thurlow and Jaworski 2012). While we largely draw on the type of data associated with 'geosemiotics' (Scollon and Wong Scollon 2003) and 'linguistic landscapes' (e.g. Shohamy and Gorter 2009; Shohamy et al. 2010), we position our work in a broader tradition of multimodality (Kress and van Leeuwen 2001), as well as visual sociology and visual anthropology. In this sense, our 'visual inquiry [of emplaced multilingualism] is no longer just the study of the [photographic] image, but rather the study of the seen and observable; it includes issues of visibility, mutual interaction and semiotics as they relate to objects, buildings and people as well as to the study of images' (Emmison and Smith 2000: ix). This is also a study of 'visuality'—the ways in which our seeing (our 'vision') is constructed: 'how we see, how we are able, allowed, or made to see, and how we see this seeing and the unseeing therein' (Foster 1988: ix; cited in Rose 2001: 6).

We have deliberately eschewed the usual airports of academic interest (Los Angeles, London, Hong Kong, New York, Amsterdam, etc.) by turning our attention instead to less obvious sites for studying the place of 'language/s on the move' (cf. Thurlow and Jaworski 2010a): the airports in our own respective back yards. Cardiff Airport (Welsh: Maes Awyr Caerdydd) and Seattle-Tacoma International Airport (Sea-Tac) have been for many years the local gateways through which we ourselves have frequently entered into the global ethnoscape; both are regional airports on the margins of powerful nations (see Figures 9.1 and 9.2). While Cardiff Airport ranks as the UK's 21st busiest airport (just over 1.2 million passengers a year), Sea-Tac ranks as the fifteenth busiest airport in the United States (with over 32 million passengers). Like most airports, they also lie outside of the city centres which they serve; in physical or territorial terms, they are doubly peripheralized from the outset.

Our goal with this chapter is to use these two airports partly as an analytic (or allegory, even) for theorizing the dialectics of centre–periphery. More than this, however, we want to use them as empirical sites or texts for tracking the place of language under globalization and the contours of multilingualism in contemporary life. With this in mind, we ask the following questions:

- Where (or when) is language at the airports?
- How are language and other semiotic resources deployed as a resource for structuring and producing these particular spaces?

Figure 9.1:
Cardiff Airport/*Maes Awyr Caerdydd*

- What languages are in evidence, how are they deployed and with/for what effect?
- How is language (or are languages) used to manage core/peripheral identities—of the nations/cities they 'serve' and of the passengers they 'handle'?

Before we turn to our ethnographic encounters with Cardiff Airport and Sea-Tac, we want to set the scene by orienting briefly to the dynamics and dialectics of centre–periphery relations and accounting for airports as (linguistic) places.

Figure 9.2:
Seattle-Tacoma International Airport

CENTRE-PERIPHERY DYNAMICS

Peter Burke (1992) finds centre and periphery a particularly productive pair of concepts for different lines of inquiry due to their opposed yet complementary nature. Burke also recognizes their ambiguity, being used both literally, in the geographical sense, and figuratively, in the political or economic sense. For example, the Marxist theory of social change considers the contrast between prosperous, industrialized nations and poor, 'underdeveloped' nations as a systemic feature of the capitalist system, with the centre, or 'metropolis', appropriating the economic surplus from its peripheries, or 'satellites', for its own economic development. In particular, Immanuel Wallerstein's (1974) spatial model of the world system is premised on the idea that the economic development of the West as the 'core', dating back to the extensive division of labour in the sixteenth century, took place at the expense of its 'peripheries', most notably the New World's slavery and East European serfdom, with other areas (e.g. Mediterranean Europe) forming the 'semiperiphery'.

Burke cites Edward Shils's (1975) idea of society's 'central value system' (what the society holds sacred) and its own central institutional system (the ruling apparatus of the ruling authorities of the society) as intimately connected, each supporting and defining the other (cf. Silverstein's 1998 'centering institutions'). Yet, while peripheries are associated with borders and frontiers, they can be seen as 'regions favouring freedom and equality, a refuge for rebels and heretics...a counterpart...to the orthodoxy and respect for authority and tradition associated with the centre' (Burke 1992: 83). And due to the permeability of borders, people on each side of a border may progressively find more in common with each other than with their respective centres (Sahlins 1989).

In likening airports to cities (or even city-states), our analysis below will evidence a number of centring political and economic forces, as well as value systems analogous to those outlined above. Along similar lines, we observe implicit and explicit shifts in linguistic usage and the valuation of languages, including their presence or disappearance from view, coming into focus and receding into peripheral 'waiting' areas.

AIRPORTS AS (LINGUISTIC) PLACES

Alongside motels, chain hotels, motorways, theme parks, refugee camps, and other similar locations, airports have been cited as a prime example of 'non-places' (Augé 1995). These spaces of mobility, epitomizing Clifford's (1997: 36) idea of 'dwelling-in-traveling', are typically said to manifest 'intense sameness' in their bland, impersonal design, and 'intense hybridity' as the nexus where vast numbers of mobile peoples and cultures intersect (Urry 2000: 63), where they 'coexist or cohabit without living together' (Augé 1995: 110 quoted in Cresswell 2006: 220). As observed by Sarah Sharma (2009: 129), so-called non-places have been disparaged for their architectural uniformity, sterility of their environments, and for their privileging of transactional interactions over personal interactions. However, Sharma rejects the idea that 'non-places' are extraterritorial spaces transcending their localities. She proposes that it is less a question of non-places displacing the local or creating asocial facelessness but rather the theorist of non-place who erases the local in their accounts.

The sense of airports' locality is also shared and particularized by the makeup of the low-wage labourers (airport cleaners, baggage handlers, security guards, and so on), often invisible to the disinterested traveller, with their ethnicized immigration flows, gendered divisions of labour, and multilingual repertoires (cf. Sassen 1996: 146–147). Airports are also recognizable as uniquely 'Amsterdam', 'Paris', 'London', 'Chicago', 'Seattle' and 'Cardiff' because of their specific geographical locations, histories, networked connections, the lived experiences of the people working and passing through them, and last but not least, their semiotic landscapes (cf. Creswell 2006: 267).

The politics of language is certainly implied in this theorizing of space. In globalized, service- and information-based economies, prestigious jobs which require standardized practices in dominant (national) languages and world lingua francas are highly remunerated or symbolically recognized as a form of distinction (Duchêne 2011). Many low-prestige and low-paid jobs (with the exception of call centre workers) require little or no use of the dominant languages which renders otherwise multilingual and linguistically highly competent migrant workers marginalized and powerless due to their inability to cope with specialized registers or literacy demands (McCall 2003; Roberts 2010). However, as explained by Duchêne (personal communication), 'front' employees at airports with national multilingual competencies and lingua francas gain access to 'visible jobs' (i.e. in direct contact with clients), but these jobs are not well-paid and have little prestige. Furthermore, the lack of competence in predictable, dominant languages works as a mode of gate-keeping, mostly for the 'lower classes' and migrants. At the same time, unpredictable language competences (or lesser-spoken languages) are used and exploited by companies capitalizing on migrants' language skills to help out with the everyday running of the institution—for instance, at airports, migrants who work as cleaners or restaurant staff, both 'invisible' jobs, may be asked to translate for passengers having problems at the transit desk. These ad hoc multilingual services facilitate the smooth functioning of the institution but are rewarded neither financially nor symbolically (cf. Duchêne and Heller 2012a).

The uses and displays of languages at airports are driven by a complex interweaving of their functionality (getting passengers through to their aircraft or destination), commercial interests (getting passengers to consume), and the dominant, centring ideologies privileging the global and national elites, their interests and well-being. One striking example of the powerful globalist linguistic ideology evident in airport spaces is the favouring of English as the language of globalization, efficiency, and 'neutrality'. For example, Amsterdam's Schiphol abandoned Dutch from much of its signage in 2001 in favour of English only signs (Cresswell 2006).[1] Yet, to borrow from Jan Blommaert's work on the sociolinguistics of scalar relations, airports are also polycentric and stratified spaces, 'where people continuously need to observe "norms"—*orders of indexicality*—that are attached to a multitude of centres or authority, local as well as translocal, momentary as well as lasting' (Blommaert 2007a: 2; more on this below). In fact, as we have shown elsewhere in the context of airline industry, different scales and orders of indexicality are simultaneously exploited in the marketing strategies of airlines seeking the symbolic and economic capital of international recognition and of a 'global reach', while also servicing their nation states' particular identity concerns (Thurlow and Jaworski 2003; Thurlow and Aiello 2007).

TRACKING THE SEMIOTIC LANDSCAPE OF AIRPORTS

In the literature reviewed so far, there is some consensus that airports are organized both as spaces of passage, transit, or flow and as spaces of containment and consumption. These broad activities are necessarily intertwined with elaborate procedures of security and surveillance (Morgan and Pritchard 2005; Sparke 2006), all of which are regulated by a combination of architectural layout, mechanical/digital technology, and vocal/visual sign-posting (cf. Cresswell 2006). As David Pascoe (2001: 201) notes, however, 'progress' through airports is usually marked as much by stasis and congestion as it is by movement and flow. This complex 'stop-start' experience of airports is important in understanding airports as simultaneously centring and decentring spaces, and for picturing the ebb and flow of languages in airports. Arguably more so than many other sites, airports are characterized by their 'between two worlds' dialectics (cf. Eggebeen 2011): coming/going, here/there, presence/absence, motion/stasis, departure/return, time/space, and, of course, centre/periphery.

It is with this dialectical quality in mind that we turn now to our analysis of Cardiff Airport and Sea-Tac. In particular, we demonstrate the role of language and languages (in the sense of multilingual uses and displays) in centring and decentring airport spaces, that is, creating focal areas/sites of engagement at different scale levels. Our data (collected in the summer of 2010) are drawn primarily from ethnographic observation and photographic recording, but supplemented with the official promotional discourse of both airports (e.g. their websites and internal documents). In tracking these semiotic landscapes and their framing, we treated the two airports as 'text types' or genres in terms of four defining moments or stages (Van Leeuwen 2005): *approach, departures, airside,* and *arrivals* (cf. de Botton 2009). In each of these communicative stages, we witness how 'centre' and 'periphery' are both static and dynamic, permanent and transient, and how they are also dialectically constituted through the deployment of various discourses, genres, and styles, including multiple language codes alongside images, interactions, bodies, and artefacts. With a special focus on mono- and multilingual displays, we mean to show how these two *regional* airports position themselves—and their passengers—as being simultaneously connected to the global (i.e. gateways to the world) and to the local (i.e. thresholds to 'home'). As agents of difference and markers of distinction, airports are purveyors of both national/regional pride and global capital (cf. Thurlow and Jaworski 2003; Thurlow and Aiello 2007; Duchêne and Heller 2012b). The periphery is centred, and established centres are drawn—sometimes quite literally—into the periphery.

APPROACH

It is in the nature of space that it is never easily located or neatly bounded (see our opening 'principles'; also Busch, this volume). Our spatial encounters with airports begin well outside the buildings themselves and long before we enter them. By the same token, our experience of an airport is also shaped by our previous experiences with other airports. Before approaching Cardiff Airport or Sea-Tac, we are already familiar with—have been enculturated into—the typical layout, bureaucratic procedures, and interactional norms of airports in general. In other words, we recognize the genre if not the local style or 'discursive content' of the airports. Our knowledge of airports—and their spatialization—is often also acquired via (old and new) media.

Strategic Centring

Many passengers will start their journey to an airport by visiting its website, perhaps to check flight arrival/departure information, to get ground transportation information, to book a parking place, or just to 'pre-visualize' this part of their trip as an exciting step towards reaching their final destination, whether going on holiday or business. Connecting to the homepages of Cardiff and Sea-Tac airports (Figures 9.3 and 9.4), the destination maps on each site immediately present an example of what we call *strategic centring*—accomplished this time by largely visual means. Neither Sea-Tac nor Cardiff is explicitly marked on the maps. By mentally completing the gestalt and filling in the 'missing' spot, however, viewers are actively engaged in a cognitive act of centring both airports—in the world (Sea-Tac) or in Europe (Cardiff). Even more crucially, the relatively small number of international (and in the case of Cardiff, national) destinations is scattered across the world/continent, implying not only the centredness but also the 'global reach' of both airports (for more examples of this visual technique at play, see Thurlow and Jaworski 2003; Aiello and Thurlow 2006). Here, the relatively peripheral and low-capacity airports are positioned as international gateways, graphically placed near the centre of the map image, with dots for destinations, and contour maps of the continents with no (or only weakly articulated) national borders, all suggesting ease of movement and access.

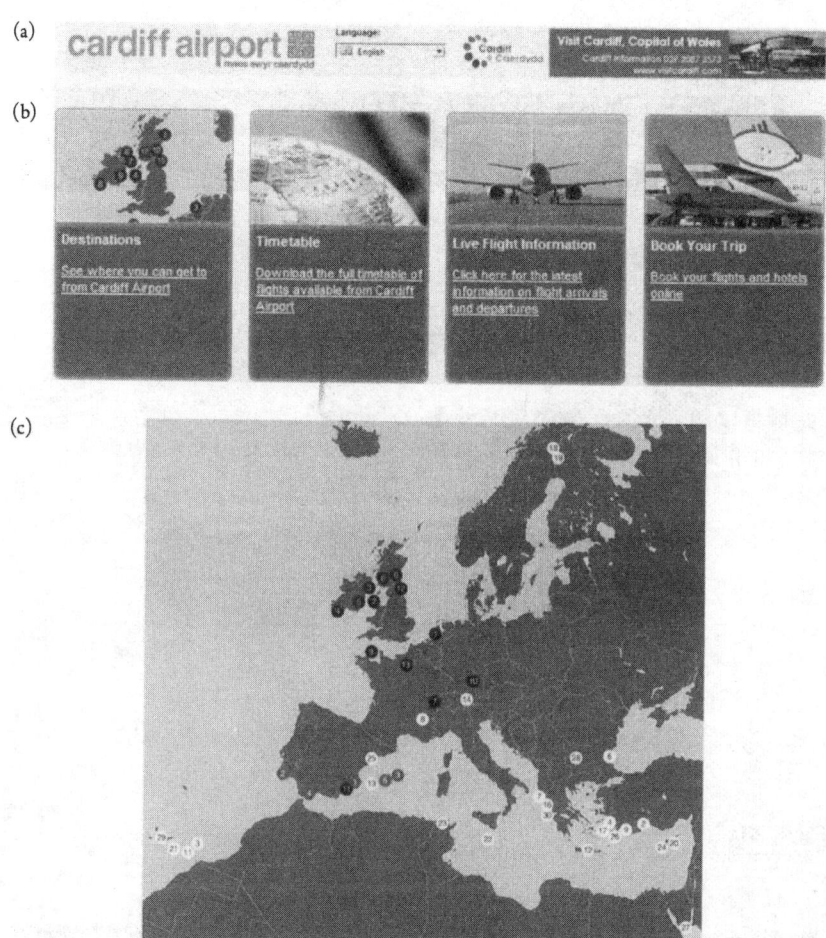

Figure 9.3:
Excerpts from Cardiff Airport website, including a route map

Gateways to the World

We have already noted how Cardiff Airport and Sea-Tac are, like many airports, located on the periphery of the cities they serve. In modern cities, one cannot fail to notice road signs scattered alongside main thoroughfares leading *out* to airports (Figures 9.5 and 9.6). While a practical necessity for those actually travelling to airports, for all those passing the signs during their daily commute to and from work, or just going about their own daily business, it is hard not to see airports as being thereby indexically centred. No matter where one may be in a city, a small arrow or outline of an aeroplane on a green sign will always point one in the direction of an airport. Like signs for city centres, and even though found on the outskirts of towns and cities, airports are their cities' new communication centres—connecting city

(a)

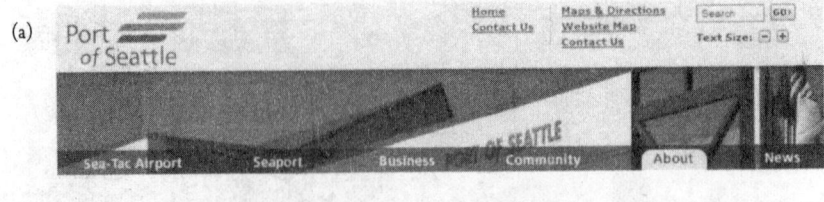

(b)

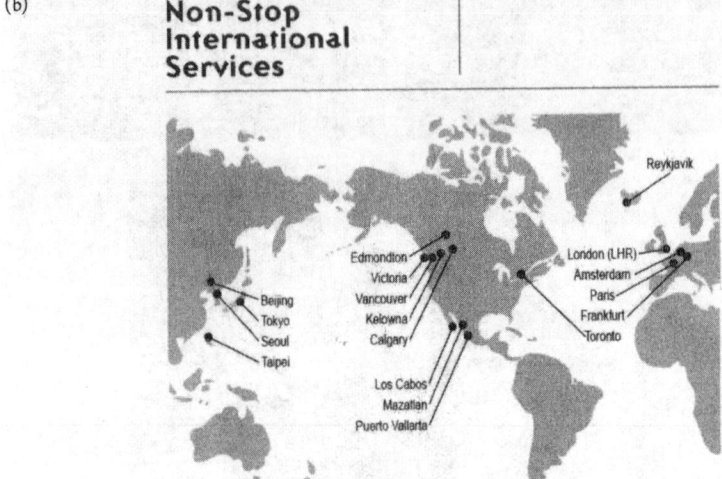

Figure 9.4:
Excerpts from the Sea-Tac airport website, including a route map

Figure 9.5:
Cardiff Airport/*Maes Awyr Caerdydd* road sign

Figure 9.6:
Road sign indicating exit for the Seattle-Tacoma airport

dwellers with the rest of the world, seeding fleeting fantasies of travel to exotic destinations, anywhere that is not 'work' (or 'home'), any place that promises a change from the routine. On most days, for most people, airports remain out of reach, but the aspirational *homing in* on airports by consuming the road signs may go on every

Figure 9.7:
Airline billboard, Cardiff Airport

day. This promise is articulated and made concrete in the kinds of marketing that occur the closer one gets to the airport (Figure 9.7) where, as with the online maps, airports look to position themselves as hubs or gateways, and airlines offer to take us there.

Global Spectacles

For all their instrumentality, airport road signs also serve important symbolic functions. The same may be said also of the indicator boards inside airport buildings (Figures 9.8 and 9.9).

Depending on the time of day, the departures board at Cardiff Airport lists distinctly non-English (or non-Welsh) places like Zakynthos, Arrecife, Enontekiö, Sharm El Sheik, Kittilä, and Fuerteventura. However déclassé these may be as tourist destinations, they still resonate as exotic, enchanted sounding places of 'infinite and immediate possibility' (de Botton 2009: 29). Charting a very different geography, Sea-Tac displays its own multilingual allusions with Kahului, Sitka, Mazatlán, Tapei-Toayuan, Incheon, and Osaka-Kansai; also, the distinctively European tones of Paris Charles de Gaulle and Frankfurt. In the mouths of locals and others passing through, the reading/speaking of these place-names obliges a shift—however fleeting—into other languages. As we hang around near the entrance to the airport terminal, we notice how arriving passengers pause, look up the boards, locate 'their' destination, re-confirm

Figure 9.8:
Indicator board, Cardiff Airport at departures

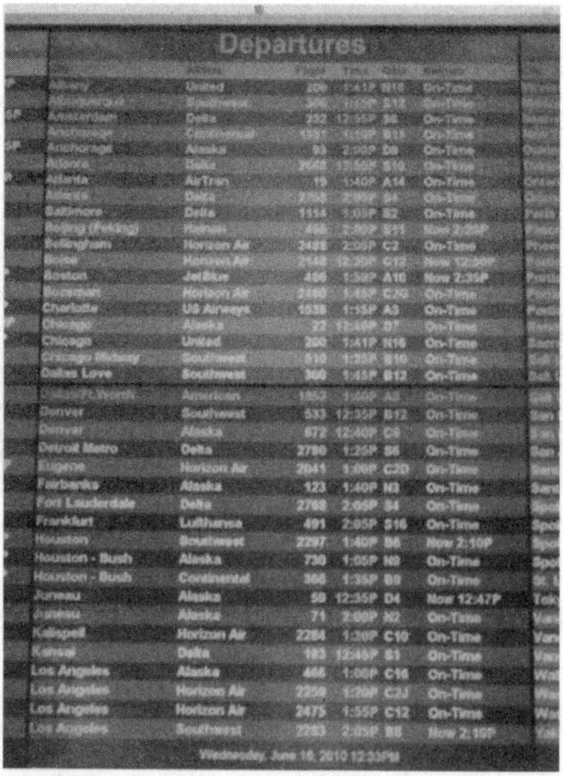

Figure 9.9:
Indicator board, Sea-Tac departures

departure time ('on time'), and seek further instructions ('Desks 03–07'); one passenger at Cardiff points at the board and says almost triumphantly to his companion
'Alicante'. These distant place-names appear as muffled, isolated soundbites, but different languages are present through them and come into earshot.

Websites and indicator boards may list a dazzling array of actual travel destinations accessible from airports, but they are also full of implied or imagined destinations. In a more glamorous—or at least, self-conscious—way, the gleaming,
polished-steel sculpture at Sea-Tac (Figures 9.10a and 9.10b) is styled as a giant
road sign indexing a myriad of international, if relatively small and unknown, destinations. Where *exactly* are Arvida, Rouen, Karlsruhe, Brno, Levola, and many others? If Sea-Tac can connect its passengers to these mysterious sounding places, and
symbolically it does by invoking their names in a spectacular display, then it appears
yet again as a fully globalized, central point on the map from which to reach even
the most 'remote' corners of the planet. The same message emanates from airline
advertisements at Cardiff either through a symbolic signpost on the steps leading
to the departure hall (Figure 9.11), or a billboard alongside the driveway leading to
the terminal building: Amsterdam, Dubai, Cape Town, Hong Kong, Cardiff, Cork,

(a)   (b)

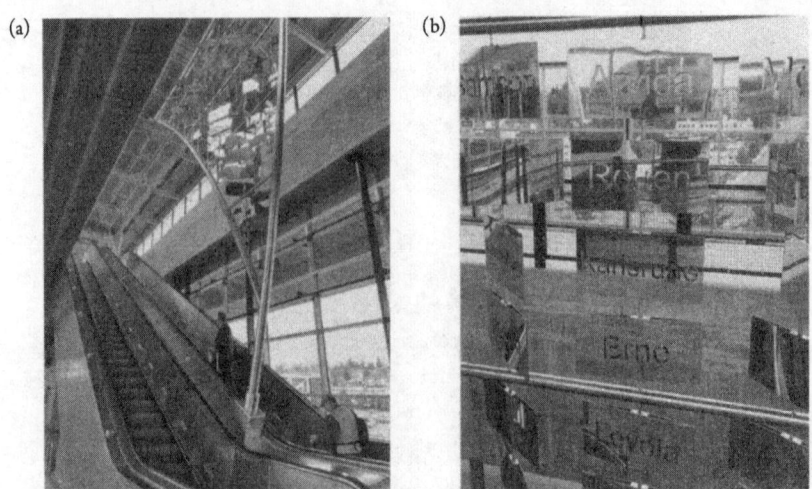

Figure 9.10:
Symbolic road signs at Sea-Tac airport (a) general view and (b) close-up

New York, Orlando. Lists are 'colony texts' (Hoey 2001), where in the absence of any visible ordering, each element is equal to all the others. In the functional and symbolic lists of destinations, the significance of each place-name is as great as the next; some are more readily recognizable than others; all, especially in their

Figure 9.11:
Airline advertisement/symbolic road sign, Cardiff Airport departures

collective promise—however illusory—of freedom of movement, reinforce the mysticism and excitement of travel and connectedness with the world.

DEPARTURES

In the 1970s, architectural design critic Robert Sommer (1974) dismissively character-ized airports as a matter of endless tunnels and funnels. Airports certainly retain much of the quintessential system of moving walkways and jetways, and the continual lining up for human 'processing'. Perhaps, however, a more contemporary way of thinking about airports is less in terms of their architectural design—which is nowadays typified by vast, glassy atria (see Edwards 2005)—and more in terms of centring and decentring processes that may emerge not only through the built environment but also through more semiotic (which includes linguistic), interactional and psychological means. With this in mind, we now head for Departures, to check-in and to clear security.[2]

Staging Centre

Movement (or lack thereof) in the airport is generically organized by a series of key communicative stages each of which is associated with a number of centring and decentring activities such as checking-in, security screening, duty-free shopping, and boarding. In most airports, particular spaces are assigned for these activities, carved out in sometimes permanent but often temporary ways. (Think here of how post hoc spaces were hurriedly created in hallways and corridors for intensified, post-9/11 security screening in US airports.) The seemingly endless hallway of check-in counters at Sea-Tac (Figure 9.12) finds its equivalent at Cardiff Airport (Figure 9.13)—albeit on a smaller scale. In both cases, different agents or air-lines sometimes have dedicated check-in zones but also share check-in counters at different times of the day (see Figures 9.14 and 9.15). Airlines therefore come to prominence in the airport by staging themselves as distinctive commercial and processing centres through a combination of fixed or transient signage (e.g. digi-tal monitors above check-in desks), banners with trademarked colours and logos, moveable stanchions and strips of carpets (a favourite semiotic marker for staging elite traveller status—Thurlow and Jaworski 2006; Figure 9.16). In the large, open space of the departures terminal, each airline stakes a claim to its own commer-cial zone which, in the case of international airlines, becomes a quasi-diplomatic zone. Cheek-by-jowl at Sea-Tac, British Airways, Korean Air, Lufthansa, Eva Air, and Air France create a little bit of Britain, Korea, Germany, Taiwan of China, and France, respectively. The same physical space can be semiotically centred and re-centered throughout the day, so that the props for staging Little Britain (i.e. two up-right banners and some Hand Baggage Allowance equipment; Figure 9.17) wait in the wings, while Little Korea (Figure 9.18) takes centre stage. Further down the line of

Figure 9.12:
Check-in area, Sea-Tac

Figure 9.13:
Check-in area, Cardiff Airport

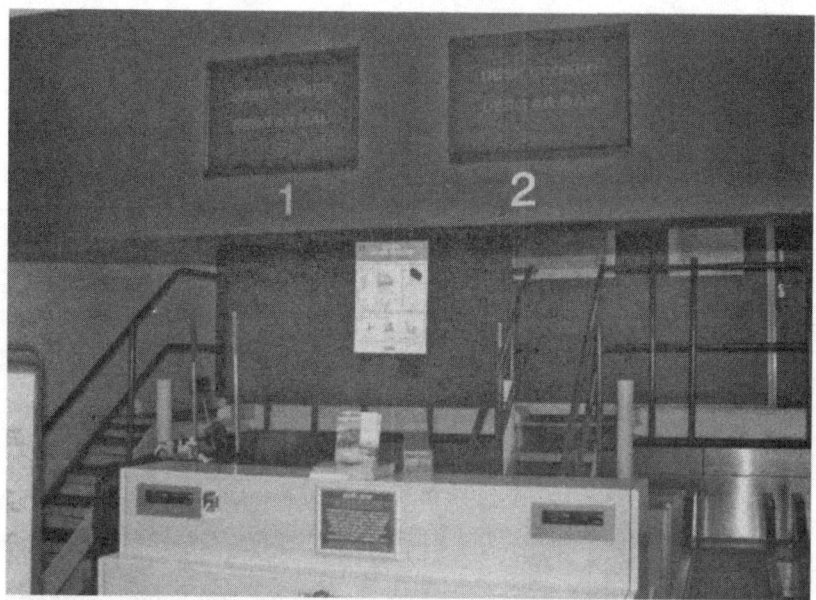

Figure 9.14:
Monitors above check-in desks, Cardiff Airport

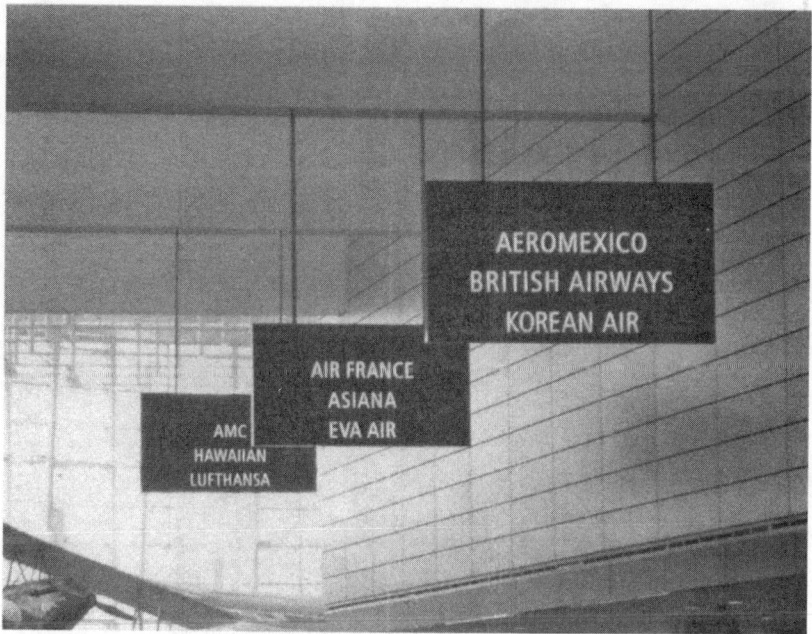

Figure 9.15:
Signs above check-in desks, Sea-Tac

Figure 9.16:
Monitors, first class banner, stanchions, carpets at Korean Air check-in desks, Sea-Tac

Figure 9.17:
British Airways sign and equipment, Sea-Tac

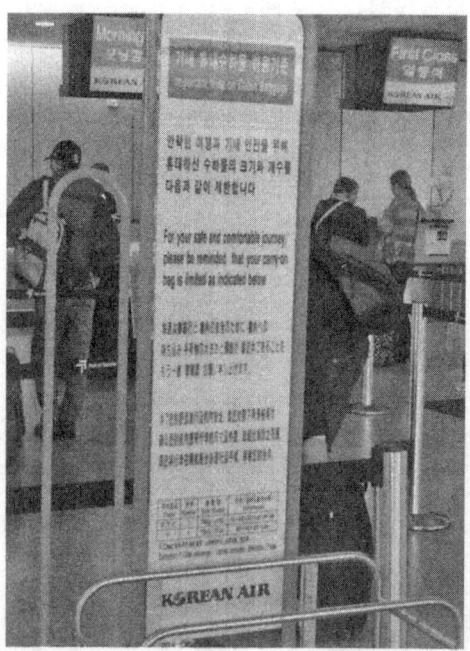

Figure 9.18:
Korean Air sign and equipment, Sea-Tac

check-in desks, Asiana and Eva Air signage wait backstage while that of Air France (not shown here) has been centred to provide appropriate setting or 'expressive equipment' for the airline's front stage performance (Goffman 1959) of checking in its passengers. At Cardiff Airport, the Manx2.com Welsh-English bilingual Hand Baggage Allowance rack (the English language side seen in Figure 9.19) sits in the corner of the check-in area waiting to be wheeled out when the passengers for its sole flight to Anglesey arrive for check-in. Through these semiotic centrings and recentrings, the airlines, their countries of origin, and the global or local destinations they service, come into and out of focus; sometimes prominent, at other times literally marginalized and muted, but always on display. The centre is thus a process of attunement as much as it is of actual space; airlines centre themselves by calling attention to themselves and by hailing passengers at relevant points in time.

Multilingual 'Touch-Spaces'

Languages are often a key resource for staging the fleeting centres of airline flag-carriers. The Korean-English displays for Korean Air's checking-in (e.g. Figure 9.18) will eventually give way to the monolingual displays for British Airways (e.g. Figure 9.19). Just as French (Air France) will give way to Korean (Asiana) and, a little later still, to Chinese (Eva Air).

Figure 9.19:
Manx2.com sign and equipment, Cardiff Airport

Languages also come into and out of focus in other polycentric spaces of departure. In the check-in zones of major US airlines (e.g. Continental, United, and American), interactive digital stands make the process of checking in available in a range of major European and East-Asian languages (e.g. French, German, and Spanish; Korean, Japanese, Thai, and Chinese—both Simplified and Traditional; Figure 9.20); Portuguese, Italian, and Greek are also available in some cases, even though Sea-Tac has no apparent cultural or commercial links with these particular languages. Elsewhere in Sea-Tac, multilingual interfaces—or 'touch-spaces'— are available in cash machines and tourist information stands (see *Arrivals* section below), just as cash machines at Cardiff Airport offer service in Welsh or English.

These different languages are brought to the fore and actualized by speakers at a moment of need, in a moment of contact. However transient computerized check-in centres may be, they exert a centrifugal pull as otherwise distant (or peripheral) places like London, Paris, Taipei, Seoul, and Frankfurt are drawn to the fore (or centre) at Sea-Tac. These transient diplomatic zones are also connected through their human geography (e.g. British ground-staff and passengers at BA check-in), the banal nationalism (Billig 1995) of their corporate

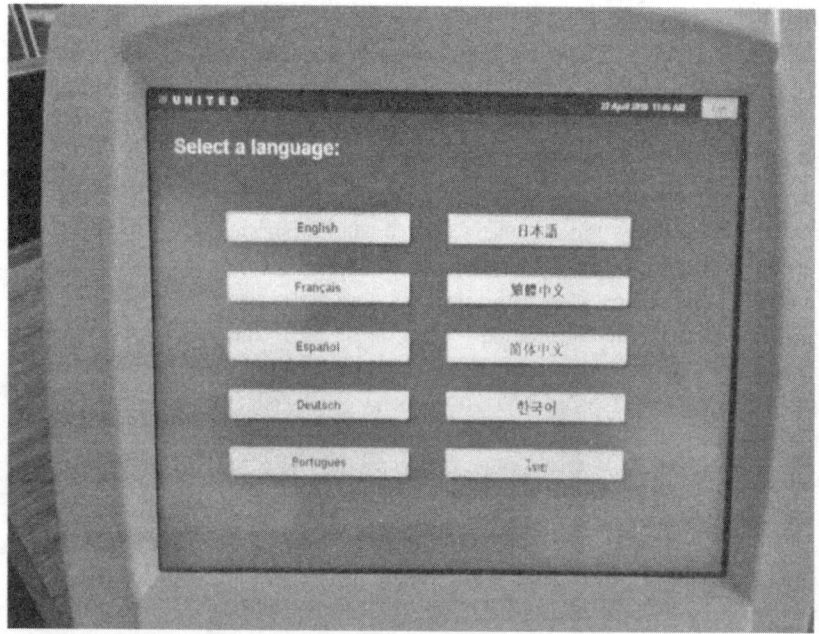

Figure 9.20:
United Airlines' automated check-in stand, Sea-Tac

displays (e.g. flag colours and national languages), and, of course, the planes waiting on the tarmac to carry off passengers. A global 'plane' or 'scape' is thereby realized.

AIRSIDE

At Cardiff Airport and Sea-Tac, 'airside' spaces are realized slightly differently. With only one terminal, these areas at Cardiff Airport are exclusively for departing passengers. This is also true of Sea-Tac's international terminal but not in its domestic terminals where departing, transferring, and arriving passengers mingle in the same spaces. In this last case, 'airside' is very much a space of coming and going, although the semiotic landscape retains a dominant orientation to the departing (or perhaps) transferring passenger.

'Glocal' Ethnoscaping

Airside spaces are, of course, at the very centre of airports' commercial activity—of restaurants and duty-free shopping. Mirroring the strategic centring on the airport websites, the world is everywhere at Sea-Tac and Cardiff Airport—at least in its most aesthetic, 'cosmopolitan-lite' (cf. Beck 2006) sense. At Sea-Tac, the commercial areas are peppered with stylized images of the globe, a ubiquitous signifier of globalization (cf. Szerszynski and Urry 2002) (Figures 9.21 and 9.22) and Cardiff has the 'WORLD' (Figure 9.23). Of course, at both airports there are opportunities to buy into the world by purchasing (or simply browsing) the usual duty-free offering of global brands, although still usually representing only a narrow slice of the world (e.g. French perfumes, Swiss watches and chocolates, Scotch whiskey, Italian scarves and ties). This semiotic landscape of brand names, logos, and shop signs, alongside the stylized globes, 'unwaved' international flags, lists of international cities/destinations, and so on, are prime examples of the visualization of what we choose to call 'banal globalization', in parallel to Billig's (1995) 'banal nationalism', Beck's (2006) 'banal cosmopolitanism', and Szerszynski and Urry's (2002, 2006) 'banal globalism'; those everyday ways that the global is performatively enacted through ordinary, seemingly innocuous textual practices and other semiotic means (see Thurlow and Jaworski 2010a, 2011).

Sea-Tac, in particular, enhances—or embellishes—its global ethnoscape with a food hall of 'exotic' restaurants with their one-word multi-languaging: *Qdoba, Maki,* and *Pallino* (see Figures 9.24, 9.25, 9.26). At Cardiff Airport, too, we can buy 'sunglasses and accessories' at the cosmopolitan sounding (or looking) *Nuance* or drink a cup of coffee at *Caffè Ritazza* (not shown here). To choose just one example (Figure 9.27), the brand names of cosmetics in one part of the Cardiff duty-free shop are arranged into a string of familiar signs: *Dior, Estēe Lauder,*

Figure 9.21:
'Globe' display and shopping area, Sea-Tac airside

Figure 9.22:
'Globe' display, 'Club Jet Duty Free', Sea-Tac airside

Figure 9.23:
The stationery-cum-confectionery store WORLD at Cardiff airside (now replaced by WH Smith)

Figure 9.24:
'Qdoba Mexican Grill', Sea-Tac airside

Figure 9.25:
'Maki of Japan', Sea-Tac airside

Figure 9.26:
'Pallino Pasta', Sea-Tac airside

Figure 9.27:
Cosmetics display at 'Nuance', Cardiff Airport airside

Lancôme, L'Oréal, Elizabeth Arden, Givenchy, Clarins, Prada, Stella McCartney, alongside a more generic 'Celebrity Fragrance' (not all these clearly visible in the reproduced image). The iconicity of these brand names exploits consumer stereotypes of Frenchness, Italianicity, or 'simply' glamour, elegance, and sophistication associated with international 'celebrity' lifestyle rather than any specific national characteristics. Pursuing their aspirational identities, targeted consumers may not even associate these brand names with any specific (national) language, or they may think of them as 'belonging' to different languages (Tufi and Blackwood 2010), a global *commercialese*. This global semiotic landscape of celebrity brand names, like the multilingual language of advertising (e.g. Kelly-Holmes 2005) interpellates (Althusser 1971) or positions its audience as cosmopolitan and transnational elite of global travellers (cf. Piller 2001; Thurlow and Jaworski 2006). Such multilingual amalgams blend into glittering 'language displays' (Eastman and Stein 1933) and a fetish of freedom and democracy or, to be more precise, neoliberal consumer choice. Thus, consumerism appears one of the key central values responsible for the organization of 'central' multilingualism of airports (cf. Shils, above).

For all its global reach, this commercial ethnoscape is also structured through its juxtaposition of the local with the global. *Seattle's Best Coffee* jostles for space (and attention) right next to the typographically authenticated *Kobo: Sushi, Salad, Udon* (Figure 9.28). At Cardiff Airport, soft-toy versions of the national emblem, a Welsh dragon (Figure 9.29), are for sale together with Welsh-themed rugby balls, teddy bears, *Penderyn* single malt Welsh whiskey, and (at a short distance away) another small department with Welsh-themed goods such as fridge magnets, rugby shirts, Welsh carved wooden 'love spoons', watches, and more soft toys. Some of these gifts are targeted at an international clientele with labels in some of the key 'central' languages (de Swaan 2001) such as English, French, German, and Italian (marked

Figure 9.28:
Localizing and globalizing brands, Sea-Tac airside

Figure 9.29:
Localizing display in duty free, Cardiff Airport airside

with corresponding 'appropriate' national flags). Others use a strategy of 'authenticating' their labels in English and Welsh (cf. Pietikäinen and Kelly-Holmes 2011). All these goods and their branding texts—Welsh single malt alongside more 'international' Scotch whiskeys and French brandies, international and local company names, souvenir labels with different and somewhat unpredictable (if limited) language choices, globes on shop signs next to maps of Wales on the fridge magnets, images of 'generic' flowers on the 'summer time' display underneath the Diageo-owned alcohol brands opposite Welsh daffodil pins, international flags and Welsh flags, Welsh dragons for sale and Welsh dragons as decoration (part of the *Penderyn* display), Swiss chocolate and Welsh fudge, together with more straightforward, commercial texts such as 'Any 2 for (+name of products and price)' speak of differently 'scaled' goods and centring forces at play—global glamour vs. shopping on a budget vs. local colour and authenticity. Duty-free stores are transpatial ('here-and-there') microcosms of 'glocalization' (Robertson 1995); they are also spaces in which the meanings and experiences of centre and periphery become very confused. Here is where Welsh people can buy dragons to take off with them to distant places as reminders *of* home, or where foreigners may buy dragons as exotic souvenirs *for* home. Indeed, we are reminded that airports are inevitably experienced as central for those who call it 'home' and as peripheral for those who call it 'away'.

Multilingual Scapes

Unsurprisingly, Cardiff Airport is a site of more visible (English-Welsh) bilingualism than the more resolutely monolingual Sea-Tac. While limitations of space preclude

Figure 9.30:
Bilingual signage, Department for Environment, Food and Rural Affairs (DEFRA), Cardiff Airport arrivals

us from a detailed discussion of this aspect of Cardiff's semiotic landscape, we will limit ourselves to just a handful of observations. Cardiff Airport is a privately owned company and has no legal obligation to orient to the Welsh Assembly Government and its 1993 Welsh Language Act stating the equality of both languages in Wales (cf. Coupland's 2010 discussion of the significance of this Act for the study of linguistic landscapes in Wales). While all state institutions in Wales are required to publish all their documents (including public signage) in both Welsh and English (as is the case with all the signs of the UK Border Agency and the Department for Environment, Food and Rural Affairs, DEFRA, around the airport; Figure 9.30), Cardiff Airport, not unlike many other Welsh-based companies in the private sector adopting the stance of 'corporate and social responsibility', strives to support and promote the use of Welsh among its staff, increase bilingual service provision for its customers, and to use the Welsh language to create a 'sense of place' for its business (cf. Cardiff Airport, 2009/2010). This extends to the (re-)placement of new (at the time of data collection) bilingual, permanent and temporary signage, audio announcements, stationary, customer satisfaction survey forms, press releases, marketing texts, and so on (ibid.). Indeed, at the time of data collection, many new signs were already on display with the bilingual 'We're evolving…' / '*Rydym ni'n datblygu…*' campaign advertised widely and included not only the linguistic re-branding but also structural improvements to the terminal building and parking facilities.

One of the key examples of the general and linguistic re-branding of Cardiff Airport is its new logo (Figure 9.1), with the clearly privileged English text over its

Welsh equivalent, and the Celtic-styled compass. While state institutions display all their signs bilingually (Figure 9.30), the presence of English as the dominant language of Wales and international travel is safely assured. This can be seen, for example, in the English-only sign 'executive Lounge', where the 'usual' space for Welsh below the main body of text in smaller font (compare Figure 9.1) is taken up by the English tagline 'a stylish departure' (Figure 9.31).

All the same, the Welsh language and Welsh iconography are present at Cardiff on a scale that makes the airport unmistakably 'Cardiff' and 'Wales' (as opposed to 'Sea-Tac', 'Heathrow', or 'Schiphol'), and the fact that the prescriptive adherence to absolute semantic and graphic parallelism between Welsh and English is lessened may overall produce effects of greater involvement with the cultural values of the Welsh language than the sterile form-focused parallelism of bilingual texts (Coupland 2010: 98). As Nik Coupland observes in his study of Welsh linguistic landscapes 'from above' and 'from below', '[c]omplementing rather than paralleling, maximizing the different cultural resources of both Welsh and English, and finding cultural value in the interplay between languages, are likely to be more productive' (ibid.).

Beyond the national–global interplay of Welsh and English bilingualism across Cardiff, far more languages are visible throughout both airports. Tucked away in a bookstore at Sea-Tac (Figure 9.32), we come across a shelf of travel magazines whose covers make colourful promises of 'elsewhere' (cf. Reh 2004 for an ethnography of 'visible writing', including books, as part of a locale's linguistic landscape; also Pavlenko 2010). Close by is another bookshelf crammed full with travel guides and 'teach-yourself' language books. It is in this repository of travel publications that a myriad of languages, or 'language potentialities', lies dormant in the relative

Figure 9.31:
'Executive Lounge', Cardiff Airport airside

Figure 9.32:
Guidebook and language self-teaching books, bookstore, Sea-Tac airside

periphery of *closed books* until an interested traveller starts browsing through their *glossaries* and *useful phrases* sections, glancing through 'foreign' politeness formulae or scripts for basic service encounters (see Thurlow and Jaworski, 2010a).

In the midst of its visual landscape of signs, brands, logos, and magazine/book covers, what is not immediately apparent—certainly not from our photographic data—is the *soundscape* of these airports. With the few exceptions of low traffic or VIP lounges, where quietude is one of the marks of *distinction* and privilege (cf. Thurlow and Jaworski 2010b, 2012), airports are by no means tranquil, silent places. Indeed, to speak of them as 'non-places' where 'people coexist or cohabit without living together' (see Augé 1995) makes more of an existential or even political claim than it does a sensible linguistic or communicative one (see above). In his critique of the 'rhetoric of ubiquity', Andrew Wood (2003) dismisses airport interactions as uniformly disconnected: 'random', 'isolated', and 'anonymous'. For us, this is equivalent to dismissing the phatic exchanges of small talk as nothing more than 'empty' or pointless (cf. J. Coupland 2010; see also MacCannell's 1989: 105 critique of Boorstin's 1964 concept of 'pseudo-places'). All across the airport but especially here in the Airside spaces, we find passengers chatting constantly with each other, whether standing in check-in lines or security check-points, in cafes or while shopping, and most definitely when they end up facing a significant delay in take-off time; ground staff ask and answer endless questions, and sometimes chat casually with passengers; flight crews mix work talk and small talk as they move swiftly towards their aircraft avoiding eye contact with waiting passengers; kitchen staff, cleaning staff, and baggage handlers, too, talk amongst themselves while working and especially during periods of relative calm between loading and unloading planes, in their backstage regions of conveyer belts and baggage carts. For all of their normative regulation of people and spaces, airports are surprising sites of agentful practice and busy interaction (most definitely awaiting a more systematic and long-term ethnography of communication). Sharma (2009) and Cresswell (2006) both argue that 'non-place' perspectives which view airports as generic, sterile, soul-less typically privilege the point of view of elites—especially the business commuter—and overlook many other people who pass through or spend their time in airports. As Creswell puts it, the airport 'is not simply a part of the life-world of the kinetic elite, but a place of shelter and livelihood. The people who service the elite are every bit as cosmopolitan' (Creswell 2006: 257).

ARRIVALS

In some ways, the spaces of arrival at airports work in parallel to—are almost mirror images of—their departure spaces. Not exactly departures in reverse, but often another set of corridors, of queuing and waiting rituals, and of centres within centres. In our visits to Cardiff Airport and Sea-Tac, we traced the geography of arriving from disembarkation, to walking towards passport control (or just the Exit), to waiting in baggage claim, and to passing through the arrivals/departure hall out to ground transportation (e.g. taxi ranks and car parks). We will keep our comments on this last stage fairly brief, using Arrivals mainly as a way to exemplify and pull together some of the recurring themes in our analysis of airports as (de-)centring spaces.

Re-Imagining Home

Welcome to your destination. Welcome home. 'Welcome to Seattle and the Pacific Northwest' (Figure 9.33). 'Bye bye airport. Hello Wales.' / 'Hwyl fawr faes awyr. Helo Cymru.' (Figure 9.34). Like Departures, Arrivals is a point of crossing, a threshold, by which airports are simultaneously gateways to a destination and places of home-coming. Always Janus-faced, they simultaneously point to 'here' and to 'there' (see Schivelbusch 1986 for a similar view on railway stations).

Throughout the arrival spaces at Sea-Tac and Cardiff Airport, this dual-purpose landscape is accomplished semiotically, as well as architecturally. As above, we find a similar mix of symbolic and functional signposting—most notably in welcome signs—where here and there must be managed. At Cardiff Airport,

Figure 9.33:
'Welcome to Seattle and the Pacific Northwest' (Lufthansa), Sea-Tac arrivals

the official Welsh Tourist Board extends its WELCOME and CROESO along with a pan-European greeting in Italian, German, Spanish, and French (Figure 9.35). Wales thereby expresses its local identity and situates—or centres—itself more internationally. At Sea-Tac, the most prominent message of welcome to

Figure 9.34:
'Bye bye airport. Hello Wales.'/ *Hwyl fawr faes awyr. Helo Cymru.*', Cardiff Airport arrivals

Figure 9.35:
Multilingual 'welcome' sign (Welsh Tourism Board), Cardiff Airport arrivals

the city and the region, is extended/sponsored by the Port of Seattle and the German airline Lufthansa (Figure 9.33). At the time, services between Seattle and Frankfurt were very new, and, with this sign, the airline was looking to make a concerted bid to centre itself visually and commercially. As such, this second welcome sign doubles as an advertisement for not only the airline but also for the world—selling to locals the global reach of Sea-Tac by enworlding their corner of the continent. Arrivals spaces therefore serve two interesting functions: they must create a distinctive sense of the local 'home culture' while reassuring visitors that they remain connected to their homes—and reassuring returning locals that they remain connected to the world at large. This can be done both literally and imaginatively. Tokens of easy or rapid connectivity—between centre and periphery (depending on your point of view)—are manifest in advertisements for international (or 'global') calling cards ('Stay in touch the easy way', 'Swipe and call') at both airports (Figures 9.36 and 9.37). Most likely directed at visitors, these tokens act as reassurances of home; for locals, they are nonetheless reassurances of elsewhere (cf. Blommaert and Dong 2010). Arrivals is an obvious space in which to imagine and stage the nation (or the city, region, etc.; cf. Anderson 1983; Billig 1995), as well as branding the place as a distinctive destination (cf. Flowerdew 2004; Jensen 2007). Inevitably, these are discursive accomplishments. At Sea-Tac, indigenous Native American 'craftwork' or other 'cultural artefacts' are encased and displayed alongside contemporary works of art by 'local artists' (Figure 9.38).

At Cardiff Airport, the seemingly endless passageway from aeroplane through baggage claim to exit is playfully but strategically staged with large red and green

Figure 9.36:
'Stay in touch the easy way', Sea-Tac arrivals

Figure 9.37:
'Swipe and call', Cardiff Airport arrivals

Figure 9.38:
Art from the Pacific Northwest, Sea-Tac

panels in English and Welsh (the playful key of the signs realized by the choice of brighter and 'cheerful' hues of red and green in contrast to the darker and more 'sober' values of the colours in the Welsh flag). The different 'stations' offer a combination of signposting, advertising, and entertainment: 'Wales this way' / 'Cymru fforda yma' (Figure 9.39); 'Our craggy coastline is 7,987 times longer than this corridor.' / 'Mae ein harfordir creigiog 7,987 gwaith yn hirach na'r corridor hwn.' (Figure 9.40); 'Wales, 23% national park[,] 0.14625% airport.' / Cymru, 23% parc cenedlaethol, 0.14625% maes awyr.' (not shown here); and many others. Interestingly, some of the signs make explicit metalinguistic comments, not only putting Welsh-English bilingualism on display, as amusing or decorative (Kelly-Holmes 2005), but as explicitly self-reflexive acts of linguascaping (Jaworski, Thurlow, et al. 2003). For example, 'Welsh also spoken in Chubut Valley, Patagonia.' / 'Hwyliodd y Cymry cyntaf i Batagonia ar gwch o'r enw'r Mimosa.' (not shown here); '"Hello" in Welsh is "helo". So helo.' / 'Helo, croeso adref.' (= Hello, welcome (back) home) (Figure 9.41). All these more or less explicitly metalinguistic displays of bilingualism, and especially of Welsh, engage in language ideological work (e.g. Woolard and Schieffelin 1994; Coupland and Jaworski 2004; Kroskrity 2004) positioning and normalizing the Welsh language as an index of the Welsh nation (especially by bringing Welsh in the linguistic landscape outside of the strictly institutional frame), subverting the mythology and hegemony of English monolingualism in Wales/United Kingdom, as well as internationalizing Welsh by pointing to its use outside of Wales ('also

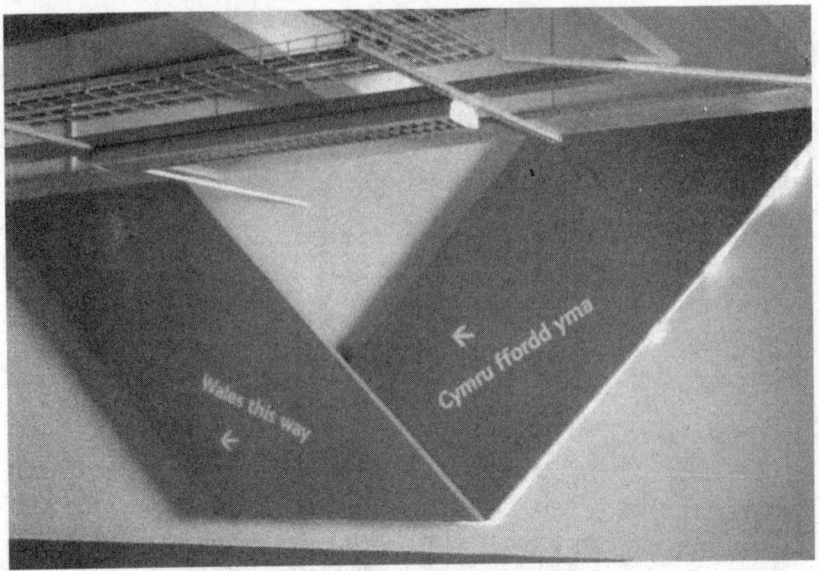

Figure 9.39:
'Wales this way' / '*Cymru fforda yma*', Cardiff Airport arrivals

Figure 9.40:
'Our craggy coastline is 7,987 times longer than this corridor.' / '*Mae ein harfordir creigiog 7,987 gwaith yn hirach na'r corridor hwn.*', Cardiff Airport arrivals

Figure 9.41:
'"Hello" in Welsh is "helo". So helo.'/'*Helo, croeso adref.*' [= Hello, welcome (back) home], Cardiff Airport arrivals

spoken in Chubut Valley, Patagonia') and inviting its international (including other British) visitors to engage in an act of code-crossing (Rampton 1995) by realizing the second part of an adjacency pair in the ubiquitous and most pervasive speech act in tourism discourse—the greeting (Jaworski 2009)—'*So helo.*' These are, again, localizing and globalizing communicative practices commonly found in other contexts of tourism and mobility, whereby languages, and especially 'small', minority languages are used as resources for creating a 'sense of place', authenticity, distinction, and exoticity of travel destinations (cf. Jaworski, Thurlow, et al. 2003; Pujolar 2006; Budach et al. 2007; Jaworski and Piller 2008; Pietikäinen 2010; Thurlow and Jaworski 2010a; Pietikäinen and Kelly-Holmes 2011).

AIRPORTS AS UNEVEN, INTERSTITIAL SPACES OF MOBILITY AND MULTILINGUALISM

[T]hese interstitial spaces... are also places of fantasy and desire, places of inclusion and exclusion, and social milieux for different groups of people. (Crang 2002: 573)

Mike Crang reminds us that airports are not easily resolved. Perhaps it is this elusive quality that warrants their status as the most emblematic spaces of globalization—even more so than their affiliation with communication technologies and human mobilities. At one and the same time, airports are spaces of mobility and immobility, elite spaces and spaces of exploitation, leisure spaces and working spaces, spaces of connection and spaces of alienation, distinctive spaces and generic spaces, and so on. Airports are also simultaneously centred (or centring) spaces and peripheral (or peripheralizing) spaces.

Drawing on Jan Blommaert's work (cf. Blommaert 2005; Blommaert and Dong 2010), we prefer to think of airports as being akin to densely populated, ethnically and nationally diverse urban neighbourhoods where different, socially stratified groups of residents and more transient dwellers, migrants and non-migrants live, work, do business, get educated, worship, relax, and so forth together or side by side. These are translocal and trans-national spaces but also locally anchored spaces, where the distribution of language codes, linguistic repertoires, and a wide range of linguistic displays vary across the 'horizontal' dimension of neighbourhood spaces (streets, businesses, cultural institutions, etc.); each of these spaces is further diversified by vertically stratified layers of scalar relations ranging from strictly local (e.g. interpersonal) to strictly global, and a range of intermediate scalar levels between these two extremes. In specific contexts of use, particular linguistic resources (standard and non-standard varieties, accents, styles, genres, and discourses, often mixed or truncated) display orientations to *orders of indexicality*, that is, socially and culturally patterned 'norms' of control, authority, and evaluation associated with these resources in their microenvironments, settings, and networks (Silverstein 2003).

Airports are sites of intense production of spatial relations which situate them not only within their local constituencies (cities, regions, nations) but also within broader global networks. Their pervasive positioning, or styling, of passengers as political, economic, and cultural subjects makes them, together with other places of mobility, particularly rich sites for critical observation and study (cf. Cwerner, Kesselring and Urry, 2009). However, as already indicated, we do not accept that this complexity is best explained by conceptualizing airports as somewhat transcendental or de-localized, and for that reason we opt out of referring to them with the somewhat misleading concept of 'non-place'. On the contrary, airports appear to us to be uniquely grounded as multiply layered spaces, both local and global, through (a) their often sophisticated and iconic architectural design (Pascoe 2001; Pearman 2004); (b) the presence and flows of human subjects with tangible biographies and aspirations (Adey 2008); (c) the interplay of globally framed but locally managed practices of mobility, business interests, and security politics (Klauser, Ruegg, and November 2008); and last but not least (d) their concentrated semioticization with spoken and written language, indexical and symbolic signage, advertisements, displays of goods for sale, exhibition/ promotional areas, works of art, that is, the totality of discourses in place (Scollon and Wong Scollon 2003), or semiotic landscapes (Jaworski and Thurlow 2010).

In paying attention to these discourses in place, we reveal airports to be places of mobility not only of people and goods but also of language and discourse. With regard to the theme of this volume more specifically, we hope to have shown how various discursive practices, including multilingual displays, are organized around different spatial norms, or orders of indexicality, how they are shaped by the polycentricity of airports, that is, multiple centres of authority producing different 'social categories, recognisable semiotic emblems for groups and individuals, a more or less coherent semiotic habitat' (Blommaert 2007b: 117). The 'coherent semiotic habitat' of the airport, like any other 'text', displays certain generic qualities that link it to other, similar text types (in this case, the global network of airports) alongside other, site-specific features anchoring each airport in a specific locality (or layered localities). To be sure, and still following Blommaert (ibid.), our wander (or *dérive*—see Debord 1995 [1967]) through Cardiff Airport and Sea-Tac surely confirms how different forms of semiosis are positioned 'as valuable, others as less valuable, and some are not taken into account at all, while all are subject to rules of access and regulations as to circulation'.

Inevitably, given the location of both airports in the United Kingdom and United States, English appears as the dominant or centralized code throughout both sites, following the centring logic and ideology of its position as the main national language of both countries, and reinforced by its role as the world lingua franca and international language of mobility. However, other codes are also present, either competing for symbolic centre-stage, or waiting in the wings for their 'moment' to be noticed, to come into our 'attention structures' (Jones 2010), to be displayed, or centred in a fleeting moment of a passenger passing through a particular area of the airport or engaging in one of the encounters with a member of staff, fellow passenger, sign, or screen. Apart from the centring of Welsh at Cardiff Airport, albeit persistently 'trailing' behind English, languages other than English are *spatialized* mimetically in terms of Wallerstein's world order, the most visible of which in our data fit de Swaan's category of 'super-central' languages: Chinese, French, German, Japanese, Portuguese, Spanish (but not Arabic, Malay, Russian, Swahili, and Turkish), with Italian, Korean (especially at Sea-Tac) a close second, and a smattering of other 'central' languages cropping up less often. However, although these languages are centred in terms of their visibility due to size and frequency of display (e.g. at airline-branded check-in areas, or on symbolic 'welcome' signs), their discourses are somewhat limited and reduced to the most rudimentary operations associated with passengers moving through the airport (e.g. organizing passengers as 'elite' or 'economy' at check-in), allowing passengers to perform basic transactions (e.g. withdrawing money from cash machines), or advertising 'ethnic' restaurants with foreign-sounding names. Together with the ostentatious brand names in retail outlets, all these codes blend into a kind of *Internationalese* (or as suggested above, *Commercialese*), spoken by few, understood by many, often devoid of any specific ethno-national associations.

In an age of intensified language commodification (Heller 2003, 2011), the global semioscape (Thurlow and Aiello 2007) is dominated by a *mélange* of relatively few but powerful genres, images, practices, and codes in a bewildering array of styles and spectacles – especially in places where it is most busily manifested (airports, shopping malls, commercial city centres, theme parks, international sporting events, music festivals, etc.). The primary orientation of the global semioscape is to *form*, hence aestheticization and realization of the poetic function in the sense of Jakobson (1960). And despite being simply a veiled manifestation of *synthetic personalization* (Fairclough 1992), its implied recipients are styled as unique and distinct from one another, and above all from the (marginalized) masses which, ironically, most of them are a part of. On the other hand, and following Sahlin (above), we suggest that people in the multilingual peripheries (Sahlin's border areas) may find more in common with one another (despite their obvious diversity) because peripheries are democratizing, egalitarian, and equalizing.

So it is in the peripheral (literal and figurative) spaces of the airports, their semiotic nooks and crannies, that we find multilingualism at its richest and most diverse, albeit, and other things being equal, lacking in symbolic capital across the board. By definition, the peripheral multilingualism of airports is frequently dormant and hidden from view. All the backstage, hushed, multilingual, and multi-accented conversations of small groups of families, fellow passengers, fellow workers passing through or dwelling at airports, languages waiting to be 'activated' by someone paying attention to them at computerized check-in, on the labels of local souvenirs, in books and magazines, testify to more chaotic and unregulated ethnoscapes.

To conclude, we return to Alexandre Duchêne's account of the otherwise 'invisible' workforce whose multilingual skills may be activated by the airport management in the moment of need (see above). In parallel to Duchêne's own example, at the KLM check-in desk at Cardiff Airport, airline staff have at their disposal two A4 sheets with four routine, security questions printed in thirteen languages, should staff and passengers at check-in be unable to find a common language, mostly English (not a frequent occurrence according to the KLM staff on duty at the time of data collection). In order of appearance, the languages on these somewhat tired, unglamorous printouts (see Figures 9.42a and 9.42b) are: ENGLISH, ČESKY/CZECH, DANSKE/DANISH, DEUTSCH/GERMAN, ΕΛΛΗΙΚΑ/ GREEK, ESPAÑOL/SPANISH, FRANÇAIS/FRENCH, ITALIANO/ITALIAN, NEDERLANDS/DUTCH, NORSK/NORWEGIAN, POLSKI/POLISH, PORTUGUÊS/PORTUGUESE, SUOMI/FINNISH, SVENSK/SWEDISH. While this list appears a little arbitrary in view of de Swaan's approximate 150 'central' languages, care has been taken to print their original names complete with appropriate diacritics. And if ever used, the printed questions are not likely to cause any communication breakdown due to the ASCII-dominated, English version of Word that was probably used for typing them up disregarding all the 'necessary' diacritics beyond the language labels. Such is peripheral multilingualism at airports. Not always in full view, not always 'perfect', and certainly not spectacular; rather humdrum but unexpectedly diverse and fully functional when needed.

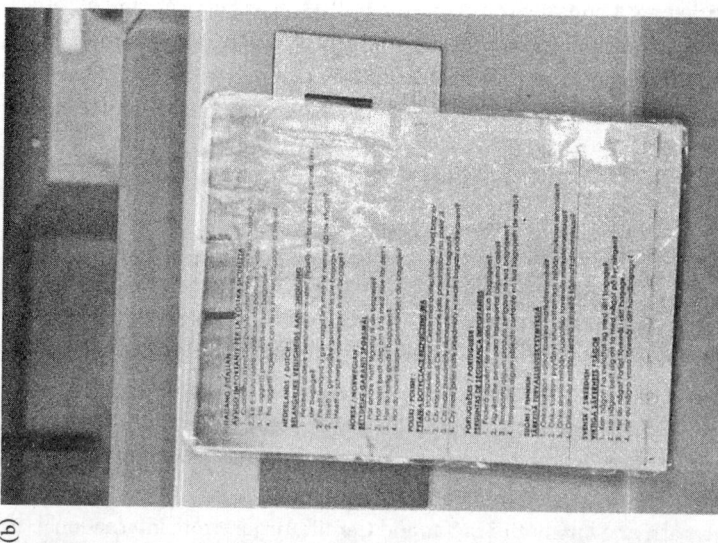

(a)

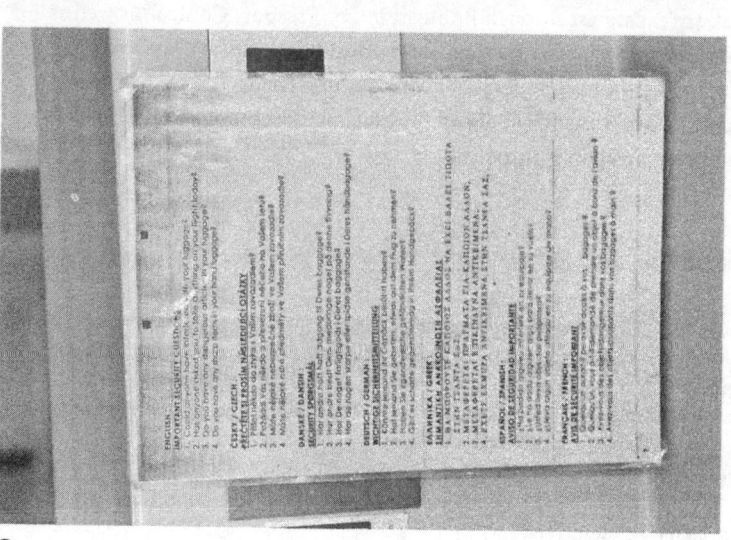

(b)

Figure 9.42a and b:
Sheet 1 of multilingual security questions at KLM check-in desk, Cardiff Airport; Sheet 2 of multilingual security questions at KLM check-in desk, Cardiff Airport

ACKNOWLEDGEMENTS

We gratefully acknowledge help and assistance with our fieldwork from both sites. Crispin thanks *Port of Seattle's* Chris Nardine for his support. Adam thanks Steve Hodgetts, Business Development and Commercial Director, Cassie Houghton, Head of Marketing, Lynne Bolton, Director of Passenger Services, and all other staff at Cardiff Airport for generously allowing access to and guidance through all areas of the airport. We also thank Sari Pietikäinen and Helen Kelly-Holmes for useful comments on the penultimate draft of this chapter. The usual caveats apply.

NOTES

1. Creswell (2006) maintains Dutch was abandoned completely on Schipol's signage. Mijksenaar, the design company responsible for Schipol's signage, in fact removed it only in the liminal airside (or runway side) spaces where passengers are either flying away from the Netherlands or have just disembarked and are heading towards the point of official entry into the country. (See http://www.mijksenaar.com/upload/pressitems/Amsterdam_Airport_Schiphol.pdf.)
2. Passengers arriving into both Sea-Tac and Cardiff Airport from international destinations must pass through Immigration or Passport Control, as well as Customs; departing passengers, however, must just clear security screening while 'passport control' is handled by the airlines' check-in agents who are, therefore, also 'check-out' agents of the State. In this sense, national borders are visibly materialized only on arrival.

REFERENCES

Adey, Peter. 2008. Mobilities and modulations: The airport as a difference machine. In *Politics at the airport*, ed. Mark B. Salter, 145–160. Minneapolis: University of Minnesota Press.

Aiello, Giorgia, and Crispin Thurlow. 2006. Symbolic capitals: Visual discourse and intercultural exchange in the European Capital of Culture scheme. *Language and Intercultural Communication* 6: 148–162.

Althusser, Lois. 1971. *Lenin and philosophy.* New York: Monthly Review Press.

Anderson, Benedict. 1983. *Imagined communities: Reflections on the origin and spread of nationalism.* London: Verso.

Augé, Marc. 1995. *Non-places: Introduction to an anthropology of supermodernity.* Trans. John Howe. London: Verso.

Beck, Ulrich. 2006. *The cosmopolitan vision.* Cambridge: Polity.

Billig, Michael. 1995. *Banal nationalism.* London: Sage.

Blommaert, Jan. 2005. *Discourse: A critical introduction.* Cambridge: Cambridge University Press.

Blommaert, Jan. 2007a. Sociolinguistic scales. *Intercultural Pragmatics* 4: 1–19.

Blommaert, Jan. 2007b. Sociolinguistics and discourse analysis: Orders of indexicality and polycentricity. *Journal of Multicultural Discourses* 2: 115–130.

Blommaert, Jan, and Dong Jie. 2010. Language and movement in space. In *The handbook of language and globalization*, ed. Nikolas Coupland, 366–385. Oxford: Wiley-Blackwell.

Boorstin, Daniel. 1964. *The image: A guide to pseudo-events in America.* New York: Harper & Row.

De Botton, Alan. 2009. *A week at the airport: A Heathrow diary.* London: Profile Books.

Budach, Gabriele, Claudine Moïse, Alexandre Duchêne, and Mary Richards. 2007. Bison, feuille d'érable et fleur de lys au Canada: Les Stéréotypes existent-ils toujours? In *Stéréotypage, stéréotypes, fonctionnements ordinaires et mises en scène*, ed. Henri Boyer, 29–45. Paris: l'Harmattan.

Burke, Peter. 1992. *History and social theory.* Cambridge: Polity.

Butler, Judith. 1990. *Gender trouble: Feminism and the subversion of identity.* London: Routledge.

Cardiff Airport. 2009/2010. Cardiff Airport Welsh language policy 2009/2010. Unpublished document: Cardiff Airport.

Clifford, James. 1997. *Routes: Travel and translation in the late twentieth century.* Cambridge, Mass.: Harvard University Press.

Coupland, Justine, ed. 2010. *Small talk.* London: Longman.

Coupland, Nikolas. 2010. Welsh linguistic landscapes 'from above' and 'from below'. In *Semiotic landscapes: Language, image, space*, ed. Adam Jaworski and Crispin Thurlow, 77–101. London: Continuum.

Coupland, Nikolas, and Adam Jaworski. 2004. Sociolinguistic perspectives on metalanguage: Reflexivity, evaluation and ideology. In *Metalanguage: Social and ideological perspectives*, ed. Adam Jaworski, Nikolas Coupland, and Dariusz Galasiński, 15–51. Berlin: Mouton de Gruyter.

Crang, Mike. 2002. Between places: Producing hubs, flows, and networks. *Environment and Planning A* 34: 569–574.

Cresswell, Tim. 2006. *On the move: Mobility in the modern Western world.* London: Routledge.

Cwerner, Saulo, Sven Kesselring, and John Urry, eds. 2009. *Aeromobilities.* London: Routledge.

Debord, Guy. 1995 [1967]. *The society of spectacle.* Trans. Donald Nicholson-Smith. New York: Zone Books.

Duchêne, Alexandre. 2011. Néolibéralisme, inégalités sociales et plurilinguisme: L'Exploitation des ressources langagiéres et des locuteur. *Langage et société* 136: 81–106.

Duchêne, Alexandre, and Monica Heller. 2012a. Language policy in the workplace. In *The Cambridge handbook on language policy*, ed. Bernard Spolsky, 323–334. Cambridge: Cambridge University Press.

Duchêne, Alexandre, and Monica Heller, eds. 2012b. *Language in late capitalism: Pride and profit.* New York: Routledge.

Eastman, Carol M., and Roberta F. Stein. 1993. Language display: Authenticating claims to social identity. *Journal of Multilingual and Multicultural Development* 14: 187–202.

Edwards, Brian. 2005. *The modern airport terminal: New approaches to airport architecture.* London: Taylor & Francis.

Eggebeen, Janna. 2011. Between two worlds: Robert Smithson and aerial art. *Public Art Dialogue* 1: 87–111.

Emmison, Michael, and Philip Smith. 2000. *Researching the visual.* London: Sage.

Fairclough, Norman. 1992. *Discourse and social change.* Cambridge: Polity.

Flowerdew, John. 2004. The discursive construction of a world-class city. *Discourse & Society* 15: 579–605.

Foster, Hal. 1988. Preface. In *Vision and visuality*, ed. Hal Foster, ix–xiv. Seattle, Wash.: Bay Press.

Goffman, Erving. 1959. *The presentation of self in everyday life.* Harmondsworth, Middlesex: Penguin Books.

Hall, Stuart. 1997. The local and the global: Globalization and ethnicity. In *Culture, globalization and the world-system: Contemporary conditions for the representation of identity,* ed. Anthony D. King, 20–39. Minneapolis: University of Minnesota Press.

Heller, Monica. 2003. Globalization, the new economy and the commodification of language and identity. *Journal of Sociolinguistics* 7: 473–492.

Heller, Monica. 2007. Bilingualism as ideology and practice. In *Bilingualism: A social approach,* ed. Monica Heller, 1–22. Basingstoke: Palgrave Macmillan.

Heller, Monica. 2011. *Paths to post-nationalism: A critical ethnography of language and identity.* New York: Oxford University Press.

Hoey, Michael. 2001. *Textual interaction.* London: Routledge.

Jakobson, Roman. 1960. Closing statement: Linguistics and poetics. In *Style in language,* ed. Thomas Sebeok, 350–377. Cambridge, Mass.: MIT Press.

Jaworski, Adam. 2009. Greetings in tourist–host encounters. In *The new sociolinguistics reader,* ed. Nikolas Coupland and Adam Jaworski, 662–679. Basingstoke: Palgrave Macmillan.

Jaworski, Adam, and Crispin Thurlow. 2010. Introducing semiotic landscapes. In *Semiotic landscapes: Language, image, space,* ed. Adam Jaworski and Crispin Thurlow, 1–40. London: Continuum.

Jaworski, Adam, and Ingrid Piller. 2008. Linguascaping Switzerland: Language ideologies in tourism. In *Standards and norms in the English language,* ed. Miriam A. Locher and Jürg Strässler, 301–321. Berlin: Mouton de Gruyter.

Jaworski, Adam, Virpi Ylänne-McEwen, Crispin Thurlow, and Sarah Lawson. 2003. Social roles and negotiation of status in host–tourist interaction: A view from British TV holiday programmes. *Journal of Sociolinguistics* 7: 135–163.

Jensen, Ole B. 2007. Culture stories: Understanding cultural urban branding. *Planning Theory* 6: 211–236.

Jones, Rodney H. 2010. Cyberspace and physical space: Attention structures in computer mediated communication. In *Semiotic landscapes: Text, image, space,* ed. Adam Jaworski and Crispin Thurlow, 151–167. London: Continuum.

Kelly-Holmes, Helen. 2005. *Advertising as multilingual communication.* Basingstoke: Palgrave Macmillan.

Klauser, Francisco R., Jean Ruegg, and Valérie November. 2008. Airport surveillance between public and private interests: CCTV at Geneva International Airport. In *Politics at the Airport,* ed. Mark B. Salter, 105–126. Minneapolis: University of Minnesota Press.

Kress, Gunther, and Theo Van Leeuwen. 2001. *Multimodal discourse: The modes and media of contemporary communication.* London: Arnold.

Kroskrity, Paul V. 2004. Language ideologies. In *A companion to linguistic anthropology,* ed. Alessandro Duranti, 496–517. Oxford: Blackwell Publishing.

Lefebvre, Henri. 1991. *The production of space.* Trans. Donald Nicholson-Smith. Oxford: Blackwell Publishing.

MacCannell, Dean. 1989. *The tourist: A new theory of the leisure class.* Berkeley: University of California Press.

McCall, Christopher. 2003. Language dynamics in the bi- and multilingual workplace. In *Language socialization in bilingual and multilingual societies,* ed. Robert Bayley and Sandra R. Schecter, 235–250. Bristol: Multilingual Matters.

Morgan, Nigel, and Annette Pritchard. 2005. Security and social 'sorting': Traversing the surveillance-tourism dialectic. *Tourist Studies* 5: 115–132.

Pascoe, David. 2001. *Airspaces.* London: Reaktion.

Pavlenko, Aneta. 2010. Linguistic landscape of Kyiv, Ukraine: A diachronic study. In *Linguistic landscape in the city*, ed. Elana Shohamy, Eliezer Ben-Rafael, and Monica Barni, 133–151. Bristol: Multilingual Matters.

Pearman, High. 2004. *Airports: A century of architecture*. London: Laurence King Publishing.

Pietikäinen, Sari. 2010. Sámi language mobility: Scales and discourses of multilingualism in a polycentric environment. *International Journal of the Sociology of Language* 202: 79–102.

Pietikäinen, Sari, and Helen Kelly-Holmes. 2011. The local political economy of languages in a Sámi tourism destination: Authenticity and mobility in the labelling of souvenirs. *Journal of Sociolinguistics* 15: 323–346.

Piller, Ingrid. 2001. Identity constructions in multilingual advertising. *Language in Society* 30: 153–186.

Pujolar, Joan. 2006. *Language, culture and tourism: Perspectives in Barcelona and Catalonia*. Barcelona: Turisme de Barcelona.

Rampton, Ben. 1995. *Crossing: Language and ethnicity among adolescents*. London: Longman.

Rampton, Ben. 2009. Speech community and beyond. In *The new sociolinguistics reader*, ed. Nikolas Coupland and Adam Jaworski, 694–713. Basingstoke: Palgrave Macmillan.

Reh, Mechthild. 2004. Multilingual writing: A reader-oriented typology—with examples from Lira Municipality (Uganda). *International Journal of the Sociology of Language* 170: 1–41.

Roberts, Celia. 2010. Language socialization in the workplace. *Annual Review of Applied Linguistics* 30: 211–227.

Robertson, Roland. 1995. Glocalization: Time–space and homogeneity–heterogeneity. In *Global modernities*, ed. Mike Featherstone, Scott Lash, and Roland Robertson, 25–44. London: Sage.

Rose, Gillian. 2001. *Visual methodologies*. London: Sage.

Sahlins, Peter. 1989. *Boundaries: The making of France and Spain in the Pyrenees*. Berkeley: University of California Press.

Sassen, Saskia. 1991. *The global city: New York, London, Tokyo*. Princeton: Princeton University Press.

Sassen, Saskia. 1996. Identity in the global city: Economic and cultural encasements. In *The geography of identity*, ed. Patricia Yaeger, 131–151. Ann Arbor: University of Michigan Press.

Schivelbusch Wolfgang. 1986. *The railway journey: Trains and travel in the nineteenth century*. Trans. Anselm Hollo. Oxford: Blackwell.

Scollon, Ron, and Suzie Wong Scollon. 2003. *Discourses in place: Language in the material world*. London: Routledge.

Sharma, Sarah. 2009. Baring life and lifestyle in the non-place. *Cultural Studies* 23: 129–148.

Sheller, Mimi, and John Urry. 2006. The new mobilities paradigm. *Environment and Planning A* 38: 207–226.

Shils, Edward. 1975. *Center and periphery*. Chicago: University of Chicago Press.

Shohamy, Elana, Eliezer Ben-Rafael, and Monica Barni, eds. 2010. *Linguistic landscape in the city*. Bristol: Multilingual Matters.

Shohamy, Elana, and Durk Gorter, eds. 2009. *Linguistic landscape: Expanding the scenery*. New York: Routledge.

Silverstein, Michael. 1998. Contemporary transformations of local linguistic communities. *Annual Review of Anthropology* 27: 401–426.

Silverstein, Michael. 2003. Indexical order and the dialectics of sociolinguistic life. *Language and Communication* 23: 193–229.

Soja, Edward. 1989. *Postmodern geographies: The reassertion of space in critical social theory.* London: Verso.

Sommer, Robert. 1974. *Tight spaces: Hard architecture and how to humanize it.* Prentice-Hall.

Sparke, Matthew. 2006. A neoliberal nexus: Citizenship, security and the future of the border. *Political Geography* 25: 151–180.

De Swaan, Abram. 2001. *Words of the world.* Cambridge: Polity Press.

Szerszynski, Bronislaw, and John Urry. 2002. Cultures of cosmopolitanism. *Sociological Review* 50: 461–481.

Szerszynski, Bronislaw, and John Urry. 2006. Visuality, mobility and the cosmopolitan: Inhabiting the world from afar. *The British Journal of Sociology* 57: 113–131.

Thurlow, Crispin, and Adam Jaworski. 2003. Communicating a global reach: Inflight magazines as a globalizing genre in tourism. *Journal of Sociolinguistics* 7: 579–606.

Thurlow, Crispin, and Adam Jaworski. 2006. The alchemy of the upwardly mobile: Symbolic capital and the stylization of elites in frequent-flyer programs. *Discourse & Society* 17: 131–167.

Thurlow, Crispin, and Adam Jaworski. 2010a. *Tourism discourse: The language of global mobility.* Basingstoke: Palgrave Macmillan.

Thurlow, Crispin, and Adam Jaworski. 2010b. Silence is golden: Elitism, linguascaping and 'anti-communication' in luxury tourism discourse. In *Semiotic landscapes: Language, image, space,* ed. Adam Jaworski and Crispin Thurlow, 187–218. London: Continuum.

Thurlow, Crispin, and Adam Jaworski. 2011. Banal globalization? Embodied actions and mediated practices in tourists' online photo-sharing. In *Digital discourse: Language in the new media,* ed. Crispin Thurlow and Kristine Mroczek, 220–250. New York: Oxford University Press.

Thurlow, Crispin, and Adam Jaworski. 2012. Elite mobilities: The semiotic landscapes of luxury and privilege. *Social Semiotics* 22 (5).

Thurlow, Crispin, and Giorgia Aiello. 2007. National pride, global capital: A social semiotic analysis of transnational visual branding in the airline industry. *Visual Communication* 6: 305–344.

Tufi, Stefania, and Robert Blackwood. 2010. Trademarks in the linguistic landscape: methodological and theoretical challenges in qualifying brand names in the public space. *International Journal of Multilingualism* 7: 197–210.

Urry, John. 2000. *Sociology beyond Societies: Mobilities for the Twenty-First Century.* London: Routledge.

Van Leeuwen, Theo. 2005. Multimodality, genre and design. In *Discourse in action: Introducing mediated discourse analysis,* ed. Sigrid Norris and Rodney H. Jones, 73–93. London: Routledge.

Wallerstein, Immanuel. 1974. *The modern world-system: Capitalist agriculture and the origins of the European world-economy in the sixteenth century.* New York: Academic Press.

Wood, Andrew. 2003. A rhetoric of ubiquity: Terminal space as omnitopia. *Communication Theory* 13: 324–344.

Woolard, Kathryn, and Bambi B. Schieffelin. 1994. Language ideology. *Annual Review of Anthropology* 23: 55–82.

CHAPTER 10

The Career of a Diacritical Sign

Language in Spatial Representations and

Representational Spaces

BRIGITTA BUSCH

INTRODUCTION: LANGUAGE AND SPACE

The notion of peripheral multilingualism establishes a relation between language and space or rather between language practices and spatial practices. In social sciences and cultural studies there has over the past decades been an increasing interest in concepts of space and spatiality. Scholars contributing to this spatial turn—such as Edward Soja (1996), Doreen Massey (2005), and Edward Said (1993)—primarily refer to the work of the French philosopher, sociologist and geographer Henri Lefebvre (1991) whose work dismisses the understanding of space as a container.

The spatial turn in the social sciences has also influenced recent work in applied linguistics, allowing interrelations between language and space to be explored from different perspectives. In the field of dialectology and linguistic geography, Viaut (2004) questions and deconstructs the notion of linguistic border referring to research in social geography. He views linguistic borders as a product of social positioning and of sharing representations of space, which results in the construction of territoriality. Drawing on semiotic theory and multimodal discourse analysis, Scollon and Scollon (2003) explore how language is materially placed in the world. They introduce the concept of geosemiotics to grasp the social meaning and indexicality of the placement of signs and discourses in the material world. Analysing language as a local practice, Pennycook (2010: 1) questions the notion of language as a pre-given system. Language, as he stresses, does not only 'happen' in particular spaces and at particular times, but contributes to organizing space and giving meaning to it. Therefore, language practices should be understood as the result of speakers' interpretation of a particular place and at the same time as reinforcing the specific reading of that place. Pennycook (2010) and Jaworski and Thurlow (2010) refer to Lefebvre's theories of spatiality to understand language practices as spatial practices. In the proliferating literature on empirical studies of linguistic landscapes (e.g. Shohamy and Gorter 2009; Jaworski and Thurlow 2010), very different approaches to space can be discerned, a common theoretical grounding—as Jaworski and Thurlow (2010: 14) deplore—is still missing.

Lefebvre (1991) defines space as a social product and underlines that every society produces its own specific space. For an analysis of the production of space (spacialization) he develops a conceptual triad which encompasses the following dimensions (1991: 33):

(1) *Spatial practice* 'embraces production and reproduction, and the particular locations and spatial sets characteristic of each social formation'. These everyday practices of appropriation of space ensure continuity and to some extent social cohesion.
(2) *Representations of space* meaning conceptualized space; discourses on space by scientists, planners, social engineers; expert knowledge—'i.e. a mixture of understanding (*conaissance*) and ideology' (1991: 41)—which conceives of space.
(3) *Representational spaces*, space lived directly through its associated images and symbols which have their source in history. It is the 'dominated—and hence passively experienced—space which the imagination seeks to change and appropriate. It overlays physical space, making symbolic use of its objects.' (1991: 39). It embodies 'complex symbolisms, sometimes coded, sometimes not, linked to the clandestine or underground side of social life' (1991: 31).

Lefebvre's concept of the social production of space defines space as perceived (*perçu*) through spatial practices, conceived through representations and theories of space (*conçu*) and lived (*vécu*) as representational spaces. These three dimensions of the social production of space do not exist independently but are dialectically interlinked. Lefebvre (1991: 132) also dedicates a chapter to the relationship between language and space in which he applies the spatial triad to language and discourse: 'Every language is located in space. Every discourse says something about a space (places or sets of places); and every discourse is emitted from a space. Distinctions must be drawn between discourse *in* space, discourse *about* space and the discourse *of* space.'

The bipolarity of centrality and peripherality which is already addressed by Lefebvre (1991) in relation to the nation-state is developed further especially by scholars in post-colonial studies who criticize the centre–periphery dichotomy as a Eurocentric concept of domination (Soja 1996). For the purpose of our concern in this volume, namely exploring the notion of peripheral multilingualism, I will rely on Lefebvre's spatial triad to approach the notion of peripherality: peripherality as produced by 'central' social practices (e.g. economic marginalization of regions and population); peripherality as a concept in spatial representations (e.g. as linked to state borders which separate the inside and the outside); peripherality as lived experience of being marginalized and excluded (e.g. as the speaker of a language other than the state language).

Investigating peripheral multilingualism from a perspective of space as a social production is more than just describing and analysing new linguistic practices in regions marginalized with respect to being far away urban centres. Focusing on questions of how peripherality was (and is) produced and how the centre–periphery binary can be displaced, this approach challenges the more static notions of linguistic practices conceived as practices tied to a specific territory. Taking the Austrian region of Southern Carinthia as an example— the homeland of a linguistic minority in a region commonly defined as borderland, rural, and structurally weak—I will examine how the seemingly static relationship between language and territory is being dislocated. Addressing the relationship between language and space I will try to apply Lefebvre's multidimensional approach in considering different aspects: spatial practices (e.g. of nation-state building) that correlate with specific language policies (e.g. of assimilation), discourse about language and space (e.g. translated into linguistic maps that draw clear-cut language boundaries), and representational spaces (e.g. interventions in the public space). The main focus will be on the third aspect, namely on the question of how changes on the economic and political macro level are translated on a micro level into linguistic manifestations in the representational space. In particular I will examine how two forms of irony, a contesting and a postmodern variant, challenge the traditional bipolar and asymmetrical language regime and give expression to growing linguistic diversification.

In the first part of this contribution, I will briefly sketch how the drawing of the national border and the resulting ethnolinguistic polarization have inscribed into the representational space the binary logics of centre–periphery and majority–minority. The second part focuses on a creative subversive intervention in public space—the addition of Slavic diacritic signs in German inscriptions—and discusses this popular campaign in the context of changing language regimes and changing connotations of the state border. The third part outlines a series of events organized by artistic and commercial actors, which takes up and comments on the fluidity of translanguaging practices under the conditions of super-diversity (Vertovec 2007).

LANGUAGE AND TERRITORY

Every social formation and every epoch produces its own idea of space; space itself has a history in Western experience (Foucault 1984). Retracing this history reveals the genesis of present conceptions of space and traces of the past in the contemporary.[1] Almost until the end of the twentieth century the drawing of the state border in 1920 has been formative for the spatial arrangement in the region of Carinthia.

After the collapse of the multi-ethnic and multilingual Hapsburg Empire, Austria was constituted as a nation-state. The programmatic orientation towards ethnic and linguistic homogeneity was initially present in the official denomination of the state as 'Deutschösterreich' (German-Austria). The new state established on the other side of the border was also defined in terms of ethnicity as the Kingdom of Serbs, Croats, and Slovenes. Within the Austrian nation-state, Carinthia was marginalized politically as a contested buffer zone, economically as a cul-de-sac far away from the industrial centres, and geographically as a zone of liminality between the 'civilized world' of settled lands and the uninhabitable mountain environment. Right from its inception, the border was reified as a 'natural' line separating the inside from the outside and loaded with mythical connotations. That which lies on the other side of the border became the construct of the fundamental, irreconcilable 'other'. What is left in the dark on the other side can thus act as a screen for the projection of fantasies, for the threatening and also the exotic and the desirable. From a Eurocentric perspective, this was, on the one hand, the 'dark continent' open for discovery and colonization, and, on the other hand, the East and the Balkans (Todorova 1999). In Carinthia the topos of the stronghold, first against the Slavic Balkans and later against the communist 'threat', dominated ideas of space. The drawing of the Austrian border had a strong impact on the daily lives of the population in the area by cutting through existing family connections and economic relations. It also altered the previous language regime in conferring on the speakers of Slovene the status of a linguistic and ethnic minority. It thereby accentuated already existing linguistic polarizations which were based on an urban-rural divide, urban centres and sub-centres being associated with the German language while the surrounding rural areas became associated with Slovene. Within the nation-state framework the linguistic minority is singled out as disturbing the imagined homogeneity. On the Carinthian side, the idea of matching the 'natural' political boundary with the linguistic one by means of forcing a process of assimilation to the German language has been a political constant over the years. On the Slovenian side the fantasy of uniting the divided nation, if not in one single state then at least culturally, has been equally cherished. In this constellation the minority in Carinthia has constantly been under suspicion of equivocation and potential disloyalty. During the Nazi regime, the use of Slovene in public was prohibited and from 1941 onwards speakers of Slovene were deported on a massive scale, with acts of resistance entailing brutal persecution.

The spatial logic that dominated the twentieth century resulted in binary oppositions between inside and outside, between centre and periphery, between majority and minority. Similarly a binary opposition between German and Slovene was constructed through language ideologies, that is, 'beliefs, feelings, and conceptions about language structure and use which often index the political economic interests of individual speakers, ethnic and other interest groups and nation-states' (Kroskrity 2005: 1). The area was not seen as a zone of language contact and transition but imagined as a language border with a clear-cut line dividing two distinct and incompatible 'language families' with their respective normative centres that watch over linguistic correctness and purity. The drawing of external boundaries separating one language from another and of internal boundaries defining the legitimate speakers of the language were argued with linguistic differences deriving from the languages' inherent laws. Gal (2001: 31–33) describes a similar language ideological process for nineteenth-century Hungary. In Carinthia, the speakers of Slovenian were perceived as being divided into a core group and a marginal group engaged in an assimilation process, whereby language was seen as a marker. Language maintenance and the Slovene standard language were linked to ethno-political consciousness whereas dialects with heavy borrowings from German counted as a sign for the willingness to assimilate. In the late 1980s the sociolinguistic situation was described as unstable bilingualism, characterized by increasing language shift from a recessive minority language to the dominant majority language and by a diglossic situation with a strict separation in function between Slovene, as a merely spoken domestic and intimate language, and German, as language of public and written communication (Österreichische Rektorenkonferenz 1989: 89-90). This constructed dichotomy between the minority and the majority language remained firmly rooted in the monolingual paradigm, in which the idea of having one single language is considered as norm. This homogenizing idea is a European 'invention' intimately linked to processes of nation-state building (Busch 2004; Makoni and Pennycook 2006).

Visible Polarizations in the Representational Space

The representational space is also structured according to the logic of binary oppositions which leave visible and invisible marks and traces. As in other peripheral border zones, there is also in Carinthia a large number of landmarks and memorial sights commemorating the history and myths of the disputed border area, the victims and the heroes of the battles. In the 1970s and 1980s several of these sites were the targets of vandalism and even bomb attacks. Particular locations still serve as stages for annual commemoration ceremonies, marches in traditional costumes, cultural events that keep the myths alive. However, in Carinthia one of the main disputes concerning language in space is about topographic signs. It was not until 2011 that a compromise was reached on this issue which has been at the top of the regional political agenda for decades. In the State Treaty of 1955, Austria entered into commitments concerning the rights of the Slovene-speaking minority in Carinthia, and among these was the obligation to set up bilingual topographic signs in the bilingual area. After protests by the Slovene-speaking minority and the Yugoslav State, the Austrian government finally decided to fulfil the obligations in 1972. The reaction from German-speaking nationalistic circles in Carinthia was immediate and thoroughly organized. In what came to be known as the Ortstafelsturm (assault on topographic signs), overnight the bilingual road signs that had been erected on the previous day were destroyed. Parts of Carinthia remained without any topographic indications for a decade, as the authorities declined to confront German-speaking nationalistic circles about the issue. A later law allowing only for very few bilingual signs was constantly criticized by minority representatives and finally suspended by the Supreme Court in 2002. In the following years a postmodern restaging of the old myth of the threatened *Heimat* by the right-wing Populist Party under Jörg Haider served to prevent a political solution.

What is at the core of the issue around the topographic signs is first of all the power of naming and renaming. Germanizing Slovene homonyms and toponyms has a long history in Carinthia. The Nazi regime first decreed and enacted the erasure of all signs in Slovene in the public space and then denied the Slovene-speaking population the right to live in this space. A master plan aimed at what is euphemistically called ethnic cleansing—replacing the deported Slovene-speaking population by resettling German-speaking families from Northern Italy—only came to a halt because of armed resistance in the area. The violent iconoclastic assault on the topographic signs in 1972 revived these traumatic experiences of violence and erasure (Kert-Wakounig 2010). The act of renaming is in itself an act of violence and imposing power. It is a symbolic act but also a performative one. In the case of toponyms, renaming can function as a landmark and support claims to a territory. In the Carinthian debate two strands of policy discourse can be discerned. From the nationally oriented German-speaking side, it was argued that Slovene toponyms could encourage the neighbouring state to uphold territorial claims. This argument is based on a concept of space that maintains the equation of language, territory, and nation. The concept of space that guides the argument of the Slovene organizations in Carinthia is different in so far as it is not based on an assumption of exclusive ownership. The argument is that bilingual signs mark a space which not only allows for the recognition of linguistic difference but also guarantees full participation in social, cultural, and economic life by respecting this 'otherness'. In Carinthia as in most European regions with officially recognized minority languages, linguistic rights are primarily framed as territorial rights. This spirit is also visible in the European Charter for Regional and Minority Languages,[2] which defines these languages in Article 1 explicitly as 'traditionally used within a given territory of a State'. In Carinthia the territorial definition of linguistic rights resulted in a complicated mosaic of laws and regulations which makes it difficult to know actually where and when Slovene can be spoken. The rights to bilingual education, to bilingual topographic signs, to the use of Slovene in administrative procedures, to the use of Slovene in court procedures are all linked in a different way to the territory of particular municipalities. There are only a few municipalities in which the whole spectrum of linguistic rights can be enjoyed by Slovene speakers. These incoherent zones with more and with less linguistic rights form a complex pattern which is part of the lived representational space.

The following two sections will deal with the process of dislocation of the inter-linked binary logics of centre–periphery, majority–minority, and German-speaking/ Slovene-speaking and of the reconfiguration of the articulation between language and space. I will explore these processes by doing a close reading of two interventions in public space which in different ways ironically comment on and transform linguistic hierarchies and practices in the representational space. Both interventions were initiated by the cultural centre UNIKUM[3] located at the University of Klagenfurt. This bilingual initiative was founded in 1986 and has since then, in cooperation with artists, organized cultural events which focus on the Austro-Slovene-Italian border area. UNIKUM is known for its conceptual art projects that comment in a critical and often satirical manner on the political situation in Carinthia. Right from the beginning UNIKUM has adopted a policy of multilingualism and has often made the unequal relationship between the regional languages a topic of its projects.

One of UNIKUM's most popular projects was the production and distribution of a set of stickers with the title 'Haček (k)lebt!—Haček živi!: Aktion zur Ergänzung von einsprachigen Ortstafeln' (Haček is alive (and sticks)!)—campaign for enhancing monolingual topographical signs) which was launched in 2002 when the debate on the bilingual topographical signs was once again high on the political agenda. Already, within a few days, stickers originating from the UNIKUM sheet (see Figure 10.1) could be seen throughout Carinthia. The art project triggered a passionate discussion in the media and the regional authorities announced that the use of the stickers in public spaces would be severely sanctioned. Nevertheless, haček stickers were placed on all kinds of public inscriptions: Figure 10.2 shows one on a topographic sign, Figure 10.3 on the door plate indicating the office of the nationalistically oriented Kärntner Heimatdienst. The success of the sticker campaign was to a large extent due to its playful character which employs strategies of irony to undermine the hegemony of monolingual German signs in the Carinthian public space. This strategy becomes apparent in several instances.

The term haček used in the title of the sticker sheet is already a deliberate choice and demonstrates a translanguaging strategy. The term translanguaging (e.g. Garcia 2009; Creese and Blackledge 2010; Li 2011) refers to a growing corpus of empirical studies which have focused attention on linguistic practices—especially among young people in urban spaces—that have also been designated by terms such as language crossing (Rampton 1995), polylingual languaging (Jørgensen 2008), and metrolingualism (Otsuji and Pennycook 2010). These studies emphasize the creative, playful, and subversive use of heterogeneous communicative resources to create meaning.

Such translanguaging practices can be identified in the way in which the term haček is employed by the initiators of the campaign. Haček stands for a diacritic sign, an inverted circumflex, which indicates when placed in the Slovene language

Figure 10.1:
The UNIKUM sheet with haček-stickers in different sizes. UNIKUM, Klagenfurt/Celovec

over the letters c, s, z the palatalized phonemes č, š, ž pronounced as [tʃ], [ʃ], [ʒ]. *Haček* is derived from *háček*, meaning in Czech 'small hook'. Whereas in Slovene this diacritic sign is called *strešica* (little roof) and not *haček*, the term is current in German—often written in the Germanized spelling '*Hatschek*'. In Austria the *haček* is seen as emblematic for Slavic languages, in Carinthia particularly for the Slovene language. In language ideological discourse it is linked to sounds that are qualified as difficult to pronounce for German speakers, as 'tongue twisting' or as 'harsh and ugly'. Although the etymology of the term '*Tschusch*' (*čuš*) is not entirely clear it does not seem to be a coincidence that there is a clustering of palatalized consonants in this ethnic slur, which is in colloquial Austrian German used as a pejorative expression for foreigners, especially of Slavic origin, in Carinthia also for Slovene-speaking persons (Priestly 1996). Although the diacritic sign which is discussed here is only part of a grapheme in the Slovene language and thus has no meaning by itself separated from the letter above which it is placed, it becomes within the Carinthian political context nevertheless an ideologically loaded sign in which different meanings and connotations intersect. Vološinov (1973: 20) speaks of the multi-accentuality of the sign, and observes the presence of conflicts

Die Haček-Maler gehen um

Immer mehr Ortstafeln und Hinweisschilder beschmiert. Exekutive und Land warnen: Das ist Sachbeschädigung! Hohe Strafen drohen.

Teurer Spaß. Eine neue Tafel kostet bis zu 800 Euro   KOSCHER

■ VON GEORG LUX

Klagenfurt, Bürgerservice, Freiheitliche: In Kärnten sind seit Wochen unbekannte Haček-Maler unterwegs. Dutzende Schilder – zuletzt eine Klagenfurter Ortstafel und das Türschild eines Villacher FPÖ-Büros – wurden beschmiert. Jetzt warnen die Exekutive und das Land (als größter Verkehrszeicheneigentümer) die Täter: Was wie ein harmloser Lausbubenstreich aussieht, ist juristisch keiner. Sondern, wie die Haček-Maler schreiben würden, Sachbeschädigung und damit strafbar!

Wer eine Ortstafel beschmiert, steht überhaupt gleich mit beiden Beinen im Kriminal. Denn zur Sachbeschädigung kommt dabei ein Verstoß gegen die Straßenverkehrsordnung, wie der Villacher Polizeijurist Arnulf Komposch erklärt. „Eine Ortstafel ist ein Verkehrszeichen und ein solches darf

> **W**enn ein Täter erwischt wird, muss er für den ganzen Schaden aufkommen.
>
> ALBERT KREINER, LAND KÄRNTEN

laut Gesetz nicht verändert werden." Pardon kennen die Gesetzeshüter keines. „Sollten wir einen Täter erwischen, wird er natürlich angezeigt", sagt Komposch. Und auch beim Land Kärnten hält man Ausschau nach den Haček-Malern, um ihnen saftige Rechnungen zu schicken.

„Bis zu 800 Euro kostet uns die Wiederherstellung einer beschmierten Tafel", so Albert Kreiner, Leiter der Abteilung Infrastruktur beim Land. „Wenn wir herausfinden, wer da am Werk war, fordern wir von den Verantwortlichen, dass sie für den Schaden aufkommen. Das ist derselbe Vorgang wie bei einem Unfalllenker, der ein Verkehrszeichen beschädigt hat." Kreiner glaubt, dass vielen Tätern nicht bewusst ist, wie teuer ihnen ihre Mal-Aktionen kommen können. Denn, so der Landes-Jurist: „Der Vandalismus am Straßenrand nimmt immer mehr zu."

Figure 10.2:
A press cutting showing the haček sign on the topographic sign announcing Klagenfurt, the capital of Carinthia. Kleine Zeitung, Kärntner Ausgabe, 26 April 2002

Figure 10.3:
The haček sign on the door plate of one of the major German national organizations. Photo J. Zerzer

and contradictions in signs that embody competing voices and interests. Removed from its usual Slovene language context and used 'out of place' in a German language context, the diacritic sign picks up yet another *ideological* meaning. It stands for contestation and resistance against the dominant discourse of monolingualism. To quote again Vološinov (1973: 23): 'In actual fact, each ideological sign has two faces, like Janus. Any current curse word can become a word of praise, any current truth must inevitably sound to other people as the greatest lie. This *inner dialectical quality* of the sign comes out fully in the open only in times of social crisis or revolutionary changes.'

The postcard-sized sticker sheet designed by UNIKUM gives in small print on the bottom of the page instructions for use, demonstrating how German words can be defamiliarized and transformed by adding diacritic signs wherever the letters c, s, or z appear:

15 praktišče Štičer (Klebefolie, geštanžt) zur Ergänžung von einšpračhigen Ortštafeln und anderen Aufščhriften in Kärnten

15 čonvenient štickerš (on adhešive foil, perforated) to čomplement monolingual topographičal šignš and other inščriptionš in Čarinthia

In the left-hand lower corner, the sticker sheet displays as 'Anwendungšbeišpiel' (example for uše) a miniature image of the topographic sign at the town exit of 'Maria Saal' modified to 'Maria Šaal'. The display of the modified topographic sign invokes images deeply anchored in the Carinthian 'collective memory'—namely those of monolingual signs being enhanced with Slovene toponyms in the quest for minority rights, as well as those of the so-called *Ortstafelsturm*, the forced removal of bilingual road signs in 1972 (see Figure 10.4).

The municipality of Maria Saal, which is given here as an example, is situated near the Carinthian capital of Klagenfurt. Although today Maria Saal is not considered to be located within the bilingual area, it has a traditional Slovene name, *Gospa sveta* (Our Lady). In German language historiography, as well as in the Slovenian language historiography, Maria Saal/*Gospa sveta* has a special place due to its history reaching back to the Celts and the Romans and due to the medieval ceremony of enthronement of the Karantanian dukes which took place nearby and included an oath of investiture in the Slovene language. In mythified interpretations this location has been constructed as a crucial site or even the cradle of Sloveneness.[4] Such locations, which play a role in nation-founding myths, are often located in peripheral and disputed areas, at the 'frontier' to the 'other'. On Slovenian dialectal maps[5] which depict the linguistic border between the German-speaking and the Slovene-speaking or bilingual territory, up to the middle of the twentieth century the border line runs right through Maria Saal. When UNIKUM started the sticker action, the mayor of Maria Saal immediately responded that bilingual topographic signs were not an issue in his municipality and that in any case there was no Slovene-speaking minority in the town.

Figure 10.4:
A picture taken during the Ortstafelsturm assault on the bilingual topographic signs. Photo H. G.
Trenkwalder

The Writing and Reading of a Diacritic Sign

Taking the example of Maria Saal does not mean a claim for the ownership of space,
but an intervention in space with a transformative character. The *haček*-campaign
points to the absurdity of establishing a reified link between language and territory.
A fine-grained analysis of how the '*haček*-ization' works allows us to understand
how with the means of translanguaging and irony, ethnolinguistic polarization can
be undermined. For the analysis I draw as a first step on Bakhtin's (1986) thoughts
on the sacred word and parody, as a second on Derrida's (1972) concept of deconstruction and thirdly on Pennycook's (2009) understanding of graffiti as a spatial
and linguistic practice.

In the modification from Maria Saal to Maria Šaal shown for example on the
UNIKUM sticker sheet, the *haček* is placed on a topographic sign. The topographic
sign itself has a range of meanings: It displays the official name of a municipality
or locality; it is a symbol of state authority and has a perlocutionary force with
regard to different administrative areas (e.g. traffic regulations). It indicates that
the state authority holds the power of naming and also indicates language policy
regulations. The wording displayed on the topographical sign is what Bakhtin
(1986: 133) defined as an authoritarian or sacred word, that is 'with its indisput-
ability, unconditionality, and unequivocality' removed from dialogue and 'retards
and freezes thought' ignoring 'live experience of life'. The addition of the *haček*

on such an authoritarian word causes an irritation in the eyes of the beholder by slightly displacing the original text and so achieving an alienation effect. It functions as a metalinguistic comment, in Bakhtin's words (1986: 133) as a parodic antibody which challenges and profanes the authoritarian word and brings it back into dialogue.

The addition of the diacritic sign makes a reference to the forgotten, denied, and repressed Slovene language: traces of Slovene are inscribed into the German toponym. The modification from Maria Saal to Maria Šaal creates a chain of signs that can neither be attributed clearly to German or Slovene. By a translanguaging gesture it transgresses the reified 'boundaries' between the two languages and the mutually exclusive constructions of identity. The addition of the *haček* is a displaced and displacing way of writing (Derrida 1972: 36). It can be seen as an act of deconstruction of the binary logic of two monolingualisms. Derrida (1972: 35) conceived the practice of deconstruction as a double gesture, whereby the first step consists of acknowledging that a binary opposition is not a relationship of peaceful coexistence but of hierarchization. The second step or gesture consists of displacing the field in which the opposition originated and in revealing what the binary logic excluded to constitute itself. In our case it points to the impossibility of a closed and 'pure' Germanness, as well as of a closed and 'pure' Sloveneness and to the existence of a marginalized and excluded other. Inscribing the *haček* into the dominant German language refers to the traces of the excluded other that leave 'a phantomatical map "inside" the said monolanguage' (Derrida 1998: 65).

Shortly after the launch of the UNIKUM *haček* campaign, stickers appeared throughout the bilingual area in Carinthia and beyond. The rapidly evolving dynamic is due to the fact that the *haček* by its form lends itself to becoming a powerful symbol. It bears all the characteristics that Chakotin (1971: 190) qualifies as important in the context of political propaganda: it is easily applicable and replicable, has a high recognition value, and when applied it transforms other signs, but is itself difficult to alter or erase. The *haček* inscriptions can be seen in the same way as graffiti: as a subversive act of reappropriation of public space in which hegemonic relations are symbolically inscribed. As Pennycook (2009: 307) stresses, graffiti 'are not only about territory but about different ways of claiming space. They are also transformative in the sense not only that they change the public space but that they reinterpret it.' From one perspective graffiti is viewed as transgressive social behaviour, as little more than vandalism; from another as the creation of a (subcultural) community using language as style (Pennycook 2009: 302). It is not only the result that matters, the presence of the sign in public space, but also the specific location where it is applied and the illicit act of applying it as an *espièglerie* in joking competition with others that 'allows for human agency and sense of play' (Pennycook 2009: 306). The addition of the diacritic sign invites the reader to engage in the language game and pronounce familiar names and words with a new parodic accent. Cunning and mockery are employed as a strategy to question deadlocked polarizations. The '*haček*ization' can be interpreted as an ironic utterance which comprehends both, the 'onlooker's gaze' and her or his distanciation from the latter. Hence, it bears a dialogic character; irony in this case is employed as a subversive strategy of self-empowerment (Böse and Busch 2007).

Moving Beyond Bipolar Logics

In contrast to the linguistic militantism of the 1970s claiming the rights of minority language speakers, the above discussed *haček*-intervention in the public space questions the very logic by which the notions of minority and majority are conceived. It cannot be seen as an isolated action but rather as an action that mirrors and represents a number of geopolitical, economic and social changes that took place from the 1990s onwards and altered the articulation of language and space. On the geopolitical level, with the end of the bipolar world division and the process of European integration, borders became more permeable and changed their connotation. When Slovenia was proclaimed an independent state in 1990, the former Austro-Yugoslav border not only changed in political denomination becoming the Austro-Slovene border but subsequently also in its geopolitical 'supra-determination' (Balibar 1997: 375) and in connotations. It was no more considered as a dividing line between two ideologically different systems and, with Slovenia's accession to the EU in 2004, became an EU-internal border. The new geopolitical situation opened an opportunity for the two peripheral regions which were separated by the border to intensify cooperation and exchange.

Almost immediately after Slovenia's EU accession in 2004, international commercial chains began to regroup parts of Austria and Slovenia to one single marketing region. One of the first was Hofer, a subcompany of the German supermarket retailer Aldi, which began its expansion into the Slovenian market in 2005. In the same year products with bilingual product descriptions and names were put on sale also in the Austrian Hofer stores. In the then current situation in which every bilingual inscription in a public place immediately aroused a heated debate, it is interesting to note that commercial language policies as the one described remained uncommented.[6]

Another change is linked to greater social and demographic mobility. Whereas moving to urban areas in the past usually entailed a language shift from the socially disregarded minority language to the dominant one, today this is not necessarily the case. An educated urban elite has emerged that retains Slovene as a family language, passes it on to the next generation and creates a linguistic environment in which bilingualism can be practised. Interpreting statistical data, demographers attest that the Slovene-speaking population has overcome its traditional disadvantaged status in the sense that its educational level has become higher than that of the monolingual segment of the Carinthian population (Reiterer 1996: 150). The growing importance of Klagenfurt as a regional centre where Slovene is also present in the local cultural and economic life has given rise to an urban vernacular, derived from the standard language and encompassing elements from different local dialects (Schellander 1988), as well as to a specific regional variety of standard Slovene (Busch 2010).

These developments contributed to an increase in the prestige and functionality of Slovene in Carinthia. This is for instance visible in the rising number of students in bilingual education: the enrolment quota for dual medium Slovene-German education in elementary school rose from the all-time low of 13.5 per cent (1976/77) to 44 per cent for the school year of 2010/11.[7] While in the 1970s, it could be assumed that all children attending bilingual instruction spoke either exclusively or mainly one of the Slovene dialects at home, today, the pattern of knowledge of Slovene is different. According to information provided by teachers nearly three quarters of students enter school without previous knowledge of Slovene. Obviously parents from German-speaking backgrounds enrol their children in dual medium schools because they consider the option to learn an additional language as an educational opportunity and not as a choice linked to ethnic identification (Wakounig 2008: 321).

A change can also be observed concerning discourses on language and space. Whereas representations of space were formerly characterized by an almost obsessive focus on the course of the political and linguistic borderline separating an imagined Germanic and Slavic space, in this period the idea of an enlarged trilingual transborder region which encompasses Carinthia, Slovenia, and parts of Northern Italy is beginning to be promoted. The trilingual slogan 'senza confini—ohne Grenzen—brez meja' which wishes away the borders is becoming emblematic for envisaged cooperation on the economic, touristic, political, and cultural level. The idea of a regional triliguality is nevertheless again based on the three national languages in the respective nation-states disregarding other regional languages such as Friulian or languages of migration. Italian, which is introduced in Carinthia as a possible third language to alter the German-Slovene opposition, is mainly used for symbolic purposes, but has also begun to play a certain role in language policy (e.g. by being promoted as a subject in school).

NEW SPATIO-LINGUISTIC CONFIGURATIONS

The above discussed developments indicate a reversal of the bipolar logics that have characterized spatial practices, representations of space and representational spaces over a long period. The increased permeability of the state border opens the way for a gradual disenclavement of the borderland and re-weights language ideologies formerly linked to the geopolitical divisions. Representations of space that were formerly determined by discourses emphasizing the polarity between two states belonging to two different ideological systems are progressively replaced by discourses presenting the enlarged region as trilingual and 'without borders'. All these phenomena of transition and discontinuity suggest the emergence of new spatio-linguistic configurations linked to processes of increasing global mobility which result in new and ever more complex social formations and networking practices beyond traditional belongings, processes for which Steve Vertovec (2007) has coined the term super-diversity. Bauman (1998) discusses globalization as a transition from national economies based on industrial production and territoriality to a globalized market based on the transfer of knowledge and information. In this context he raises the question of peripherality in terms of a 'progressive spatial segregation, separation and exclusion' (Bauman 1998: 3). While the 'time/space compression' (Bauman 1998: 2) interlinks the increasingly global and extraterritorial elites in the centres, other regions are marginalized and 'localized' as no-man's-lands because they are excluded from the relevant communication flows. In structurally weak regions such as Carinthia, the fear of being left with the marginalized locals is omnipresent and frequently compensated for by different kinds of political activism, characterized by Bauman (1998: 3) as neo-tribal and fundamentalist.

In some domains it seems, nevertheless, that peripherality is not just a disadvantage but can also be turned into an advantage (see e.g. McLaughlin, this volume; Coupland, this volume). One aspect often mentioned in this context is the possibility of drawing on the idea of the periphery as a counter-world to the central areas (as Pietikäinen and Kelly-Holmes; Jaworski and Thurlow; and others in this volume point out). Precisely because of its quality of peripherality, it can be perceived as possessing values such as authenticity and unspoiltness, values which can be commodified. In peripheral areas such as the South of Carinthia, in the last few years there has also been a certain inward movement that has slowed down the demographic drain. This counter-movement is, on the one hand, due to a rising number of jobs which are now less tied to specific locations (e.g. in the IT sector). On the other hand, traditional small-scale economic structures which were preserved can provide a certain basis of subsistence when complemented by other activities (e.g. in the field of cultural work or soft tourism). Finally, the temporary placement or long-term stay of asylum seekers and refugees in municipalities of Southern Carinthia can also be seen in connection with the municipalities' location near the border.

Speakers on the Move

Increased mobility of the inhabitants, their participation in translocal networks of communication, as well as social ties and partnerships that reach far beyond the confines of the greater region, have led over the past decade to a linguistic diversification that resembles small-scale language regimes and linguistic practices described up to now mainly for urban areas. In one of the rural border municipalities, Eisenkappel-Vellach/Železna kapla Bela, a citizens' initiative,[8] promoting social integration and language learning organized in tandem pairs and conversation circles, counted among the 2,500 inhabitants more than fifteen languages other than Slovene and German, among these the languages of former Yugoslavia, as well as Turkish, Kurdish, Hungarian, Italian, French, English, Polish, Farsi, Ukrainian, and Russian.

As far as Slovene is concerned, the sociolinguistic situation that was traditionally framed in terms of language maintenance versus language shift, standard versus dialect has become far more differentiated. What was almost unthinkable some twenty years ago has become an everyday experience: there are learners of the minority languages and therefore there are speakers of 'Slovene with an accent' (Busch 2010). This includes individuals learning Slovene as children or as adults, in formal or in informal contexts and with different language backgrounds. The motivations are equally varied: for some it means returning to a 'lost' family language, for others acquiring a new family language within a linguistically mixed partnership; some learn Slovene for professional or economic reasons; for immigrants with a Slavic language background it often proves to be the first language of social contact in the new environment. There is very little recent sociolinguistic research into the developments in Carinthia. One recent, as yet unpublished study,[9] carried out among learners and alumni of bilingual schools indicates changing self-perceptions: most of the young people interviewed do not define themselves in terms of membership of an ethnic or linguistic group. They stress their participation in different spaces of communication in which they make self-confident use of their heteroglossic linguistic resources and present themselves as polyglot and as rooted. Their linguistic practices of language crossing and translanguaging as means of style and stylization resemble what has been described earlier by Rampton (1995) and other authors for urban areas.

The Alphabet Soup

The intermingling of the local and the global, of codes, registers, and styles that refer to different linguistic spaces, was the topic of another event organized by the UNIKUM cultural initiative a few years after the haček-campaign. It is again the diacritic sign on the letters c, s, and z that plays a central role. For this UNIKUM project a local enterprise began to produce a special version of pasta for alphabet soup adding the letters č, š, and ž to the so far 'monolingual' alphabet. The pasta was packed and labelled as 'buhštabenzupe' (see Figure 10.5). 'Buhštabenzupe' figures as a transliteration of the German word 'Buchstabensuppe' (alphabet soup) into a 'Slovenized' spelling. Unlike the haček campaign, where the Slovene diacritic sign was inscribed into German words and names, in the buhštabenzupe case, hybridity is foregrounded. The package information sheet accompanying the pasta details the contents as 'Buhštabenzupe—gewürzt und veredelt mit slowenischen Š, Č und Ž-Nudeln' (seasoned and enhanced with Slovene Š, Č, and

Figure 10.5:
The alphabet soup with the supplementary 'Slovene' letters č, š, ž. Photo G. Pilgram, UNIKUM

Ž pasta). The commercial slogan consists of two parts in the two languages: '*Z dvoječnim okusom! Zweisprachig schmeckt besser!*' (With bilingual flavour! Bilingual tastes better!). The local Carinthian pasta enterprise profited from the joint action with UNIKUM which served as a promotion campaign for the local pasta manufacturer, spreading its brand name. It discovered a market niche for custom-made products—one of their next clients being Jörg Haider's right-wing party BZÖ. The at best pragmatic and market-oriented attitude of the commercial partner is in clear contrast to the cultural and socio-political ambitions of UNIKUM.

As with the *haček* project, the *buhštabenzupe* project was very popular and a series of events took place not only in Carinthia but also in Vienna where small tasters with alphabet pasta were distributed at the International Book Day bringing questions of peripheral multilingualism right into the centre. To launch the *buhštabenzupe*, a series of events where alphabet soup was cooked and served was organized. These events also featured a jazz music and poetry performance in the style of slam poetry by the well-known Carinthian author Jani Oswald. His poems written for the *buhštabenzupe* events[10] revolve—as in the following extract of a poem named 'composition'—around the topics of cooking, mixing, stirring up, spicing, and savouring.

composition

	Nicht allein das
ABC	bringt den Menschen in die Höh
	bei
A and O	da käuft man so
	keifft
soso tatà	tàta pápa čudovito črkovito župo
X4U	and nix for me
	ist wie etwa
A-A-A	tripple Ah
	Papá isst Buchstabensuppe
	kar tako
	psst ach nur so
	Suppé, Franz von
	schon von
	črkovita Tscherkowitter
	Čajkovskij
	Tschudowitter
Pjotr	Ilijič
Čuš	windischer

Using techniques such as transliteration, alliteration, onomatopoeic word creations, and different kinds of wordplay and puns, Jani Oswald draws on a broad range of linguistic resources and discourses referring to the local and its commodification (hooks 1992), as well as to the repertoire of cultural and economic globalization.

As in the *haček* project, in the *buhštabenzupe* project irony serves as a means to undermine ethnolinguistic categorizations and polarizations. But whereas in the first project language policy activism was a core concern, the second foregrounded hedonistic and culinary aspects and used a postmodern variant of irony combined with a rather arbitrary use of quotations (Rorty 1989; Colebrook 2004). There is reference to a globalized repertoire in which Slovenian is one of the elements, an element of distinction that functions in a postmodern sense as symbolic capital. Linguistic heterogeneity in this context is seen as a resource for constructing socially interpretable and interpreted styles (Auer 2007).

The *buhštabenzupe* events can be interpreted following bell hooks (1992) as a cultural commodification which she refers to as 'eating the other': messages of social change are not taken up for their content but rather as an arbitrary element of style. In fact, the *buhštabenzupe* events are meant to be both: the commodification and the ironic commentary on commodification. In the postmodern variant of irony, it is not the origin of the quotation that matters, but its appearance as a reference as such. For the commercial project partner this form of quotation lacked the dimension of self-empowerment, the quotation rather served as an eye-catcher, as a free-floating signifier without a signified.

CONCLUSIONS

Like Lefebvre, Michel Foucault (1984: 1) sees space as historically conditioned, as having itself a history in Western experience which needs to be retraced. Developing a larger historical picture, Foucault, in 'Of Other Spaces' (1984), explains that space in the Middle Ages was seen as a hierarchical ensemble of places in which every person and every thing had its emplacement, while in the Modern Age space becomes an infinitely open space, and extension was substituted for localization. In his text (1984: 1), he sketches a present-day (bearing in mind that he was writing in the late 1960s) understanding of space that anticipates the conditions of globalization and super-diversity: 'We are in the epoch of simultaneity: we are in the epoch of juxtaposition, the epoch of the near and far, of the side-by-side, of the dispersed. We are at a moment, I believe, when our experience of the world is less that of a long life developing through time than that of a network that connects points and intersects with its own skein.'

If every era has its own understanding of space, then there is also a specific understanding of the connection between language and space linked to that specific moment in history. Space cannot simply be seen as a container that encompasses particular languages or language practices. Language comes into play on all three levels described by Lefebvre: on the level of spatial practices, of representations of space (discourses on space) and of representational spaces (space lived directly through its associated images and symbols). Language practices are themselves spatial practices and space is also constituted through language practices. Language ideologies are often linked with representations of space (e.g. monolingualism as the norm with nation-state ideologies). And, language is present as signs and symbols in the representational space, for example, visible in the form of topographic signs, invisible in the naming of places and locations.

The peripherality of European border regions is determined by different connotations that define the border as hermetic or permeable, as a zone of contact or of separation. The nation-state ideology has for a long period led to a conception of state borders as lines unambiguously separating the inside from the outside which also resulted in politics of linguistic homogenization within the state territories: state borders were ideally supposed to be reified as 'natural' separations between distinct national languages. Contesting linguistic homogenization could be interpreted as a sign of ambiguity or a lack of loyalty towards the centres: 'peripheral' speakers who were not willing to assimilate to the dominant language were frequently considered as 'not quite ours' or 'not ours at all'. Such forms of repeated Othering, of identification and misidentification due to 'suspicious' language practices, contributed to establishing and to reinforcing discursive categories of ethnolinguistic belonging which exerted a formative and constitutive power on the speaking subjects.

Analysing the situation in Southern Carinthia, shows that speakers of a language traditionally labelled as a minority language can no longer be unambiguously territorially localized or ethnically identified, and that they see themselves as multilingual subjects with complex and changing linguistic repertoires rather than as bilinguals oriented towards competing centres. The main focus has been on the transition from modernity, linked to the logics of territorial extension, to postmodernity, characterized by simultaneity, networking and the deterritorialization of linguistic practices.

Focusing on spatial representations and representational spaces, the co-presence of different notions of space and different discursive formations on language in space, connected to different moments in history, become obvious. As Heller and Labrie (2003: 16) observe for the context of French in Canada, different types of competing discourses on linguistic diversity can be discerned in different phases of history, but are today also simultaneously present: the traditionalist (*traditionaliste*), the modernizing (*modernisant*), and the globalizing (*mondialisant*). In the Carinthian context I identified the co-presence of different discursive formations on language and space: a traditional ethno-territorial discourse which is restaged in a postmodern version; a discourse of multiculturality which finds its expression in the idea of an enlarged trilingual region; and finally a postmodern emphasizing a glocalized form of linguistic diversity.

NOTES

1. This overview draws on my earlier sociolinguistic work on the situation in Carinthia (Busch 1999, 2003a, 2003b).
2. *European Charter for Regional or Minority Languages*, European Treaty Series 148 (Strasbourg: Council of Europe Publishing, 1992).
3. http://www.unikum.ac.at/.
4. A Slovene Tourism Agency, for example, proposes guided tours to 'the cradle of sloveneness and our first statehood' (*zibelka slovenstva in naše prve državnosti*). http://www.alpetour.si/index.php?page=alpI_raziskuje&item=168&predmet_id=&drzava_id=&id=133, accessed May 2011.
5. See, for example, Fran Ramovš, Karta slovenskih narečij v priročni izdaji, Cankarjeva založba, Ljubljana, 1957.
6. The data that this chapter is based on were collected in the framework of research projects carried out between 2006 and 2011, financed by the Austrian Ministry of Education and Culture and by the Austrian Office for Minorities at the Chancellery (Volksgruppenabteilung im Bundeskanzleramt) (Busch 2010; Busch and Doleschal 2008).
7. All data in this paragraph according to press information and reports by Landeschulrat für Kärnten (Carinthian school authority).
8. http://www.gesk.at/de/sprachentauschboerse.
9. Unpublished study financed by the Austrian Office for Minorities, carried out 2011 by B. Busch and G. Gombos, Gelebte Mehrsprachigkeit: Eine

qualitative Untersuchung der Schulerfahrungen von AbsolventInnen des mehrsprachigen Kugy-Zweiges des BG/BRG für Slowenen und ihres Umgangs mit Mehrsprachigkeit.

10. Jani Oswald, *Frakturen* (Klagenfurt/Celovec: Drava, 2007).

REFERENCES

Auer, Peter. 2007. *Style and social identities: Alternative approaches to linguistic heterogeneity.* Berlin, New York: Mouton de Gruyter.

Bakhtin, Mikhail. 1986. From notes made in 1970–71. In *Mikhail Bakhtin: Speech genres and other late essays,* ed. Caryl Everson and Michael Holquist, 132–158. Austin: University of Texas Press.

Balibar, Etienne. 1997. *La Crainte des masses: Politique et philosophie avant et après Marx.* Paris: Galilé.

Bauman, Zygmunt. 1998. *Globalization: The human consequences.* Cambridge: Polity Press.

Böse, Martina, and Brigitta Busch. 2007. The political potential of multi-accentuality in the exhibition title 'gastarbajteri'. *Journal of Language and Politics* 6: 437–457.

Busch, Brigitta. 1999. *Der virtuelle Dorfplatz: Minderheitenmedien, Globalisierung und kulturelle Identität.* Klagenfurt, Celovec: Drava.

Busch, Brigitta. 2003a. Changing borders, changing identities: Language and school in the bilingual region of Carinthia. In *Transcending monolingualism: Linguistic revitalisation in education,* ed. Lena Huss, Antoinette Camilleri Grima, and Kendall A. King, 243–257. Lisse: Swets & Zeitlinger.

Busch, Brigitta. 2003b. Shifting political and cultural borders: Language and identity in the border region of Austria and Slovenia. *European Studies: A Journal of European Culture, History and Politics* 19: 125–144.

Busch, Brigitta. 2004. *Sprachen im Disput: Medien und Öffentlichkeit in multilingualen Gesellschaften.* Klagenfurt: Drava.

Busch, Brigitta. 2010. Slowenisch in Kärnten—Sprache jenseits ethnischer Kategorien. In *Grenzverkehr/ungen: Mehrsprachigkeit, Transkulturalität und Bildung im Alpen-Adria-Raum,* ed. Werner Wintersteiner, Georg Gombos, and Daniela Gronold, 174–188. Klagenfurt: Wieser.

Busch, Brigitta, and Ursula Doleschal. 2008. Mehrsprachigkeit in Kärnten heute. *Wiener slavistisches Jahrbuch* 2008: 7–20.

Chakotin, Serge. 1971 [1939]. *The rape of the masses: The psychology of totalitarian political propaganda.* New York: Haskell House Publishers.

Colebrook, Claire. 2004. *Irony.* New York: Routledge.

Creese, Angela, and Adrian Blackledge. 2010. Translanguaging in the bilingual classroom: A pedagogy for learning and teaching? *Modern Language Journal* 94i: 103–115.

Derrida, Jacques. 1972. Positions. Interview by Jean-Louis Houdebine and Guy Scarpetta (1971). *Diacritics* 2: 34–43.

Derrida, Jacques. 1998. *Monolingualism of the other; or, The prosthesis of origin.* Stanford, Calif.: Stanford University Press.

Foucault, Michel. 1984. Des espaces autres, Hétérotopies. *Architecture, Mouvement, Continuité* 5: 46–49. English translation: Of Other Spaces, Heterotopia. http://foucault.info/documents/heteroTopia/foucault.heteroTopia.en.html 04.09.2011.

Gal, Susan. 2001. Linguistic theories and national images in nineteenth-century Hungary. In *Languages and publics: The making of authority,* ed. Susan Gal and Kathryn Woolard, 30–46. Manchester: St. Jerome Publishing.

García, Ofelia. 2009. Education, multilingualism and translanguaging in the 21st century. In *Multilingual education for social justice: Globalising the local*, ed. Ajit K. Mohanty, Minati Panday, Robert Phillipson, and Tove Skutnabb-Kangas, 140–158. New Delhi: Orient BlackSwan.

Heller, Monica, and Normand Labrie. 2003. Langage, pouvoir et identité: Une étude de cas, une approche théorique, une méthodologie. In *Discours et identité: La francité canadienne entre modernité et mondialisation*, ed. Monica Heller and Normand Labrie, 9–41. Cortil-Wodon: Editions Modulaires Européennes.

hooks, bell. 1992. *Black looks: Race and representation*. Boston: South End Press.

Jaworski, Adam, and Crispin Thurlow. 2010. Introducing semiotic landscapes. In *Semiotic landscapes. Language, image, space*, ed. Adam Jaworski and Crispin Thurlow, 1–40. London: Continuum.

Jørgensen, J. Normann. 2008. Polylingual languaging around and among children and adolescents. *International Journal of Multilingualism* 5 (3): 161–176.

Kert-Wakounig, Sonja. 2010. Dvojezični napisi na Koroškem—Od pogroma do konference o konsenzu. Opis in ocena dogodkov od leta 1972 do 2007. Diplomarbeit, Fakultät für Kulturwisschenaften. Klagenfurt/Celovec: Universität Klagenfurt.

Kroskrity, Paul A. 2005. Language ideologies. In *Handbook of pragmatics*. On-line version. Amsterdam: Benjamins.

Lefebvre, Henri. 1991. *The production of space*. Malden: Blackwell.

Li, Wei. 2011. Moment analysis and translanguaging space: Discursive construction of identities by multilingual Chinese youth in Britain. *Journal of Pragmatics* 43: 1222–1235.

Makoni, Sinfree, and Alastair Pennycook. 2006. *Disinventing and reconstructing languages*. Clevedon: Multilingual Matters.

Massey, Doreen. 2005. *For space*. London: Sage.

Österreichische Rektorenkonferenz, ed. 1989. *Bericht der Arbeitsgruppe 'Lage und Perspektiven der Volksgruppen in Österreich'*. Vienna: Böhlau.

Otsuji, Emi, and Alastair Pennycook. 2010. Metrolingualism: Fixity, fluidity and language in flux. *International Journal of Multilingualism* 7 (3): 240–254.

Pennycook, Alastair. 2009. Linguistic landscapes and the transgressive semiotics of graffiti. In *Linguistic landscape: Expanding the scenery*, ed. Elena Shohamy and Dirk Gorter, 302–313. London: Routledge.

Pennycook, Alastair. 2010. *Language as a local practice*. Abingdon: Routledge.

Priestly, Tom. 1996. On the etymology of the ethnic slur *Tschusch*. *Journal of Slavic Linguistics* 4 (1): 109–132.

Rampton, Ben. 1995. *Crossing: Language and ethnicity among adolescents*. London: Longman.

Reiterer, Albert F. 1996. *Kärntens Slowenen zwischen Minderheit und Elite: Aktuelle Tendenzen der ethnischen Arbeitsteilung*. Klagenfurt: Drava.

Rorty, Richard. 1989. *Contingency, irony and solidarity*. Cambridge: Cambridge University Press.

Said, Edward. 1993. *Culture and imperialism*. London: Vintage Books.

Schellander, Anton. 1988. Sodobni slovenski jezik na Koroškem: vprašanja govornega sporazumevanja, jezikovnega znaja in jezikovne rabe v dvojezični situaciji. *Obdobje. Sodobni slovenski jezik, literatura in kultura* 8: 261–275.

Scollon, Ron, and Suzie Wong Scollon. 2003. *Discourses in place: Language in the material world*. London, New York: Routledge.

Shohamy, Elena, and Dirk Gorter, eds. 2009. *Linguistic landscape: Expanding the scenery*. New York, London: Routledge.

Soja, Edward W. 1996. *Thirdspace: Journeys to Los Angeles and other real-and-imagined places.* Cambridge, Oxford: Blackwell.

Todorova, Maria. 1999. *Die Erfindung des Balkans: Europas bequemstes Vorurteil.* Darmstadt: Primus Verlag.

Vertovec, Steven. 2007. Super-diversity and its implications. *Ethnic and Racial Studies* 29: 1024–1054.

Viaut, Alain. 2004. La Frontière linguistique de la ligne à l'espace: Élémentes pour une schématisation. *Glottopol* 4: 5–22.

Vološinov, Valentin Nikolaevich. 1973. *Marxism and the philosophy of language.* New York: Seminar Press.

Wakounig, Vladimir. 2008. *Der heimliche Lehrplan der Minderheitenbildung: Die zweisprachige Schule in Kärnten.* Klagenfurt: Drava.

CHAPTER 11

The Peripheral Multilingualism Lens

A Fruitful and Challenging Way Forward?

HELEN KELLY-HOLMES AND SARI PIETIKÄINEN

This volume represents an attempt to understand in more depth the relationship between language (multilingualism) and space/place (the periphery), by focusing on sites of peripheral multilingualism. From the many and varied contexts examined in the volume, the common features of such sites can be seen as follows: they are areas conceived of and designated as minority language spaces; they are places and spaces of geographic, economic, and historical peripherality, and they are witnessing increasing commodification of that peripherality—particularly in relation to tourism; they exhibit a high dependency on authenticity and cultural legitimacy; they are the sites of pragmatically driven and often innovative multilingual practices; and they are subject to complex and complicated language ideological processes, which involve, on the one hand, a maintenance of monologic ideologies and, on the other, a contestation and rejection of such ideologies.

These are sites where we can observe language shift(s), and also language flows, and because of this complexity, one of the aims of the volume, as outlined in the introduction, has been to bring together these two ways of understanding sociolinguistic processes. Our desire was to try to create a dialogue between system/modernist/structuralist and repertoire/postmodernist/post-structuralist approaches, because, as the contributions to the volume show, both are needed and both are in evidence, and in fact, they both rely on each other. In this final chapter, we would like to reflect on some of the possibilities afforded by examining multilingualism and the periphery and also some of the challenges presented, and, at the same time, to highlight possible future research directions.

First, the focus has been on areas and localities which are identified both as minority language spaces and also as geographically and historically peripheral in relation to some notional centre. These two essentialized features provide the common context or frame within which practices, ideologies, and processes have been examined in this book. The focus on peripherality and on minority language status relies, of course, on a system or structuralist approach. It explicitly acknowledges the existence of—and more than that exploits—binary oppositions such as majority/minority and centre/periphery. It necessarily involves a freezing in time of relations and their categorization and description in terms of prevailing ideologies. However, in order to identify the contestations, playfulness, and creativity, it is first important to identify how the context for these phenomena was created and has been sustained. As Rampton (2006) points out, just because post-structuralist language practices are being analysed and valorized increasingly in the contemporary era does not mean that structures cease to exist. All the contributions to the volume, however, recognize the danger in relying just on the structuralist account, which would mean that 'peripheral multilingualism' becomes simply another synonym for 'minority language'. Thus, combining the focus on peripherality with an understanding of the dynamics of the centre–periphery relationship can be a fruitful way forward for combining 'language as system' and 'language as practice' approaches to the study of multilingualism.

The focus on the dynamics of the centre–periphery relationship not only shows how processes of peripheralization come about but also how they can change, as discussed by Heller in this volume. Such an approach allows for the possibility of movement; not just mono-directional or even bi-directional movement, but poly-directional. The periphery–centre lens also allows, as the many cases in the volume show, for the possibility of stability and movement occurring simultaneously and codependently. Centrist norms and ideologies are a necessary platform from which to launch creative play. As Jaffe (2006: 51) points out, many minority language movements have reached a certain maturity in recent years, having achieved recognition, resources, and in some cases markets for these languages, their speakers, and their products. In some minority language contexts, as illustrated in the volume, there is now something to rebel against, after many years of 'centring' and normalizing in the form of acquisition planning and status-planning initiatives. Norms are known and established, so there is a possibility to subvert and play with them. Many fights (for language rights, revitalization, status, etc.) have been won or partially won, although with several exceptions, and to an extent, the need to present a homogeneous front to the outside world may not be necessary at all times. Irony, mockery, and hybridity, valued in the contemporary era, have become a resource for multilingual identity and practices. Endangerment discourses (Heller and Duchêne 2007) and heritage discourses can be simultaneously both resisted and exploited, as many of the contributions to the volume show.

In addition, it is not just that new practices are emerging, as the contributions show. We seem to be moving from 'erasure' (Irvine and Gal 2000) to 'display' in terms of peripheral multilingualism. Thus, it is not just the case that diverse and mixed linguistic practices and 'incomplete' linguistic repertoires which were erased and rendered invisible by centrist ideologies (both in the periphery, by language rights activities and minority language movements, and in the centre, by the state, media, education, etc.) are no longer required to be hidden; as many of the contributions to the volume show, they are also increasingly highlighted, paraded, and commodified. In such a situation, the speaker with an 'unbalanced' repertoire, no matter how limited, has something to offer and something that can be valorized in particular sites and contexts (e.g. tourism and crafts, as indicated in the contributions to the volume). In the current era, the ability to draw on a range of 'transidiomatic practices' (Jacquemet 2005) which can be manipulated in multimodal ways is arguably more valuable than being the ideal monolingual, 'pure' speaker. What is 'real', as Mireille McLaughlin tells us in her chapter, is now valued as much as what is 'pure' in certain contexts and for certain purposes. Keeping a methodological and theoretical footing in the 'language as system' approach reminds us, of course, that 'bilingualism as deficit' discourses persist alongside 'bilingualism as added value' (Jaffe 2006) ones; that monolingual ideologies both dominate and coexist with and also codepend on monolingual discourses; that peripheral normativities (Blommaert et al. 2005) often make sense in juxtaposition to central norms; and that discontinuities occur in the midst of continuities.

As many of the contributions to the volume show, much of what drives peripheral multilingual practices is a pragmatic concern with getting things done, and the goal-directed nature of tourism and related domains, which create a space for 'linguistic flexibility' as Alexandra Jaffe and Cedric Oliva, this volume, call it. This reflects a valorization, which could then be reflected in other domains, leading to an 'upscaling' (Blommaert 2007). However, as all of the contributors make salient, display or fetishization, or even use for instrumental purposes, does not always contest and overthrow prevailing language ideologies. Commodification can be destabilizing (da Silva, McLaughlin, and Richards 2006), but can also be restabilizing. By using the linguistic resources for certain commodified purposes, existing linguistic regimes may simply be reinforced—a sign in the language, a brand name, a piece of pasta, a visual can be simply, in Brigitta Busch's words, a fleeting and free-floating signifier, a small bit of colour to brighten up monolingual norms. Or, it could challenge such ideologies. Or perhaps do both; simultaneity, as Brigitta Busch and Crispin Thurlow and Adam Jaworski remind us in their contributions, being the contemporary experiential mode.

Coupland (2003) tells us that authenticity is valued in the contemporary era perhaps more than in previous eras, given the present discursive regime. All of the contributions to the volume show us that authenticity matters in sites of peripheral multilingualism—whether this is commodified authenticity or unmediated authenticity (Coupland 2003), centripetal or centrifugal authenticity (Pietikäinen, this volume). Ownership, Jaffe (2006) points out, has taken over from competence in discourses about minority languages for the simple reason that competence is too excluding and in the end possibly self-defeating for minority language revitalization, since it can alienate people who live in and support peripheral minority language communities, and who feel ownership over the culture and the authenticity, using it as 'a source of creative identity' (Jaffe 2006). It is therefore just as possible in the current regime for the potter who moves his business from Dublin to the Irish-speaking periphery to 'own' and use Irish as a commercial resource (as Helen Kelly-Holmes describes), as it is for the Welsh-speaking natives in Glanporth, who Joan Pujolar reports on, to exhibit their 'real', 'living' bilingual community for tourists. It seems clear, however, that all the cases discussed in the volume are more or less authentic in some way or other, in line with Nikolas Coupland's (2003) criteria. Indeed, as his contribution to the volume shows, tracing authenticity—in the form of the provenance, meaning, and legitimacy of 'Welsh tea'—through time and space is a far from straightforward process. As the contributions to the volume highlight, trying to pin down what is and is not authentic is not the point of a peripheral multilingualism approach; instead, the focus needs to be on what is authentic for whom (producers and consumers) and why (for commodification, identification, etc.). The cosmopolitan spaces and visual/aural multilingualism of the airport, as Adam Jaworski and Crispin Thurlow, point out are both very fake and highly real, just like the Inari Sámi lassoing display in tourism space, described by Sari Pietikäinen.

The contributions to the volume also show us that peripherality, like many modern categorizations previously thought to be preordained, is now not just acknowledged as socially constructed, but is also possibly becoming a verb (cf. Cameron 2005 in relation to gender categorizations), something we can do, in the 'performance' era (Pennycook 2003; cf. Pietikäinen, forthcoming; Pietikäinen and Kelly-Holmes 2011 in relation to minority languages). It is clear then that the performative potential of peripherality thus creates both a challenge and an opportunity for sites like those examined in the volume. If use of these resources is uncontrolled, polycentric, bottom-up, and completely fragmented (Pietikäinen 2010), even globally dispersed, what are sites of peripheral multilingualism to do in order to wrest back control of this authenticity? What kinds of processes and types of 'boundary maintenance' (Barth 1969 in Kroskrity 2000: 340) are undertaken to keep claims to authenticity and ownership—both in terms of identification and commodification? As Pujolar (2006: 82) puts it, 'What strategies do minorities and their elites develop to protect their own sources of value and legitimacy in the new economy?' In a similar vein, da Silva, McLaughlin, and Richards (2006: 184) pose the difficult question that highlights this tension: 'In the new economy, which performances of language, culture and identity are rendered legitimate?' These questions, which have resonance for all the contributions in the volume, are certainly something to grapple with in future examinations of peripheral multilingualism. In addition, while authenticity in cultural tourism has traditionally been seen as 'anti-urban' (Prentice 2001), involving retreat to peripheral sites such as those examined in the volume, this is clearly changing. Industrial heritage tourism, architectural tourism, and movie tourism are all competing in the cultural tourism and authenticity stakes. Sites of peripheral multilingualism are thus in competition for 'authenticity', and the ways in which they compete are extremely revealing in terms of understanding the sociolinguistics of contemporary multilingualism.

Finally, the contributions to the volume show how the current dynamics and dialectics of language, space, and place emerge from adopting a peripheral multilingual approach to multiple sites; from the 'non-places' of airports and websites to the 'hyper-places' of tourist destinations, whose names are indexical of escape and beauty, the centre–periphery lens points to a fruitful and challenging way forward for our understanding of multilingualism as a dynamic/static, flexible/fixed phenomenon in minority language spaces and beyond.

REFERENCES

Blommaert, Jan. 2007. Sociolinguistic scales. *Intercultural Pragmatics* 4: 1–19.

Blommaert, Jan, Nathalie Muyllaert, Marieke Huysmans, and Charlyn Dyers. 2005. Peripheral normativity: Literacy and the production of locality in a South African township school. *Linguistics and Education* 16 (4): 378–403.

Cameron, Deborah. 2005. Language, gender and sexuality: Current issues and new directions. *Applied Linguistics* 26 (4): 417–431.

Coupland, Nikolas. 2003. Sociolinguistic authenticities. *Journal of Sociolinguistics* 7 (4): 417–431.

Da Silva, Emmanuel, Mireille McLaughlin, and Mary Richards. 2006. Bilingualism and the globalized new economy: The commodification of language and identity. In *Bilingualism: A social approach*, ed. Monica Heller, 183–206. Basingstoke and New York: Palgrave Macmillan.

Heller, Monica, and Alexandre Duchêne. 2007. Discourses of endangerment: Sociolinguistics, globalisation and social order. In *Discourses of endangerment*, ed. Alexandre Duchêne and Monica Heller, 1–13. London: Continuum.

Irvine, Judith T., and Susan Gal. 2000. Language ideology and linguistic differentiation. In *Regimes of language: Ideologies, polities, and identities*, ed. Paul V. Kroskrity, 35–83. Santa Fe, N. Mex.: School of American Research Press.

Jacquemet, Marco. 2005. Transidiomatic practices: Language and power in the age of globalisation. *Language and Communication* 25: 257–277.

Jaffe, Alexandra. 2006. Minority language movements. In *Bilingualism: A social approach*, ed. Monica Heller, 50–70. Houndsmills: Palgrave Macmillan.

Kroskrity, Paul V., ed. 2000. *Regimes of language: Ideologies, polities, and identities*. Santa Fe, N. Mex.: School of American Research Press.

Pennycook, Alastair. 2003. Global Englishes, Rip Slyme, and performativity. *Journal of Sociolinguistics* 7 (4): 513–533.

Pietikäinen, Sari. 2010. Sámi language mobility: Scales and discourses of multilingualism in polycentric environment. *International Journal of Sociology of Language* 202: 79–101.

Pietikäinen, Sari. Forthcoming. Multilingual dynamics in Sámiland: Rhizomatic discourses in language change. *International Journal of Bilingualism*.

Pietikäinen, Sari, and Helen Kelly-Holmes. 2011. Gifting, service, and performance: Three eras in minority-language media policy and practice. *International Journal of Applied Linguistics* 21 (1): 51–70.

Prentice, Richard. 2001. Experiential cultural tourism: Museums and the marketing of the new romanticism of evoked authenticity. *Museum Management and Curatorship* 19: 5–26.

Pujolar, Joan. 2006. *Language, culture and tourism: Perspectives in Barcelona and Catalonia.* Barcelona: Turisme de Barcelona.

Rampton, Ben. 2006. *Language in late modernity: Interaction in an urban school.* Cambridge: Cambridge University Press.

INDEX